MW01283952

Dawn of Sunday

New Studies in Theology and Trauma

Series Editors:

Joshua Cockayne
Scott Harrower
Preston Hill
AND
Chelle Stearns

Forthcoming Books in the Series:

Formerly Published Books in the Series:

Dawn of Sunday

The Trinity and Trauma-Safe Churches

Joshua Cockayne
Scott Harrower
Preston Hill

CASCADE *Books* · Eugene, Oregon

DAWN OF SUNDAY
The Trinity and Trauma-Safe Churches

Copyright © 2022 Joshua Cockayne, Scott Harrower, and Preston Hill. All rights reserved. Except for brief quotations in critical publications or reviews, no part of this book may be reproduced in any manner without prior written permission from the publisher. Write: Permissions, Wipf and Stock Publishers, 199 W. 8th Ave., Suite 3, Eugene, OR 97401.

Cascade Books
An Imprint of Wipf and Stock Publishers
199 W. 8th Ave., Suite 3
Eugene, OR 97401

www.wipfandstock.com

PAPERBACK ISBN: 978-1-7252-9104-1
HARDCOVER ISBN: 978-1-7252-9103-4
EBOOK ISBN: 978-1-7252-9105-8

Cataloguing-in-Publication data:

Names: Cockayne, Joshua, author. | Harrower, Scott, author. | Hill, Preston, author.

Title: Dawn of Sunday : the Trinity and trauma-safe churches / Joshua Cockayne, Scott Harrower, and Preston Hill.

Description: Eugene, OR: Cascade Books, 2022 | Series: New Studies in Theology and Trauma. | Includes bibliographical references and index.

Identifiers: ISBN 978-1-7252-9104-1 (paperback) | ISBN 978-1-7252-9103-4 (hardcover) | ISBN 978-1-7252-9105-8 (ebook)

Subjects: LCSH: Post-traumatic stress disorder—Religious aspects—Christianity. | Spiritual healing. | Psychology, Religious.

Classification: BV4910.45 D53 2022 (paperback) | BV4910 (ebook)

05/19/22

To those who reached to us and to those we love from the dawn of Sunday: David; Francis and Lysbeth Fong; Silvia Chaves and Beatirz Buono; Chad Griffin and the Schmutzers.

"Why do you keep filling gallery after gallery with endless pictures of the one ever-reiterated theme of Christ in weakness, of Christ upon the cross, Christ dying, Christ hanging dead? Why do you stop there as if the curtain closed upon that horror? Keep the curtain open, and with the cross in the foreground, let us see beyond it to the Easter dawn with its beams streaming upon the risen Christ, Christ alive, Christ ruling, Christ triumphant.

"For we should be ringing out over the world that Christ has won, that evil is toppling, that the end is sure, and that death is followed by victory. That is the tonic we need to keep us healthy, the trumpet blast to fire our blood and send us crowding in behind our Master, swinging happily upon our way, laughing and singing and recklessly unafraid, because the feel of victory is in the air, and our hearts thrill to it."

—MICHELANGELO, 1564

Contents

New Studies in Theology and Trauma

New Studies in Theology and Trauma is a series of entry-level mono-graphs in Christian theology, engaging trauma. The series showcases work at the intersection of trauma and theology from emerging scholars in this new discipline. Each volume will be approximately 60,000–80,000 words long according to the topic at hand. Monographs in the series are aimed at exploring: (i) how trauma studies and trauma theory can inform theological method, (ii) how theology can be used as a frame for under-standing trauma, (iii) and how churches and faith communities can facili-tate theologically informed, effective trauma care.

Recent neuroscience has confirmed that surviving traumatic violence leaves lifelong scars in the brain and body, and that "the body keeps the score." This persistent reality of trauma poses a unique challenge to Chris-tian communities and churches. Thankfully, many of these communities have begun to recognize that trauma and abuse do not happen "out there" but are horrors that occur within our own ranks, with many Christians call-ing out for justice for victims that have hidden in the shadows far too long. Christians cannot avoid confronting trauma that is tragically manifesting within our own church communities. When trauma is perpetrated by pas-tors and Christian leaders, this threatens to undermine a Christian witness to the gospel. As a result, trauma is raising the stakes on theological truth-claims made by Christians. This leaves a door wide open for Christians to explore the intersection of theology and trauma.

Given the emerging state of literature on theology and trauma cur-rently, there is a need to solidify the intuitions shared by scholars in the many disciplines of theology and biblical studies and signal a constructive and generative approach for the future of this growing field. The present series seeks to fill this need by offering a series of monographs grouped around a *double witness*: a witness to the laments and losses involved in surviving trauma and a witness to God's ongoing presence and agency in the aftermath of violence. By promoting a double-witness approach in this series, authors engaging theology and trauma will be provided a coherent and fruitful platform for witnessing both the wounds of trauma and the healing in recovery for communities today.

We have started this series because trauma calls for faithful and generative witness, which is why we have selected the Australian lyrebird as the symbol for our series. The lyrebird is able to listen carefully to sounds of its surroundings, then repeat these back in concert with new voices as part of a broader song. This new song is unique in that it faithfully reflects the original sounds into a new context of richer harmony. Likewise, empathetic listening that faithfully witnesses the wounds of trauma while remaining open to renewed hope within a larger frame is the core idea of the New Studies in Trauma and Theology series.

Series Editors:

Joshua Cockayne, Scott Harrower, Preston Hill, and Chelle Stearns

Acknowledgments

Thanks to Rebecca Muir from Ridley College (Melbourne, Australia), and Capt. Rev. Warwick Fuller from Fort Bragg (North Carolina, USA) for providing helpful feedback on a final draft of the book. Your insightful work greatly improved the manuscript. Thanks to Michael Thompson for believing in this project and the larger series to which it belongs, New Studies in Theology and Trauma. Thanks also to TheoPsych/Blueprint 1543 for inspiring and supporting us in engaging the psychological sciences in our work on traumatology. We wish to thank the various international forums where we have been able to present the material and receive feedback, including the Australian Anglican Diocese of Tasmania, the Anglican Diocese of Canberra and Goulburn, and the Mission School of Ministry (USA). Also, thank you to those students who have eagerly received this material and offered insightful feedback, especially Preston's counseling students specializing in trauma therapy in the School of Counseling and Preston's theology students in the School of Ministry at Richmont Graduate University and the Richmont Institute of Trauma and Recovery (USA). We must also thank the members of the reading group from St Andrews who discussed Scott Harrower's book, *God of All Comfort* in 2019: Emilie Grosvenor, Hannah Craven, Karen Kiefer, Chelle Stearns, and Rachel Anne Clinton-Chen. Relatedly, we wish to thank the Logos Institute, which generously funded the 2019 Theology and Trauma Conference that made many of these connections possible.

Preface

This book started as a conversation between three scholars across three continents around a shared passion for the church and a desire to see her flourish. After reading Scott's book *The God of All Comfort* in St Andrews in Scotland, Josh and Preston began to talk about how the profound trinitarian lessons in Scott's work might help to address the growing need in the church to address the effects of trauma. In engaging with Scott, we found a like-minded dialogue partner who shared our hope that churches might become trauma-safe environments. Between us, we have a wealth of experience in theology, ministry, and pastoral care in a variety of contexts. Some of us have firsthand experience of the damaging effects of trauma and we have walked alongside many others who are recovering from trauma. Preston in particular is a survivor of childhood trauma who lives with a PTSD diagnosis.

Whether we realize it or not, our churches are full of those who have experienced and are living with the aftereffects of horror and trauma, whether as survivors, carers, or perpetrators. The central question of this book is simple: *How can our churches become open to the Trinity such that they are trauma-safe environments for everyone?* The solution is more complex. It will take time to unpack just what the problem is, and how the church might respond to this problem. Our hope is that in allowing the experiences of others to shape our own approach to ministry, we might all gain a greater appreciation for the profound love of God revealed in the work of the persons of the Trinity. We do not pretend to have all the answers, but our hope is that our reflections on these issues might help to start new conversations in your own context. Wherever we have missed the mark, we eagerly invite you to join us in offering new insights and perspectives. We are all on the journey of becoming trauma-safe and we all need one another to do this work well.

The discussion of horror and trauma that proceeds might in places feel intense and too heavy to dwell on for long periods. We invite you to take it at a pace that is right for you. And our prayer is that you come away with a deeper and broader understanding of what it is to live in relationship with God the Trinity.

Part 1

Understanding Trauma

1

A Crisis of Horrors

As many of us know all too well, "The world is full to overflowing with pain. It is a relentless source of dismay for a person of faith to struggle with the omnipresence of radical, destructive suffering."[1] Perhaps these words ring true to your own experience of life; through no fault of your own, life seems to be an endurance of one trial after another, with seemingly no respite. The suffering of life's horrors, the mundane as well as the grotesque, threaten to disrupt all sense of meaning and purpose in our lives. Along with the preacher of the book of Ecclesiastes, we shout in unison, "meaningless, meaningless, everything is meaningless!" (Eccl 1:2). Our hope of a life of purpose with God is all too often undermined by experiencing precisely the opposite: "in my vain life I have seen everything; there are righteous people who perish in their righteousness, and there are wicked people who prolong their life in their evildoing" (Eccl 7:15). This sense of horror and meaninglessness is only compounded by the sense of threat so many of us feel when looking at the world.[2] Most of us have the eerie sense that the world is becoming an increasingly treacherous place to live.[3] This is a crisis we cannot avoid; a growing awareness of the widespread occurrences of horrors and the traumatic effects these generate.

This sense of unsafety is slowly drip-fed by our constant exposure to bad news—scientific research, media reports, personal experience all slowly eat away at our hope and self-confidence. The physical sciences offer us apparently indisputable facts about the chaotic and inherently unpredictable nature of our existence; life is stranger and more dangerous than we

1. Farley, *Gathering Those Driven Away*, 5.
2. Dudley, "Where And Why The World Is Getting More Dangerous."
3. Mannion, "Most people think world is more dangerous."

thought. Medical sciences tell us that any one of us might be at risk of life-destroying cancers, deadly viruses, or mental breakdowns at any minute. Social sciences warn us of the unpredictability of human behavior, putting even our daily commute, or evening run, at risk of attack from the violence of fellow human beings.

Media outlets lure us into footage and interviews that show off abandoned and abused children, stabbings, bombings, assaults, and lots of people of whom we should be very afraid. Sometimes we recognize our kin and personal experiences and history in these events. Seeing footage of savagely beaten faces reminds some of us what our own blood tastes like, and even worse, what it tastes like when our own people have done this to us. We have been profoundly wounded and shaped by this hurt as its memories haunt us and shut us off from other people. Life is lived with sad limps and lisps that were not ours by birth or by choice but are the result of the heinous actions of other people. Tremendous evils are committed against people, animals, and the Earth, and it seems as though there is little that we can do to remedy this.

Given these facts, our lives seem random, dangerously weird, and even nonsensical. More personally, and painfully closer to home, our own experiences and relationships are bruised by the blows of conflict and pain; sometimes they include sickening experiences of despicable and deadening deeds—life is horrific. We have lived evidence that life hurts, and worse still we have had the experience of knowing that there is no one who really can help. People come and go, scarring and scaring each other. Making matters worse, the suffering that befalls many in this life comes from the very places that supposedly offer the antidote. How can there be new life with the God of all comfort amid the pain of trauma and horror?

This depiction of life's radically destructive suffering does not capture everyone's experience of life. Many of us stamp our feet incredulously upon hearing the words of Ecclesiastes and reply: "No! Life is filled with moments of profound meaning, purpose, and beauty." While many suffer, life is not a relentless source of dismay for everyone, pain is not always overwhelming, and horrors do not provide the last word. Many of us have not suffered in profound and difficult ways—we have experienced loving homes and nurturing friendships. In the church, we have experienced communities of protection, light, and wholeness. However, even in these best-case scenarios of the church, most of us have experienced awkward or difficult interactions with other members. Sometimes people who have endured severe harm may come across as odd, or difficult. For example, they may avoid eye contact and conversation with others; or quite the opposite, they might overshare, and we simply don't know what to do or say in response. By the same token, survivors of trauma often struggle to know what to do or say: they may come across as too intense or have a lower tolerance than most for relational disruptions.

Take for example the stories of Luc and Martine. When Luc would go forward to receive the Lord's Supper, he seemed very jittery and nervous. He was in a rush to receive it, concerned that he might miss out. Standing in front of the minister to receive the bread seemed like an eternity to him. When he received the bread, he would squeeze it in his palm, crushing it, pressing down hard in order to feel that it was really there. His hand would shake at times, yet he was not shaking it in anger. Whilst receiving the common cup, Luc would keep his eyes open, and would insist on holding on to it himself.

The intensity of his participation in the Lord's Supper surprised and even scared some people. For this reason, and others, most people avoided him and never included him in social gatherings. No one was keen to invite him to regular Bible studies. Luc was passively excluded from the life of the local church. He sat at the back of the church for years, hoping for meaningful interactions with other Christians. He would try to initiate conversations with other people, but these were cut short by disinterest or interruptions from others. Attending church was a profoundly alienating experience, and it gradually became overplayed with a deep sense of shame. Four years later he stopped attending church services. He built his own chapel in his garage as a way to maintain faith, with the hope of opening it up to others who were not actively welcomed in churches either. He takes the Lord's Supper alone each week. For him it is as much a lamentation with Christ as it is a celebration.

Martine also struggled with a similar combination of intense feelings and isolation, as Luc did. However, for her the experience of events in formal church services was far different. She would arrive slightly late in order to avoid having to talk to people who she felt would not be able to understand what she had experienced. Every week, during the sermon, for reasons she did not understand, tears would flow down her cheeks. As the tears flowed, she would sniffle and have to blow her nose, which unfortunately drew unwanted attention to her. She grew used to people leaving empty seats around the spot where she usually sat. The minister was only interested in "productive people" who could fill in slots on church rosters; after all, he would joke, he had to keep his church-franchise going, didn't he? The isolation and shame in church services mirrored her shame and isolation in the wider community. To whom could she speak about her confusing experiences of crying during sermons?

The stories of Luc and Martine speak to the ways in which horrors that have been suffered make themselves known in indirect ways through the relationships that survivors hold in the present. But even those of us who have been fortunate enough to live mostly stable and safe lives are not immune to this crisis of evil. Visiting friends in hospital, attending their funerals, or being reminded of their absence is sad, horrific, even terrifying. Seeing the pain, suffering, and wounds of others has an unnatural feel to it, that things should not be this way. We are haunted in the moments and days after direct exposure to human wretchedness, as disturbing thoughts and fears plague our sense of safety, community, and hope because we worry about what will happen tomorrow, or what will eventually happen to our parents, our future spouses, or our children. Why would you bring a child into this kind of world? What possible good could our lives serve? Naturally, we do not experience all of these at the same time or to the same depth—we each experience different intensity of wounding by others, various shades of disappointment, hurt, shock, and fear.

But evil's invasion into our lives is not lessened by the degrees to which we feel it. This invasion of evil into our bodies, souls, relationships, agency, and morality is a tragic given in a world wandering east of Eden. Like any infection, evil's invasion into our communities and very being has widespread consequences. We face an unprecedented crisis of horrors and trauma; appalling things happen, and we are left to deal with the aftermath.

Ultimately, there are no bystanders in confronting the reality of life's suffering. As the Apostle Paul is keen to stress, within the community of faith, there is no suffering that does not involve us all: "If one member suffers, all suffer together with it; if one member is honored, all rejoice together with it" (1 Cor 12:26). The reality of suffering, trauma, and horror is a reality that we must all confront in some way. This confrontation may involve walking through the immense pain and trauma we have suffered directly and personally. Or, perhaps, the stories in this book may open our eyes for the first time to the vast amounts of pain and suffering experienced by our fellow human beings. But if we take Paul's emphasis on the life of community seriously, then not only is our suffering a shared suffering, but our response must also be a shared response. Whether we encounter horrors directly or not, the reality we must face is that our communities are filled with those who suffer the destructive force of horror. All too often, our communities not only allow such atrocities to occur, but actively participate in creating these horrors; the frank reality is that the church is a mixed bag of horror survivors and horror makers.

This book seeks to confront the reality of life's horrors, but this does not mean that it speaks only to survivors of horrors. The diversity of experiences, of life's meaningless and meaningfulness, of its brokenness and its wholeness, of its pain and its joy, are not competing realities. No one of us stands from a neutral standpoint and corrects the other. Rather, we all stand in a shared crisis of horrors, and a shared crisis of the traumatic aftermath caused by horrors. The central question we ask, then, is this: faced with the reality of this crisis, how will the church respond today? While the reality is bleak, the church dares to "hope against hope" because of the nature of God and of the body of Christ. We can think of our reason for hope in terms of death and resurrection. Like the story of Jesus, our stories hold the tension of standing between Good Friday and Easter Sunday, between brokenness and beauty. An ancient Christian hymn reflects this truth: "In the midst of life, we are in death." And yet, the story of the Trinity, Christ, and the church tells us that there is something better than feeling stuck in death or wanting to return to life as it was before. We don't long for resuscitation; we long for resurrection. With Christ and in him, we long to stand at the boundary between Holy Saturday and Easter Sunday, with one foot on either side, looking the bleak reality of horrors and trauma full in the face while remaining open and postured toward the light of healing and recovery just over the horizon. The metaphor of remaining in the dawn of Sunday means that we seek to understand the stakes of horrors and trauma in order to facilitate recovery in the church. In dwelling on these issues, we hope that we might reflect more deeply on the question of how our churches can become *trauma-safe* environments. That is, we seek to explore how the church can facilitate God's healing from the effects of horrors of this life.

We can explore this hopeful work because we are realists about God. God the Trinity does not sit back and watch the world crumble. God the Father mourns with the suffering of his people (2 Cor. 1:3; 1 Pet 5:7), God the Son experiences our very humanity, suffers alongside, and prays for us (Heb 4:15–16; 7:25), God the Spirit renews and draws us together as one in

7

Christ (1 Cor 12)—God the Trinity brings hope and healing to the church through suffering as a protest against horrors. There is no horror too great from which God cannot bring goodness and beauty. Thus, while we seek to take seriously the reality of life's despair, we also seek to provide a Trinitarian, and ultimately ecclesiological, vision of recovery that is rooted in hope.

We must keep our eyes open, defiant in hope, to the reality of God the Trinity in the face of the present horrors and trauma. For the good news is that the Trinity can bring healing to this *crisis of horrors and trauma* through the work of the church. The bad news is that this will not be an easy process for the body of Christ. In what follows we outline a general approach for how the church might cooperate with God's grace for the sake of restoring and healing people and communities.[4]

Wounded Sheep Need Good Shepherds

So, how can the church channel the Trinity's response to a person or community's loss of flourishing in the wake of horror and trauma?[5] If you come to this book looking for an easy and very quick answer to this question, then in all likelihood you will leave disappointed. The wounds inflicted by trauma are profound, and the process of recovery is lifelong. Many ministry workers will lack the patience and resilience to pastor those who are recovering from such experiences. Perhaps, you might think, some people are not worth the personal and emotional cost of pastoring. In a congregation filled with difficult problems and challenging pastoral situations, you might think, we need to find the right places to invest our time and energy, or else risk burning out entirely.

It is difficult to square this response with the radical message of love we find in the pages of Scripture. Consider one of Jesus' most told parables (adapted suitably for our purposes here):

> Suppose one of you has a hundred sheep and loses one of them. Doesn't he leave the ninety-nine in the open country and go after

4. This model is a variant of the one offered in Harrower, *God of All Comfort*, 27–28.

5. By "flourishing" we mean the phenomenon that has to do with God's images living life to the full as relational, moral, creative, and perceptive beings. The goal of flourishing is to love God and in so doing to love others and oneself. Flourishing in this broad perspective clearly involves both objective standards, since flourishing is circumscribed by an ultimate relation to God's intention for shalom, as well as the subjective criteria of seeing this shalom instantiated in individual and collective human experience. See Harrower, *God of All Comfort*, 8–12.

the wounded sheep until he finds it? And when he finds it, he joyfully puts it on his shoulders and goes home. Then he calls his friends and neighbors together and says, "Rejoice with me; I have found my wounded sheep."

Do those of us in ministry take the vocation of shepherding seriously? Are we prepared to love God's children at their most broken and damaged? We might not always get it right, but the model of shepherding we find exemplified in Jesus calls us to at least try. We cannot be content to care only for the ninety-nine. Reflecting more deeply on this parable also shows us that there is rarely a one-size-fits-all solution to such problems; lost sheep get wounded in many different ways. Releasing a sheep that is snagged in barbed wire will require a different tack than helping a sheep traverse boggy ground. Moreover, shepherding requires a knowledge of the particular sheep and their particular wounds. And returning the sheep to the fold is not the end of the task; nursing the wounded animal to recovery takes skill, care, and time. Shepherding those wounded from the force of horrors is similar in many ways. While we recognize that those recovering from trauma experience a loss of safety, the outworking of this will be different in each person and recovery will be different in each case. What works for some will be more challenging for others. All too often the church is content for its response to such problems to be merely surface level, welcoming for the sake of appearances, but lacking a depth of pastoral care that is needed to attend to those wounded by trauma.

When the church falls into a surface response to survivors of horrors for the sake of appearances, this response is known as giving someone "ScoMo's handshake." In the wake of the 2019 bushfires, the Australian Prime Minister, Scott Morrison—ScoMo—was photographed meeting some members of the public who had their homes and livelihoods destroyed by the fires. One image sticks vividly in the mind—that of the prime minister grabbing the hand of an unwilling woman who survived the fires.[6] He grabbed her hand, yet she did not really want to shake it as a sign of fellowship because she was frustrated at the government's lack of action in responding to the disaster—including the fact that Scott Morrison did not return immediately from his holiday in Hawaii when the fires began to rage.[7] He took her hand anyway, shook it awkwardly, then appeared to run off in shame. "ScoMo's handshake" was a perfect photo opportunity,

6. *Guardian News*, "Scott Morrison's attempts to shake hands in Cobargo rejected."

7. BBC News, "Australia fires."

for him, but used the woman for his sake, and against her wishes and what may have helped her.

When I (Preston) watched the video of this interaction, my whole body cringed with a PTSD response. What must it have felt like for that woman to have her hand taken (against her consent!) by a man with so much power? To have her request for help denied, and her protest against being touched ignored? Most painfully, how would all this feel if she had a traumatic past herself? The handshake, which is ironically a sign of respect and cooperation, was inflicted on an unwilling and resistant victim of horror. The lady in question, Ms. McDermott, understood that: "He just wanted photos. He walked off on me." She continued: "I would have had utmost respect for him, for any leader, if they had just sat down with us and discussed [what we needed]."[8]

ScoMo's handshake aimed at creating the image of a politician who cared, masking an unwillingness to meet this woman where she was, and trying to hide the fact that greater government support had been given to wealthy areas than poorer ones. At bottom, ScoMo's handshake was deceitful and took advantage of a vulnerable person for the sake of propping up the reputation of a regime that appeared to have responded lazily and selectively to the survivors of the fires. The church must avoid, at all costs, a "ScoMo" response to trauma. We cannot be a community that welcomes survivors with gestures and words, but that lacks the depth of care to shepherd the wounded with all their complexities. If we shepherd for our own self-interest, with the intention of covering up our past failings in this area of Christian care, we will eventually cause more harm than good; the good shepherd lays down his life for the sheep. So, a good shepherd encounters people in their particularity (they leave the ninety-nine to find the one), they take time to respond, and they seek to love unconditionally and sacrificially. Those who have been shepherded by Jesus are called to be like him; one of Jesus' final commands to his disciples before his death is that we are to love one another: "This is my commandment, that you love one another as I have loved you. No one has greater love than this, to lay down one's life for one's friends" (John 15:12–13). Echoing the description of himself as the

---

8. Drevokovsky, "Bushfire victim slams Scott Morrison for walking away." The Prime Minister's lack of empathy for trauma survivors was again on view in the wake of allegations of sexual assault by his own staff in the Australian Parliament offices. This shows that Morrison (and his leaderships circles) did not develop in empathy, or change his ways, after previously failing to care for the fire survivors. See Waterford, "Scott Morrison's handling of Brittany Higgins rape allegations lack empathy."

Good Shepherd (John 10), Jesus tells his disciples that they are to do likewise. The church's members, especially its leadership, have the task of imitating Jesus as a shepherd. This is more than daunting. But as we have described it so far, it is also incomplete. The task of shepherding can be done, but it cannot be done alone. The good shepherd's love of his sheep must first be rooted in the Trinity. Jesus says: "I am the good shepherd; I know my sheep and my sheep know me—*just as the Father knows me and I know the Father*—and I lay down my life for the sheep" (John 10:14–15). Christ the Good Shepherd has a relationship with his sheep as well as with the Father, and his love for the sheep is rooted in the love between himself and the Father. The eternal relationship of holy love between the Father, Son, and Spirit is the fountain from which divine love flows to creatures like us. The Good Shepherd loves the sheep because his divine nature is holy love. He also loves the sheep because the Father, Son, and Spirit share a desire and vision for the world—a world in which people love each other: "My command is this: Love each other as I have loved you. Greater love has no one than this: to lay down one's life for one's friends" (John 15:12–13). Christians, and especially those in vocational ministry, are called to follow the ways of the Good Shepherd. People who shepherd Jesus' flock must also have a profound relationship with God the Father: a relationship of knowing him and being known. Engaging the Father and being engaged by him is the starting point for loving others well and offering the Father's gift of eternal life in the aftermath of trauma. Jesus' command to love must be understood as a call to love others in union with, and in tune with, the Trinity. "As the Father has loved me, so I have loved you; abide in my love . . . When the Helper comes, whom I will send to you from the Father, the Spirit of truth who comes from the Father, he will testify on my behalf" (John 15:9, 26). We are invited to minister in the context of the perfect love found between the Persons of the Trinity—through the presence and testimony of the Holy Spirit, we abide in the love of the Son, and of the Father.

Jesus' words on sending the Helper in John 15 are followed soon after by his prayer for all disciples, "that they may all be one just as the Father and the Son are one" (John 17:21). The work of the Holy Spirit in the world is to bring about this unity between people such that we might all be one in the body of Christ (1 Cor 12). Ministry in the church must not lose sight of the fact that true unity is the work of the Persons of the Trinity. This does not mean that the "institution of the church" and "the church" are identical; there is much about the human structures of the church that we are called to lament. Instead, we must recognize that our schemes for humanly imposed unity will only take us so far; we need to find ways of channeling the love of the Persons of the Trinity, rather than getting in the way of God's perfect love.

But Jesus does not call us to channel the love of the Trinity all on our own. Jesus also models for us what it looks like for a full member of the human race to channel triune love in a world of trauma. Before praying for the Holy Spirit to come "that they may all be one" Jesus first declared to the Father, "As you sent me into the world, I have sent them into the world" (John 17:18). Our ministry in the church of shepherding trauma survivors is possible because Jesus is "the great Shepherd of the sheep" (Heb 13:20) who shows us that effective trauma care always starts with empathy: "For we do not have a high priest who is unable to emphasize with our weaknesses" (Heb 4:15). Empathy is profoundly precious to trauma survivors, because it is hard to trust someone with your wounds if you know they can't relate from their own experience. This does not mean that no one can minister to trauma survivors unless they have survived trauma themselves. Through empathy, anyone is able to be emotionally open to knowing the experiences of trauma survivors, not being afraid of being affected by their stories, but maintaining a desire to witness their wounds for the sake of their healing. Embodying empathy simply means that if we are to be made one in the Spirit as a church that responds to trauma by engaging the love of the Father, we must turn our eyes to Jesus, who perfectly models the work of the Trinity in healing the wounds of trauma, beginning with empathetic understanding. Although we may never empathize with trauma survivors as fully as Jesus, we must continually express that we have a desire to understand the wounds of trauma as much as we are able.

Even if we recognize that the church's unity comes from the work of the Trinity and not ourselves, it doesn't follow that we can do nothing to bring about love and unity in the world. Being a channel of the love that we have received from the Trinity shapes the kind of ministries and good we may do in the communities we serve—or not. Consider the contrast between two ministries within a mere mile from one another. When he began working as the pastor of his parish, Rev. Tracy was disappointed in what (not whom) he found: a blue-collar congregation that included a proportion of people who were not able to work full-time or volunteer many skills at church. Rev. Tracy's basic feeling towards the people of the parish was irritation: he was annoyed that they weren't upper-middle class like he was, that they did not have robust energy levels, that they found work tiring, and worst of all, they seemed to expect him to "just stand there and listen to them drone on about their sad and shabby lives" at the same time as they were not that interested in helping with the menial jobs involved in running a church. No one would volunteer to empty the bins on Sunday evening, and Rev. Tracy was ropable about it. Over the course of a couple of years Rev. Tracy did his best to "move people on," by which he meant "move people out," if they were disruptive, needy, or not really interested in hearing his sermon illustrations about overseas travel and expensive hobbies. What Rev. Tracy wanted most of all was a bright looking congregation, with shiny people in it, so that he could get invites to sparkly dinner parties with articulate highfliers—"you know, people of high net worth." Lamentably, for Rev. Tracy, people mattered more when they have "high net worth" relative to banks, country clubs, and to himself. He was driven by a deep need to control people and to fit in at the nicer end of town. This meant that his congregation were not safe with him: they were either valued because of the labor they could offer (i.e., used as a means to an end), or were subtly excluded and squeezed out in the hope that nicer looking people would arrive one day and not be scared off by "grimy types." Rev. Tracy was ordained, but was not a channel of God's kindness. He represented and embodied a form of secularized pseudo-Christianity.

Nearby, Rev. Lewis was having a burger with Barbara and Batch. They wanted to get married. Rev. Lewis wanted the very best for them and their families; he loved them and would help them. It didn't matter that they lived in a rented caravan. Being prone to jealousy and gluttony meant they were far from perfect, yet they were God's children, of infinite worth to God and therefore to Rev. Lewis. Listening to them, praying for and with them, Rev. Lewis suggested some ways forward that they might consider. He was driven by understanding God's deep love for people and care for them despite the appalling social structures and sins that wreak havoc in our lives. For the overflow of God's love, and from loving God, Rev. Lewis continually cared for those people placed in his hands in the Boronia neighborhood. There was something different and surprising about this older man; his motives, manner, and goals were otherworldly in the best sense of the word. He was part of a fuller, deeper, and more caring kingdom, one which is "righteousness, peace and joy in the Spirit." Rev. Lewis was a channel of God's grace and renewing power, as well as an embodiment of what God's safe, holy love can look like, even in trailer parks.

The contrast between these two ministry styles and their foundations is stark, yet they are true stories. In the coming chapters, we will outline how God can restore to survivors a sense of safety, a sense of self, and a place within community so that we can be like Rev. Lewis and support God's divine work in people's lives.

Encountering Stories

The hope and difficulty of recovery from horrors is impossible without attending the real stories of people interacting with one another in the world. Stories are integral to our communities as human beings; our stories of past memories are the cement that bind our families together. The narratives of fiction and film provide common ways of thinking and expressing the sentiment of our cultures and societies. Stories speak to us in ways that even the most carefully crafted prose cannot. While the most profound theological and philosophical texts can make us think in ways previously unavailable, stories present us with worlds to inhabit and to make sense of our own experience. Stories are also profound in allowing us to enter into the psyches of others; they provide a kind of personal knowledge that is not captured in the meaning of propositions. Rather, in the encounters that occur between ourselves and those painted by the narrative, we come to know them in a way that is similar to our knowledge of other persons in everyday experience.

The power of hearing other people's stories is illustrated by those times when people who know each other online through games finally meet up and get to know one another. Whereas a pair of gamers may know each other online as their gaming tags and an avatar of a monkey, when they meet to get to know each other offline, they meet a person who has a particular narrative. Getting to know the person and their story is a deeper form of knowledge than knowing someone's avatar and gaming name. In this book we want to get beyond dealing with the problems of trauma at a surface "avatar and gamer tag" level; we want to hear from people and their stories for the good of other people and the renewal of their stories.

Our contemporary popular culture has often been quicker to realize this fact than the church. Netflix is filled with stories of dystopian worlds, serving to narrate on the current state of our society and offer responses of its own. We consume hours of zombie-themed dramas, which point out that those humans who remain in the wake of pandemics are often dangerous and threatening to one another, even more so than the zombies. Movies like *Joker* make us fear that we are all potential Jokers in the making, given the "perfect storm" of abusive relationships, the poverty cycle, and the contempt of others. Documentaries on serial killers terrify us with the threat of the most perverse violence we could possibly imagine. These stories infiltrate our minds with narratives of uncertainty and hopelessness.

We cannot just think *about* horrors as some detached theological or sociological category to make sense of the world and we cannot build theological frameworks with which to understand God's response to horrors while remaining detached. We must allow ourselves to encounter the horrors of our fellow human beings, in all their messy particularity. While it may be harrowing to hear the depths of human experience, in hearing the stories of real suffering we see glimpses of the world that no amount of argument could persuade us of. Our exploration of horror therefore must hear from those who have lived through and survived horrors so that we may encounter something of their experience. Empathy, mercy, and mourning must always precede our response to horrors. This tenuous paradox of empathy and hope is exemplified in a story from Serene Jones, who tells of her work leading a women's self-defense class for survivors of domestic violence:

> I encountered this group of tough women several years ago when I helped to lead a women's self-defense class that met on Thursday nights in the all-purpose room in the parish house basement of my church . . . The last meeting of the self-defense class, as it happened, coincided with Maundy Thursday. In the UCC tradition, we mark this day in a service that celebrates the Last Supper and tells, in gory Gospel detail, the long tale of Christ's betrayal . . . That evening, I was surprised when four women from the class appeared at the church's front door and slipped into back pews just in time for the start of the service. Two sat alone, two together, and as they lost themselves in the growing darkness of the liturgy, they all wept, silently, profusely . . . But when it came time to leave, they seemed neither diminished nor depleted: to the contrary, they seemed thankful to have been there, to have heard the story, and to have cried together . . . Rather than provoking fear, the story-ritual had nourished them . . . That nourishment flowed from a strong, positive connection they felt with Jesus in the midst of his passion. Far from cultivating a victimlike reaction, their identification with him appeared to lift them up by bringing them down, and to strengthen their spirits by drawing forth tears . . . Mari's comment

struck me as significant: "I get it," she had said. "He gets me. He knows."[9]

We seek to hear the stories of those who have grappled with the profound existential questions that occur in living through horrors, to hear their stories of recovery in tandem with God's speech into—and works within—this situation, in order to gain theological insight from the ways in which the God of all comfort has brought new life from deep pain.

We must also acknowledge, however, that trauma doesn't fit into tidy definitions—while thinking of the world as made up of "good guys" and "bad guys," or "victims" and "perpetrators" may fit a certain narrative, the reality is that horror is more complex than this. Many of those who are horror makers are themselves survivors and victims. Unless we are prepared to encounter the range of human experience, we cannot begin to comprehend the ways in which trauma and horror have affected our common humanity.

Just as stories help us to identify the extent of our crisis, they must also inform our response. The church cannot be content to allow serial killer dramas and dystopian TV series to tell our story for us. A church defiant in hope must learn to acknowledge the reality of life's horrors while telling the beautiful story of our redemption through the work of the Trinity; we must find ways of understanding our place in this good news narrative that do not negate the severity of horror, but also do not give in to the nihilism of our culture. We tell our story boldly and hopefully but with empathy and compassion, knowing that *good* news will take a whole lifetime to transform us. Throughout the book our encounters with experiences of horror are therefore brought into the healing context of life with the God of all comfort that we find in the pages of Scripture.

Confronting the reality of horrors may provide us with a bleak and desperate diagnosis of our world. Yet, such a diagnosis cannot be the final word. While many may feel removed from God's life-giving presence, the Trinitarian God does not sit back and watch the world crumble. God the Father mourns with the suffering of his people, God the Son experiences our very humanity and suffers alongside us (Heb 4), and God the Spirit draws us together as one in Christ (1 Cor 12)—God brings hope through suffering. There is no horror too great from which God cannot bring goodness and beauty. Thus, while we seek to take seriously the reality of life's despair, we also seek to provide a vision of recovery that is rooted in hope.

9. Jones, *Trauma and Grace*, 75–77.

The paradox of taking despair seriously while hoping defiantly is given powerful voice in the story of Andrew, an adult male survivor of childhood sexual abuse, who describes his healing experience of "warm tears":

> In therapy I learned to face my brokenness, and several things happened: I walked away from the "victory only" crowd, I found a richer drama in the theology of lament, and I began to accept my own tears. Very few people were willing to hear my messy story. I had been part of a church that never mentioned sexual abuse—no one named it for survivors, and it became clear that my testimony would never be welcomed . . . I had another breakthrough when my counsellor asked me to reflect on the past months. I told him, "My tears flow warm and free now." . . . I wasn't crying anymore, I was weeping. My counsellor smiled and comfortingly said, "You've absorbed the toxin." . . . I had a graduation that day, and those words were the best commencement speech I'd ever heard . . . Because I live in a twisted and selfish world, I will walk with a limp for the rest of my life. Some pain remains. But the faith I now enjoy has been "freshly caught." I own it. It has been deeply refined. I journey with the God of the limping-in-between.[10]

The triune God of grace witnesses our sorrow, joins us in "warm tears," and makes the hope of his healing known in the caverns of our horrors and trauma. But for the tears to flow and the healing to come, we first have to learn, like Andrew, to face our own brokenness. "There is no other way to the Sunday of his joy and victory, and ours, than through his and our Sabbath of sorrow and defeat."[11] Let us now turn to confront the reality of horrors and trauma.

10. Schmutzer et al., *Naming Our Abuse*, 83, 85, 120.
11. Lewis, *Between Cross and Resurrection*, 426.

2

Horrors, Trauma, and Recovery

I f there is one thing to know about horrors and trauma, it is that it often feels impossible to navigate the aftermath. Horrors and trauma are by nature profoundly disorienting. The combat veteran Tim O'Brien describes the disorientation of horrors and trauma this way:

> War has the feel—the spiritual texture—of a great ghostly fog, thick and permanent. There is not clarity. Everything swirls . . . Order blends into chaos . . . The vapors suck you in. You can't tell where you are, or why you're there, and the only certainty is over-whelming ambiguity. In war you lose your sense of the definite . . .[1]

O'Brien gives powerful voice with these words to the disorienting altera-tions of consciousness that occur for persons who survive horrors and trau-matic events. This swirling chaos in the aftermath of horrors and trauma is all too often like Lucy's travels in *The Voyage of the Dawn Treader* to the Dark Island, also chillingly called the Island Where Nightmares Come True. C. S. Lewis paints a haunting picture of a scene where the sailors of the Dawn Treader furiously paddle to escape this dark, chaotic island of nightmares coming to life:

> Drinian's hand shook on the tiller and a line of cold sweat ran down his face. The same idea was occurring to everyone on board. "We shall never get out, never get out," moaned the rowers . . . The stranger, who had been lying in a huddled heap on the deck, sat up and burst out into a horrible screaming laugh.[2]

1. Quoted in Herman, *Trauma and Recovery*, 53.
2. Lewis, *Voyage of the Dawn Treader*, 193–94.

In the middle of such disorientation, in the middle of how horrors and trauma feel like the entry into an island of nightmares, it often feels like all we can do is to whisper with Lucy, "Aslan, Aslan, if ever you loved us at all, send us help now."[3]

Like Tim O'Brien's "great ghostly fog" and Lucy's narrow escape from the Dark Island, recovery from horrors and trauma require that we acknowledge that making a start feels overwhelming and difficult. Before we are ready to confront the reality of horror and ask how the church might respond to this reality, it will help to be clear on precisely what the problem is. "Trauma," "horror," "suffering" are all concepts that are used vaguely and imprecisely; it can sometimes be difficult to identify what horrors and trauma are, let alone what we can do about them. If we don't know what the problem is, it will be difficult to identify a response. Imagine going to see the doctor and before you've had chance to sit down, let alone open your mouth and describe your problem, a course of antibiotics is thrust into your hands: "Take three times a day with food; make sure you finish the course; if there are any problems ring the number on the packet. Next patient please!" Or, suppose your doctor was a little more patient than this and waited to hear you tell her that you were feeling "a little under the weather," before proceeding to prescribe strong painkillers. We would be worried about the efficacy of this doctor's treatment. Likewise, if the church is to take seriously its need to respond to life's horrors, we must not do this blindly or glibly—we must not assume that we understand if we haven't taken the time to listen and reflect. In other words, we need a diagnosis and an understanding of the pathologies before we can work with God's medicine for the wounds we have suffered.

First, consider the difference between the reality of horror and our response to it. *Horror,* at least as we use the term, refers to any damage or evil done to one person by another. *Trauma response* describes the survivor's unique responses to horrors. Why is the difference important? The reality is that people respond to particular horrors in varying ways. For some, a violent assault on their own person may generate trauma responses, whereas for others, the experience of witnessing horrific events in others may trigger trauma responses, while still other people will suffer neither response from the same experiences. Both horrors and trauma responses always involve the person; the person is always at the center of our concern. The difference lies in the vantage point. Horrors are third-personal, whereas

3. Lewis, *Voyage of the Dawn Treader,* 194.

trauma responses are first-personal. That is, you might think of horrors as "event-centered" whereas trauma responses are "experience-centered": the former describes all manner of persons in catastrophe, whereas the latter describes what it is like for a particular someone to suffer a catastrophe *from their perspective*. It is important to note that "trauma response" doesn't mean that these experiences are within our control; experiences of trauma occur in the person as an involuntary, preverbal, precognitive reaction to an event of overwhelming violence.[4] Moreover, "trauma response" does not imply a decision one makes *after* a horror is over; rather, survivors respond to their horrors both *during the event* and *after the event*. This means that trauma has a "double-structure," or more pointedly, is a "double-wound."[5] The survivor is confronted with a horror (the traumatic event) in which they are powerless, and as a result, develop a trauma response during the event *that continues even after the event is over*. This "suffering that remains" is the defining trait of traumatic stress.[6]

Trauma responses are resilient adaptations to impossible situations. Trauma responses are the mind and body's attempt to mitigate the fall-out from horrors. The problem, however, is that there is no "one-to-one" correspondence between horrors and trauma responses. Each horror may trigger a cascade of traumas or not. In addition, the nature of the events (sudden vs. chronic, by a stranger vs. a trusted family member), as well as a person's previous history, also shape the kind of responses that it triggers in the mind and body. Despite these predictors, the truth is that we just don't know why some people have traumatic responses and others don't, because avoiding a trauma response has nothing to do with one's inner moral courage. If the horror is great enough, anyone and everyone will develop a traumatic response, and it is difficult to say what amount of preparation could avoid such a response. Traumas are, by definition, *overwhelming*: you can't prepare sufficiently to withstand them. In this sense, developing a trauma response is not in any sense a sign of weakness or failure, but of profound resilience and adaptation in the face of impossible circumstances. But difference in response doesn't change the nature of the initial horror. So, we need to keep these two concepts distinct when we think about what exactly the problem is.

4. Van der Kolk, *Body Keeps the Score*, 39–102.

5. Rambo, *Spirit and Trauma*, 7; Caruth, *Unclaimed Experience*, 3.

6. Arel and Rambo, eds., *Post-Traumatic Public Theology*, 3.

In what follows, we outline our psychological-theological model for describing horrors, trauma responses, and the key connection between the two.[7] We seek to draw together insights from theology, psychology, and medical literature to give a clear account of these concepts. The theological description of both horrors and trauma responses is carried out relative to God the Trinity's creative and redemptive goals for each human being. We are all images of God with creative, moral, and relational capacities; from the perspective of redemption, we are oriented towards becoming images of Christ in union with God. This creation-redemption framework is the reference point for the work that follows. In light of the paradigms that we offer in what follows, we will explore how to work towards recovery from horrors and traumas *together with the Trinity and the church.*[8]

Horrors

Horrors may be immense events or cumulative thickets of smaller commonplace ones. Often, they are a dark combination of both. Immense horrors are usually one-off events such as a physical assault or a rape. Commonplace horrors are also events, although these events sustain a prolonged pattern of chronic abuse and neglect. As such, they are subtle and covert, but are no less capable of devastation in the long run than immense horrors. Examples include being subjected to ongoing controlling behaviors in which one's domestic captor restricts time with friends, access to money, or the ability to take initiative in terms of family and educational opportunities. Targeted verbal, emotional, or physical abuse are also examples of commonplace horrors. They are common in that people suffer them in the ordinary course of life, and, considered in isolation, no one of them seems as overtly disruptive as, say, the case of physical assault. For example, one instance of bullying in the workplace may not generate the need for immediate psychiatric intervention. The problem is that commonplace horrors are common, and what makes them horrors is their cumulative effects as

---

7. This model is a revision and extension of the proposals in Harrower, *God of All Comfort.* However, due to our concern for brevity and in order for this present book to be less of a technical work and more widely read, we have left some of the finer distinctions and discussions to that work.

8. In what follows we assume the use of best practice medical and psychological care in tandem with what we propose. This present work aims to integrate the finest resources and practices from medical and theological sciences for the sake of providing excellent Christian care for one another.

sustained frequent events. "Prolonged exploitation" is a way to capture the essence of commonplace horrors.[9]

Sadly, another reason why we refer to them as commonplace is that they are more likely to be tolerated or go unchallenged by witnesses such as the workmates of the person being bullied; whereas immense horrors like a severe physical assault are less likely to be tolerated by witnesses who have the capacity to intervene in them. The cumulative effects of these events undermine a person's moral, relational, and creative capacities. Psychiatrist Judith Lewis Herman writes that "survivors of prolonged abuse develop characteristic personality changes, including deformations of relatedness and identity."[10]

Perhaps we find the language of deformation too strong or too shocking. Our shock drives home the point—sustained commonplace horrors are horrors because they have devastating effects on survivors. Survivors may develop symptoms across the entire breadth of their attitudes, interactions, and approaches to "work, the world, man[kind] and God."[11] Naturally, we do not take the language of deformation to be pejorative, nor as an evaluation of the person—survivors are not deformed people, however, the coping strategies they currently employ may be. The effects of trauma are deformed, not the person. The trauma experience is a deformation but the person who suffers it is categorically not. Negative coping strategies such as self-medication, or avoidance of intimacy, are the focus of the deformation language used by trauma specialists. The language of deformation also brings home the point that something has been lost, and therefore the events, the coping mechanism deformations, and their symptoms require intervention and a long road to recovery.

Complex Post Traumatic Stress Disorder is a common category used to identify the effects of commonplace horrors such as domestic abuse. Complex PTSD "involves challenges with shame, trust, self-esteem, identity and regulating emotions. [It] has different coping strategies. These include alcohol and drug use, self-harm, over- or under-eating, over-work etc., [and] affects emotional and physical health, wellbeing, relationships and daily functioning."[12] Though these affects strongly parallel the impact of PTSD related to intense once-off events, the difference between complex

9. Herman, *Trauma and Recovery*, 122.

10. Herman, *Trauma and Recovery*, 119.

11. Emmanuel Tanay, cited in Herman, *Trauma and Recovery*, 120.

12. Blue Knot Foundation, "What is Complex Trauma?"

PTSD and noncomplex PTSD is that whereas noncomplex PTSD mostly tends to revolve around fear, alienation, shame, and memory dissociations related to more tangible encounters, complex PTSD hides in the shadows of how a survivor's earliest or deepest bonds of attachment have harbored developmental heartache and created dysfunctional styles of relating that profoundly shape the survivor's personality into the present.[13]

The significance of complex PTSD for overwhelming and impairing a person's perception of the world and making moral and creative decisions has been highlighted in many legal and medical cases, such as the case of Sally Challen, a woman recently acquitted of murdering her husband after years of experiencing abuse.[14] Sally suffered years of manipulation, having her spending monitored, travel curtailed, and was insulted frequently in front of family and friends.[15] Psychiatrists judged that years of suffering such abuse culminated in "an abnormality of the mind that substantially impaired her mental responsibility for her acts."[16] Culminative thickets of horrors might seem insignificant, but over a long period of time, they might still result in severe disorder. The culminative effects of years of suffering and abuse eventually rose to the level of an immense horror of suffering complex PTSD, which in turn had devastating consequences.

Often times, commonplace horrors can occur within our family of origin, which then sets the stage for immense horrors to occur in other related contexts. Consider the story of Daniel Gorski, an adult male survivor of childhood sexual abuse. Daniel tells the story of how he endured chronic relational dysfunction within his family of origin as his father and mother consistently denigrated his masculinity:

> I was the youngest of six kids—a sister followed by five boys. As the baby, I was sometimes regarded as a spoiled brat by jealous siblings when they felt I was treated with favor. My parents used to say that had they had a second girl, they would have stopped procreating. Usually uttered in a moment of anger over the latest explosion of fraternal masculinity, that statement holds painful subtexts and implications for me . . . What followed was a commitment not to exhibit "boy traits" that would cause trouble.[17]

13. Herman, *Trauma and Recovery*, 248–61. See also Herman, *Trauma and Recovery*, 115–29; Van der Kolk, *Body Keeps the Score*, 149–68.

14. Faulkner, "Coronation Street."

15. Burns, " 'My mum killed my dad with a hammer but I want her freed.'"

16. Burns, " 'My mum killed my dad with a hammer but I want her freed.'"

17. Schmutzer et al., *Naming Our Abuse*, 32.

Daniel continues to recount that the cumulative commonplace horror of having his last born masculinity silenced under the shadow of his older siblings caused him to aspire to an imaginary ideal of chivalry, gentleness, and self-sacrifice. Daniel then tells how the fantasy of being a "good boy" left him vulnerable to being preyed on by his Catholic priest. The post-traumatic fallout of the sexual abuse constituted an immense horror for Daniel. He had experienced a cumulative commonplace horror in his family of origin. He then experienced an immense horror as a survivor of sexual abuse and developed complex PTSD.

Immense horrors are perverted and damaging actions by at least one person upon another. As species of evil, they are profoundly wounding *events* and have *necessary* consequences in any image of God. Horrors are true and real events regardless of how we (or those who may deny their impact) perceive them subjectively; in other words, horrors are objective events with effects in space and time.[18] Horrors affect us on a number of levels: on the emotional, intellectual, spiritual, and bodily registers. For example, on an emotional level we are shocked by horrors and want to pull back in disgust from them because intellectually we sense that they are per-versions of nature and prevent us from flourishing in ways that we would have otherwise.

An instance of a horror could be a physical assault such as a stabbing. The assault is sourced in a malevolent and sinful will towards the assaulted; it involves someone acting in ways contrary to their nature as an image of God; the blade's puncture literally introduces a wound into one's body and the loss of one's physical integrity; the body experiences something for which it was not designed by God. The blade's puncture becomes an undeniable part of personal history. The immediate consequences of the stabbing, such as staggering, bleeding, and nearly dying are literally written in blood into one's physiological, psychological, spiritual, and social story. Parts of one's body are lost and cannot be replaced; in addition, there are long-term health implications to be recovered from. As a result of these events and consequences, neither the survivor nor the perpetrator can ever go back to their previous course of life as it was before the stabbing.

---

18. What follows is a revised version of the taxonomy outlined in Harrower, *God of All Comfort*, 24–45. It is dependent on the work of a number of scholars, including Aquinas, *Summa Theologiae*, vol. 8, 1a qq. 44–49 and vol. 18, 1a2ae 18–21; Herman, *Trauma and Recovery*; Fahy, *Philosophy of Horror*; Carroll, *Philosophy of Horror*; and Rambo, "Spirit and Trauma."

Life cannot be as it was before because the reality of being brutalized and surviving the attack has objective consequences: there is a physical wound that may or may not heal, scarring and physical complications for the body. There are emotional, social, spiritual, and intellectual wounds too. Further subjective consequences are also generated: these are what we refer to as "trauma responses," which we unpack in more detail shortly.

In a nutshell, what makes this act of being stabbed a *horror* is that it is an unnatural and uncanny event and with real consequences for both the victim and perpetrator. Because it is real despite how we or others may perceive it, it is an objective event. Likewise, the trauma response is objective in the sense that it begins inside the event of the horror. But the horror is a horror *universally* for whoever experiences it, even if others minimize or deny its impact. Trauma does not share this universal quality because trauma is an incredibly particular experience that is always unique to the perspective of the person who experiences it. This means that horrors are distinguished from trauma responses because trauma responses are consequent to horrors and varied in their effects. In other words, horrors generate trauma reactions.

We can be more specific here in defining an immense horror. Immense horrors can be identified by examining (i) their effects on the person, and (ii) whether they aim at a person's good.

First, immense horrors have permanent *effects* on those who suffer from them. These effects are permanent and irreversible, stemming from the fact that what has been lost by disruption or destruction cannot be fully restored. While some sense of progress might be made in recovering from horrors, one can only move forwards; the past self cannot be regained. Recall the character of Gollum from *The Hobbit* and *The Lord of the Rings*. Gollum was afflicted and assaulted by all manner of visible and invisible beings, with the result that he becomes a ghostly and ghastly version of a hobbit. The effects on Gollum are a parallel to what horrors do to a human person: they whither the person. This is not to say that human survivors of horrors become grotesque in the way that Gollum did. They are not deformed. Rather, horrors profoundly undermine the relational, moral, and creative inheritance of a person made in the image of God. Horrors at the hands of others inhibit a person's enjoyment of their robustness as an image of God because they disrupt the natural processes of flourishing morally, relationally, and creatively as God intended. What makes a horror a horror, then, is that the survivor will not flourish in the same way as if the horror had not occurred. But paradoxically, this is also precisely what makes recovery so beautiful and subversive to evil's intent. To be sure, the image of God is not and can never be lost in a survivor; yet, they will not flourish as God's image as if there had never been any horror. From now on, their flourishing as God's image will take a "horror-surviving shape," or, as Marilyn McCord Adams puts it, "going to hell and back with God is one shape that an overall beatific intimate relationship with God can take."[19] Those of us who are privileged to witness such a subversive transformation of horrors into unthinkable beauty can only stand in awe at the courage and resilience of survivors who brilliantly image God through their suffering. The course of their lives is permanently sidetracked, and although this new track will be unimaginably good when joined to the work and will of the triune God, it will not be what it would have been had the horror never occurred. To illustrate this, consider the story of Wendy told by her friend Serene:

> It had been raining all morning, and the earth gave way softly as Wendy and I dug into it with spoons from her kitchen. We were quite a sight: two women, huddled under a black umbrella in the corner of a yard, digging . . . and crying. Wendy had been bleeding for three days, and she looked ghostly; she had just miscarried an eight-week pregnancy (her fourth) and was grieving not only this present pain but her dimming hope of ever having children. In her grandmother's handkerchief she had collected a few small remnants of her loss—a combination of bloody tissue and dashed dreams. We placed these in the earth and tried to think of something to say, but words would not come . . . She told me, ". . .I find myself walking around my kitchen bleeding away a life that I quite intentionally chose to make . . . and I am completely powerless to save it . . . I cannot stop the blood, Serene. It keeps pouring out of me and then washing away, lost. I cannot staunch its flow; it seeps out through the pores of my will which so ardently fight to stop it."[20]

Wendy's experience of suffering several miscarriages has left a traumatic mark on her hope of bearing children. No new child can replace the ones she has lost. We can imagine that even if Wendy were given the joy of a healthy child who came to play on the very grass where the unborn sibling was buried, something of the sorrow of her miscarriages would remain.

19. Adams, "Plantinga on 'Felix Culpa,'" 137.
20. Jones, *Trauma and Grace*, 127, 155.

Wendy's love for her children as a mother who brightly images God can only be honored in light of the horrors she has survived. Horrors have effects on survivors that must be recognized and honored.

Secondly, horrors do not *aim at a person's good*. It is here that the *theological* nature of horrors adds something to a clinical diagnosis. For the problem of immense horror is not found *only* in the person's response to these events; horrors are bad not only because they are experienced as so but because they are distortions of something holy. The profanity of horror is that it aims at disrupting or destroying life and flourishing in a person or community. In other words, while human beings bear the image of God and were made to live in fullness of relationship with God, horrors aim at undermining or destroying God's good purposes. We are also made to live in relationship with one another, in communities that reflect God's goodness and draw us into deeper relationship with God. An immense horror undermines an individual's God-given right to fully flourish in community with God and with their fellow human being.

Typically, these profane acts of horror-making are intentional, although not always. Horror-makers sometimes intend on destroying goodness by elevating their own interests and pleasure above that of others. Forces of evil and demonic powers also play a role here. As well as individual horror-makers having an intent which aims away from a person's goodness, there are other agents of malevolence at work in the world. While we will not dwell in much detail here, it is important to acknowledge there is demonic and evil intent behind many of the acts of horror in our world; horror arises through a twisted or distorted will in which God's good creation is subjected to the powers of evil. Consider the story of psychologist Dan Allender, who tells about how his work with survivors of childhood sexual abuse has caused him to change his opinion about the significance of demonic forces:

> When I wrote *The Wounded Heart*, I believed evil existed but it was not my calling to directly address its presence or consequences. If asked then what my therapeutic approach was, I'd say I simply didn't want to consider the presence of evil other than in systemic and impersonal terms. Then I changed. How? By listening to my clients. Through their stories I have come to the conclusion that evil is very much at work in the world, in our mind, and in our body.[21]

---

21. Allender, *Healing the Wounded Heart*, 35.

In addition to noting that horrors are rooted in someone's malevolent will, whether human or demonic, sometimes horrors may also be rooted in neglect or misguided goodwill. It is also important to see here that an act can be aimed not at a person's good, while arising from seemingly good intentions. Many cases of religiously induced trauma seem to be of this category. Take, for example, the tragic story of a male member of a biblical fundamentalist church who was encouraged in the name of godly discipline to punish a small child to the point of physical abuse for a period of hours:

> The little girl in the diapers, would not receive her discipline. She cried and cried and [he] kept hitting her, trying to make her tears stop. "I wasn't sure of myself," he recalls, "so I kept calling [a fellow church member]. I'd say, "She's doing the same thing. I don't know what to do." He told me, "You spank her till she breaks." So I spanked her and I spanked her and I spanked her. I was crying. She was crying. Her parents were crying. I called again. He said: "Spank her till she breaks." But [she] didn't break, and after four hours, [he] couldn't continue.[22]

While some parents and caregivers justify their abusive actions as something that is *good for the child*, it is important to see that these acts are still cases of immense horror because they clearly do not, in fact, aim at a child's good. In other words, people with good intentions can be mistaken about the goodness of their actions and can be the cause of immense horror, because they have a deluded and distorted sense of what goodness is.

In a nutshell, the horror of horrors is that we become *less able and available for good relationships, works, wonder, and worship* than what we could be. This absence of fullness might also lead to a number of other consequences. For instance, pain may be associated with the direct and indirect losses brought about by horrors; this pain acts as a withering force upon a person's vitality as well as a reminder of their wounds. The affected person may also be less available and able to help other image bearers and communities to flourish. Lastly, as we explore in more detail shortly, one distinguishing feature of *immense* horrors is that they always generate trauma responses in the individual. One way of knowing whether commonplace horrors have risen to the level of immense horror, then, is to consider the effects on the individual.

22. Greven, *Spare the Child*, 37.

Trauma Responses

Whereas our definition of horrors focuses on the necessary damage it does to a person or community and the ways in which actions can undermine a person's flourishing, our definition of trauma responses aims to focus and keep our attention on the survivor's unique experience of the horror and its effects. In order to understand trauma responses, going back to our example of the stabbing may help to illuminate.

The event of the stabbing is connected with evil in that the agency of the perpetrator and the damage to the survivor are both real evils—real absences of good natural things in both the horror-maker and the survivor. So, there is the event and the subsequent trauma, yet evil pervades them both. The survivor's response, the trauma response, however, is distinct from the event. It is distinct from the event because, unlike the stabbing, it cannot be perceived externally but only through the survivor's experience. This response is not voluntary but is generated by the resilience of the survivor's body, spirit, and mind as the survivor experiences and perceives the horror of gathering all these faculties together to confront an impossible set of circumstances. A trauma response is a stress reaction to horrors. According to the American Psychiatric Association's DSM-5, it is a response to any "exposure to actual or threatened death, serious injury, or sexual violence."[23]

This stress reaction occurs to varying degrees regardless of the kind and type of triggering event: the horror may be mostly internally perceived or externally experienced. A trauma response is very natural and understandable: being sensitive to this response may be a helpful step for post-traumatic growth.[24] However, our response to horrors may become stressfully problematic and develop into a number of forms of PTSD, which are some of the most powerful and problematic effects of evil. The problems it generates include spiritual problems, which is why a spiritual ministry is needed in addition to a biomedical one. As noted above, whereas a number

---

23. American Psychiatric Association, *Diagnostic and Statistical Manual of Mental Disorders: DSM-5*, 830, cited in Carlson, "Lament," 50.

24. Writing about the five elements that contribute to post-traumatic growth, Seligman notes that understanding our response to trauma and the subsequent questions it raises is not problematic nor pathological but helpful. Firstly, "to *understand the response to trauma itself*: shattered beliefs about the self, others, the future. This is, I want to emphasize, the normal response to trauma; it is not a symptom of post-traumatic stress disorder, nor does it indicate a defect of character." Seligman, *Flourish*, 162.

of people speak about "a trauma" as the event that is traumatic or of trauma in general terms, we prefer to distinguish the event (horrors) and the first-personal experience of the event for survivors (a trauma response).

The trauma response to a horror largely has to do with the overwhelming nature of the event from the perspective of surviving it. It is overwhelming because it is wholly unnatural and goes against our human makeup: we were not designed to cope with horrors. The images of God were designed for wholeness, relationship, wholesomeness, and flourishing. We were made for the best of the cosmos, not its worst. However, in this life we are confronted with some of the worst potential that lies in people. The uncanny and unnatural nature of horrors means we find them overwhelming.

Because horrors are overwhelming events, our brains are unable to integrate the event into their way of understanding and coping with the world. As a result, horrors and trauma create what psychiatrist Judith Herman calls "alterations of consciousness."[25] In terms of perception, "trauma results in a fundamental reorganization of the way mind and brain manage perceptions. It changes not only how we think and what we think about, but also our very capacity to think."[26] Memories of the event continue to haunt the person, as the brain constantly tries to comprehend and integrate what occurred—but cannot. For this reason, "trauma . . . carries the individual beyond the shock of the first moment. The trauma is a repeated suffering of the event, but it is also a continual leaving of its site. The traumatic reexperiencing of the event thus carries with it . . . the impossibility of knowing that first constituted it."[27]

There is an indirect aspect to trauma responses. Their effects on people and groups cannot be mapped in a clear, linear, and causal manner. There are unforeseen and surprising consequences to trauma responses. Thus, the full impact of trauma will never be fully understood. The stress reaction to horrors involves an excessive response in which its intensity and scope of impact exceeds one-to-one correlations.[28] Consider the story of Leah, a young woman with a traumatic past who experienced a traumatic response during her church's eucharistic celebration. As the pastor began

25. Herman, *Trauma and Recovery*, 1.

26. Van der Kolk, *Body Keeps the Score*, 21.

27. Caruth, "Introduction," in *Trauma*, 10.

28 Carr integrates the indirect aspect of trauma responses in his definition of what he calls trauma, which is "an overwhelming, haunting experience of disaster so explosive in its impact that it cannot be directly encountered and influences an individual/group's behaviour and memory in indirect ways." Carr, *Holy Resilience*, 7.

the administration of communion with bread and wine, "Leah's body grew rigid. Her nail-bitten fingers began to twist the folded order of worship paper in her lap, her face assumed a frighteningly blank look, her fear was cold and palpable." A friend of Leah's was intrigued and disturbed that what she thought would be the most vulnerable and nourishing portion of their church service had become a moment of excruciating terror for Leah. The next week Leah told her friend what it was like for her to have this traumatic response:

> It happens to me, sometimes. I'm listening to the pastor, thinking about God and love, when suddenly I hear or see something, and it's as if a button gets pushed inside of me. In an instant, I'm terrified; I feel like I'm going to die or get hurt very badly. My body tells me to run away, but instead, I just freeze. Last week it was the part about Jesus' blood and body. There was a flash in my head, and I couldn't tell the difference between Jesus and me, and then I saw blood everywhere, and broken body parts, and I got so afraid I just disappeared. I thought the bathroom might be safe, but even it scared and confused me. I forgot my name. I forgot the hot and cold.[29]

The indirect consequences of trauma responses include how the survivor tries to cope as they live in its shadow of horrors. Because the survivor will anticipate more events like the one they repetitively reexperience, they will naturally try to protect themselves from further horrors. However, these protective behaviors can be maladaptive.[30] Negative coping behaviors such as unwarranted withdrawal from others, anxious or insecure attachments to other people, self-medication, and engaging in high-risk behaviors often accompany trauma responses. These often compound the real losses of self and community in the wake of horrors. We may unwittingly ingrain and compound evil's complex stains and deformities in our lives.

The primary experience of horrors, as well as the trauma responses, generates problems to do with alienation or fractured-ness. The alienation stems from the violation of the person's sense of how the world should work and their place in the world. The alienation caused by the perpetrator's sinfulness and actions occurs on a number of registers. The first is that survivors are alienated from a robust sense of wholeheartedly embracing and freely trusting their instinctive drive to act and flourish within safety.

29. Jones, *Trauma and Grace*, 7.
30. Van der Kolk, *Body Keeps the Score*, 92.

Secondly, they are alienated from an integrated and secure sense of themselves. And thirdly from meaningful and engaged relationships with other people. Trauma threatens safety, fragments one's sense of self, and isolates one from the joys of life in community.

Dealing with the three issues is essential to recovery from trauma. Our proposals on recovery will therefore concentrate on: (1) recovering a sense of safety with God and flourishing from within this relationship, and (2) rediscovering a vital connection to God's community and flourishing through meaningful engagement within it and with the world.[31]

---

31. These points integrate Trinitarian theology with psychiatrist Judith Lewis Herman's foundational work on recovery from trauma, and are a development of earlier work in Harrower's *God of All Comfort*.

3

Losing Safety and Losing God

Attachment and Community:
Flourishing with Others

U nderstanding the nature of trauma and horrors is a good place to start in building a trauma-safe church, but the discussion is still too general. If we are to minister like the Good Shepherd, who recognizes every sheep in the fold and understands the sheep's wounds specifically and individually, then we must do more to understand the damage of trauma. Reflecting on the erosion of safety in the midst of trauma will help us to see more clearly the wounds that survivors live with.

Our flourishing as human beings is bound up in our sense of safety. For example, if we are hypervigilantly looking over our shoulders for the next source of threat, we cannot be at rest. The disruption caused by trauma experiences aims at undermining this sense of security and trust.[1] Consider the words of Susan Brison, as she lived in the aftermath of her assault and attempted murder:

> I was no longer the same person I had been before the assault, and one of the ways in which I seemed changed was that I had a different relationship to my body. My body was now perceived as the enemy . . . but . . . body and mind had become nearly indistinguishable. My mental state (typically depression) felt physiological, like lead in my veins, while my physical state (frequently, incapacitation by

1. By saying that trauma "aims at" undermining security we are indicating the teleological aspect of trauma in a broader Christian frame of reference. For more on this, see Harrower, *God of All Comfort*, ch. 3.

fear and anxiety) was the incarnation of a cognitive and emotional paralysis resulting from shattered assumptions about my safety in the world. The symptoms of PTSD gave the lie to the latent dualism that still informs society's most prevalent attitude to trauma, namely, that victims should buck up, put the past behind them, and get on with their lives. My hypervigilance, heightened startle response, insomnia, and the other PTSD symptoms were no more psychological, if that is taken to mean under my conscious control, than were my heart rate and blood pressure.[2]

Recovery of a visceral sense of safety is key to our flourishing. But we cannot regain this sense of safety in isolation; our security as human beings is bound up in our relationships with others. Both psychological science and Trinitarian theology show us that we need a strong attachment to a trustworthy person and the healthy behaviors that go with this in order to flourish.

There are four dimensions to reestablishing a sense of safety, given the insights of attachment theory. These are:

(1) establishing bodily safety,

(2) being safely loved,

(3) having safe boundaries, and,

(4) regaining big picture safety.

Without these four elements it will not be possible to recover a robust sense of safety in the wake of trauma. *Establishing bodily safety* focuses on retraining the body so that it does not anticipate harm where there is none. *Being safely loved* and *having safe boundaries* refer to our relational safety; recovering safety means becoming those who can be accepted by others and feel free to love others back. This can only happen when we feel safely loved in the context of safe boundaries. And *regaining big picture safety* requires regaining a global sense of security; that of feeling part of a universe which is not aimed only at destruction and loss.

We must acknowledge that this recovery is far from easy; an openness to others is a vulnerable posture to adopt, especially for those who know all too well that community is often the context in which safety is undermined. Yet precisely because horrors and trauma occur in community with others, our recovery must also take place in the context of relationship. Like

2. Brison, *Aftermath*, 44.

a doctor who tries to heal a broken arm by placing a cast on the leg, our efforts at recovery from horrors and trauma are misplaced if attempted in isolation from others. "It cannot be reiterated too often: *no one can face trauma alone.*"[3] Healing must happen where the wound has occurred: in relationships and in community with others and God. It will be helpful to dwell on the role of attachment in both the destruction of safety, as well as its recovery.

Establishing Bodily Safety

Before looking at the role of attachment in the loss and recovery of safety we must first acknowledge the primary role of the body in this recovery: "Recovery still begins, always with safety . . . safety always begins with the body. If a person does not feel safe in her body, she does not feel safe anywhere."[4] Like the primacy of our relationships with others in both establishing and losing safety, traumatic events always call bodily integrity into question. In fact, modern neuroscience shows that "the body keeps the score" in traumatic events, meaning that traumatic memories and sensations of past terror are quite literally "imprinted" on our skin.[5] More often than not, survivors feel the ongoing terror of their traumatic stress primarily as a bodily discomfort that feels nearly impossible to put into words. The fear involved in having survived horrors and living in the aftermath is felt for survivors in ways that cannot always be put into words and do not always manifest in the explicit beliefs of survivors. This is because there are some things that are just too horrible to consciously recall, put into words, or remember in a coherent way. Our bodies bear the deep wounds of trauma. Because trauma causes a "freeze" response deep in the "gut" of survivors, the terrors of traumatic memory get stored at a deeper level than rational thought. Trauma therefore does not operate like normal memory. In normal memory, there is a coherent beginning, middle, and end. In traumatic memory, it is a garbled mess of incoherent sensations that feel terrifying and have no narrative context. Traumatic stress is stored in human memory as a kind of fragmented, subconscious, embodied fog that feels so scary because, despite being so ambiguous and difficult to put into words, it is viscerally disruptive in the form of gut-wrenching sensations. The reason

3. Herman, *Trauma and Recovery*, 153, italics original.
4. Herman, *Trauma and Recovery*, 266, 269.
5. Van der Kolk, *Body Keeps the Score*.

why trauma feels so unsafe in this way is because the memories of terror are stored in the most basic, primitive level of human interaction where the wound of trauma has occurred, namely, *in the body*.

We will go into greater depth on the role of the body throughout our subsequent chapters. For now, it is imperative that we recognize that "traumatized people feel chronically unsafe inside their bodies: The past is alive in the form of gnawing interior discomfort. Their bodies are constantly bombarded by visceral warning signs."[6] This means that if we are to create trauma-safe churches, we must acknowledge that secure attachments and safe relationships do not happen in a vacuum: safe relationships are always enacted in a robustly *embodied* way that facilitates the empowerment of the other. Judith Herman summarizes well when she says that "helplessness and isolation are the core experiences of psychological trauma. Empowerment and reconnection are the core experiences of recovery."[7] That is, the powerlessness of surviving a traumatic event destroys a sense of safety because the survivor's autonomy over their own body and identity are called into question by the violence of another. This is precisely the opposite of what we were made for by God, namely, the exhilarating liberation and empowerment involved in owning our bodies, ourselves, and actively enjoying the freedom of safe relationships with others. In chapters 8, 9, and 10, we will offer some practical guidelines for how to make our churches places of bodily safety.

Being Safely Loved and Having Safe Boundaries[8]

Before we can reflect on the next two dimensions of safety (being safely loved and having safe boundaries), we must first understand the nature of human relationships that these dimensions seek to recover.

It is now widely recognized that one of the best ways to understand the role of connection with others for a sense of safety is through what is called "attachment theory." Over the last century, psychological science has shifted from viewing people as self-contained blank slates to viewing people as profoundly connected with others and shaped by relationships

6. Van der Kolk, *Body Keeps the Score*, 96–97.

7. Herman, *Trauma and Recovery*, 197.

8. We are happy to acknowledge that parts of this section are heavily influenced by Justin Barrett's lectures at the TheoPsych 1 Seminar, Fuller Theological Seminary, July, 2019.

from the very start of life.[9] As a result, we can recognize that even the tiniest infants experience a profound "interpersonal world" that is affected by a sense of connection (or "attachment") with their parents.[10] These early experiences have an enormous impact on how we relate to others as adults. It affects the friends we adopt, the spouses we choose, and the way we parent our own children.[11]

This shift to a relational psychology has led researchers to study the spectrum of impacts on behavior and health that stem from whether or not someone had (and has) unhealthy or healthy affection and caregiving attachments to other people. This way of thinking about human relationships assumes a certain understanding of what human beings are and how they operate, namely that we are programmed to seek bonds and relationships of affection with others (this applies to both receiving caregiving and also to being caregivers).[12] Psychologists tell us that human beings have an innate drive to value and relate to other people. For example, psychological data suggests that babies and toddlers have a basic orientation to relate to persons.[13] They look for faces and people in their environments, and they prefer people over other features of their environment such as shapes and colors.[14] In the absence of people, babies and toddlers get upset—really upset. They protest against this absence by crying and calling for attention. Being away from Mom or Dad—or worse, being lost without Mom or Dad—is their greatest fear. Leonard Shengold makes this point eloquently in his description of childhood abuse as a kind of "soul-murder" that calls basic family trust into question: "Without the inner picture of caring parents, how can one survive? . . . Every soul-murder victim will be wracked by the question 'Is there life without father and mother?'"[15]

The importance of relating to others is driven home by the fact that the best way to comfort a distressed child is to have another person comfort

9. Mitchell and Black, *Freud and Beyond.*

10. Stern, *Interpersonal World of the Infant.*

11. Most recently (and perhaps most excitingly), the force of our attachments with others have been confirmed by advances in neuroscience, where we can literally see our interpersonal connections occurring in the brain through tools such as fMRI brain scans. See Schore, *Affect Regulation and the Origin of the Self;* and Fosha et al., eds., *Healing Power of Emotion.*

12. Heard et al., *Attachment Therapy with Adolescents and Adults,* 218.

13. Barrett, *Cognitive Science, Religion, and Theology,* 64–67.

14. Barrett, *Cognitive Science, Religion, and Theology,* 64–67.

15. Shengold, *Soul Murder,* 315.

them, preferably their parents. As a result, even adults faced with trauma "spontaneously seek out their first source of comfort and protection. Wounded soldiers and raped women cry for their mothers, or for God."[16] Crying out "Mommy!" when faced with terror is not only understandable: it is completely natural. This research strongly suggests that from the outset of our lives, we are all made with an instinctive drive to seek out and relate to other people. In other words, it is *natural* for people to seek out other people and believe they are better off with other people around.[17] We were made to connect with others. Because this is a natural tendency that does not have to be learnt, we can observe that humans are naturally and instinctively wired to need and dynamically receive other people into their lives.

The drive for attachments of affection and caregiving means that there will be tremendous stress if these needs are not met. We know that the strength and reliability of the bonds we make with other people (especially our caregivers) in childhood profoundly shapes the kinds of relationships we are able to have in adulthood. Lacking strong relationships in childhood can lead to anxiety in forming relationships with others, or even an attempt to avoid meaningful relationship altogether.[18] In the end, a lack of strong relationship with others can undermine our sense of safety and security about ourselves in the world. Strong bonds create deep trust; by the same token, safety is scarce where friendships are few. In spite of all this, our innate drive for relationships is also incredibly positive because there is enormous scope for flourishing when these needs *are* met.[19]

All of this research raises important questions about the importance of relationships for human flourishing. The importance of attachments confronts us with our radical vulnerability and reliance on others. It confronts us with the joys and terrors of needing one another. Psychologists ask: "How does it come about that human beings seem to want to survive with wellbeing and enjoy using and developing their skills and talents in company with others who share the same interests?"[20] For it's not just babies, but human beings of all ages who need secure attachments to other people

---

16. Herman, *Trauma and Recovery*, 52.

17. Barrett, *Cognitive Science, Religion, and Theology*, 59.

18. Bowlby, 1969/1982, xi–xii, cited in Barrett, *Cognitive Science, Religion, and Theology*, 217.

19. Heard et al., *Attachment Therapy with Adolescents and Adults*, 218.

20. Heard et al., *Attachment Therapy with Adolescents and Adults*, 3.

because this provides us with a necessary sense of safety and security.[21] A sense of safety and security is so important that it is "one of life's natural forms of . . . happiness."[22] In other words, the human need for healthy, morally committed relationships with other people is not just a romantic notion about how nice people are. It is a basic component of human being.

We are relational beings who thrive and celebrate life when we are with other people and are focused on them. We might put it like this:

> Very little that is positive is solitary. When was the last time you laughed uproariously? The last time you felt indescribable joy? The last time you sensed profound meaning and purpose? . . . Even without knowing the particulars of these high points of your life, I know their form: all of them took place around other people.[23]

This observation is backed up by numerous experiments. For instance, it has been shown that eating chocolate with others is more pleasurable than eating it alone,[24] and that experiencing pain with others (especially with friends) can lead to a deeper sense of community and cooperation with them.[25] Beyond wanting to relate positively to visible persons, humans are also naturally inclined to seek after invisible persons. Developmental studies in children show that the interpersonal nature of human existence is not limited to physical beings but also includes beliefs about spiritual beings.[26] For example, many people have imaginary friends as children, which is an extension of sensing that there are invisible beings to whom we are related.[27] The thought that we might be related to invisible beings by choice and friendship lines up well with our instinct that invisible agents such as gods and angels actually exist. Whether visible or invisible, the others with whom we relate have a nearly immeasurable impact on our flourishing. We were made for healthy, secure attachments with other people and with God.

---

21. Knabb and Emerson, "Attachment Theory and the Grand Narrative of Scripture," 828.

22. "But it could equally be called love, security, gratitude, self-esteem, and any number of other labels for positive emotions." Mikulincer and Shaver, "Adult Attachment and Happiness," 834.

23. Seligman, *Flourish*, 20.

24. Boothby et al., "Shared Experiences Are Amplified."

25. Boothby et al., "Psychological Distance Moderates Amplification of Shared Experience"; and Boothby et al., "Shared Experiences Are Amplified."

26. For more on this, see Hay, with Nye, *Spirit of the Child*.

27. Barrett, *Cognitive Science, Religion, and Theology*, 67.

So, then, safety is essential to human flourishing and our relationships of attachment with others is one of the key factors in this sense of safety. This leads us to consider the next two dimensions of safety: Our attachments with others are determined by the right combination of (i) being safely loved and (ii) having safe boundaries. Without feeling safely loved and having safe boundaries in our relationships, we become insecurely attached and lose our sense of safety with others. And without a sense of safety, recovery from horrors and trauma becomes nearly impossible.

We can see the significance of attachments for safety by looking at the story of creation. In Genesis, we find an abundant God who makes Adam and Eve for intimate communion with one another and with God. We read that they were "naked and unashamed" (Gen 2:25). We then read the tragic story of the fall in which Adam and Eve open their eyes, realize they are naked, and the "cover-up" begins. By relishing the beauty of Adam and Eve's original vulnerability, the image of covering nakedness with fig leaves helps us to better understand the losses involved in hiding from God and one another. This shows us that we can only understand the tragedy of horrors and trauma against the backdrop of original benevolence and goodness. Just as we can only understand horrors in light of the backstory of God's "Edenic ideal," so too the debris and aftermath of trauma can only be understood in light of how we were made for healthy attachments.[28] Learning about healthy human attachments helps us understand what is at stake when trauma threatens a sense of safety.

What's more, because we are so profoundly shaped by our early attachments in a way that creates certain styles of relating in the present, creating safety after trauma will always involve tending to the particular ways that our wounds manifest uniquely *to us*. This is why there is no "one-size-fits-all" approach to trauma care: my wounds have to be seen as *my* wounds, and your wounds have to be seen as *your* wounds. And we cannot know our traumas unless we are willing to know how trauma manifests as attachments gone wrong. Part of what makes horrors and trauma so unbearable is the intricate ways they are unrepeatably expressed according to each person's unique past (and present) relationships. In this sense, creating a trauma-safe church requires that we be willing to zero in on the unique stories of each individual seeking safety. What was *your* mother like? What was *your* father like? How did your relationship with them leave *you* open or sheltered to horrors and trauma? How does this disrupt or enrich *your*

28. Harrower, *God of All Comfort*, 7.

relationships in the present? While the majority of answers to these questions need to be tended in a professional therapeutic setting, we have to be able to hold these tensions in our churches and in our relationships. This requires a basic understanding of the difference between secure and insecure attachments according to attachment theory.

Put simply, attachment theory posits what we have been exploring: we flourish based on feeling safe in our connections with others. We feel safe with others when we know that we are (i) being safely loved with (ii) safe boundaries in place.[29] Psychologist Dan Allender describes feeling safely loved with safe boundaries by looking at the parent-child relationship: "Beginning with the first day of life outside the womb, every child is asking two core questions: 'Am I loved?' and 'Can I get my own way?' These two questions mark us throughout life, and the answers we receive set the course for how we live."[30] Being safely loved is the sense of connection we feel when we know that we are seen by another and that someone else is "in tune" with our needs. It answers the question "Am I loved?" When parents are attuned to their children, powerful emotional connections are created that "permit one human to 'be with' another in the sense of sharing likely inner experiences on almost a continual basis. This is exactly our experience of feeling-connectedness, of being in attunement with another. It feels like an unbroken line."[31] Safely loving someone means resonating with the feelings of another because you want to share life with them. Being in tune with the emotions of others creates connection.

But being safely loved on its own can overstimulate us and leave us exhausted. We also need the experience of safe boundaries. A safe boundary answers the question "Can I get my own way?" The truth is that no matter how much we thrive on connection with others, we need the counterbalance of being differentiated from others. We need to know that when another is seeing us and loving us, they are not overwhelmed by our needs. When a parent is containing their child with a safe boundary, they can hold the screaming child in their arms with all the squirming and writhing, and say, "You are not too much for me." In this sense, the establishment of safe boundaries brings a sense of dignity and honor by respecting the boundaries of relationship. We therefore experience healthy attachments when we

---

29. Also called "attunement" and "containment." See Stringer, *Unwanted*, 171.

30. Allender, *How Children Raise Parents*, 21.

31. Stern, *Interpersonal World of the Infant*, 157.

can let go of control and allow those we love to be their own persons, even in the midst of being attuned to them.

With the right balance of being safely loved with safe boundaries, a relational dance is created that allows for what psychologists call "secure attachment."[32] The good news is that you don't have to be the perfect parent or person to have or create secure attachments. In fact, there are no such things as perfect parents or persons. All that is required is that we be "good enough" for secure attachments.[33] In these securely attached settings, children feel confident that their needs will be met, and their boundaries will be honored. As a result, they feel free to move about, to explore the world, to take risks, and to try new things because they know that mother and father will be there no matter what happens. There is a sense of safety and belonging that provides an antidote against all of life's uncertainties.

Insecure attachment is the loss of safety that occurs when safe love and safe boundaries are out of whack. Psychologists have identified two main types of insecure attachment, with a recent third added.[34] First there is "avoidant" attachment. You might think of this as no love, all boundaries. In this environment the other person one wishes to be close to is distant, formal, unavailable, and usually critical of the desire for connection. Persons in this environment of neglect learn how to thrive in isolation, pretending that they have no need, since no connection is available. As a result, they learn to grit their teeth and white-knuckle through life "dealing but not feeling."[35] Avoidantly attached people have learned how to live when connection doesn't seem possible.

"Anxious/ambivalent" attachment is kind of the opposite of the avoidant style. It is all love, no boundaries. Anxious/ambivalently attached people have learned that connection is possible, but there is a constant fear of losing the connection because there are no boundaries to safely contain it. The other person to which one desires connection may be attuned to your needs, but the care is unpredictable, so the love doesn't feel contained with safe boundaries. Sometimes it is there, sometimes it isn't; there is no *container* or regulated structures to create safe boundaries. This environment creates a situation where people are "feeling but not dealing" in that they are hypervigilantly watching and waiting for connections to go wrong.

32. Bowlby, *Secure Base*.
33. Van der Kolk, *Body Keeps the Score*, 113.
34. Mikulincer and Shaver, *Attachment in Adulthood*, 25.
35. Van der Kolk, *Body Keeps the Score*, 116.

Because there are few safe boundaries in this style of relating, persons in an anxious/ambivalent attachment have learned how to take connection and love when possible while mitigating intrusive and controlling caretakers who are almost overinvested to the point of emotional exhaustion.[36]

The third type of attachment is the most heartbreaking and has emerged with the rise of trauma studies. It goes by the frightening name of "disorganized" or "chaotic" attachment. Chaotic attachment is essentially no love and no boundaries. Persons in this environment not only feel no hope for connection with others, but also they are threatened by the ones with whom safety is desired. This style of attachment tends to go with high levels of addiction, situations of extreme substance abuse, and chronic childhood neglect and violence.[37] Chaotic attachment is also called "disorganized" because the survivor of abuse in these circumstances feels constantly on edge watching for threats, while simultaneously cutting off feeling in order to avoid pain. The situation is, in essence, a post-traumatic style of attachment that oscillates between avoidance and anxiety.[38]

The four types of attachment—secure, and avoidant, anxious/ambivalent, and disorganized/chaotic (the three insecure types)—are helpful concepts for navigating the beauty and brokenness of our relationships with others and with God. Moreover, the ways that safe love and safe boundaries determine these attachments and styles of relating can help us to create trauma-safe environments that restore safety by appropriately tending to one another's needs in love while honoring one another's boundaries.

Losing Connection and Trust

Insecure attachment is a great description of what life is like in the aftermath of trauma. One of the destructive forces of trauma is that it undermines the sense of safety involved in secure attachment. There are two primary ways in which a loss of being safely loved and safe boundaries impact on our capacity to flourish. First, they undermine our attachment to other human beings. Second, they undermine our attachment to God. We take each of these in turn. Judith Herman summarizes the relational fragmentation of trauma this way:

36. Allender, *Healing the Wounded Heart*, 97.
37. Allender, *Healing the Wounded Heart*, 98.
38. Van der Kolk, *Body Keeps the Score*, 117–122.

> Traumatic events call into question basic human relationships. They breach the attachments of family, friendship, love, and community. They shatter the construction of the self that is formed and sustained in relation to others. They undermine the belief systems that give meaning to human experience. They violate the victim's faith in a natural or divine order and cast the victim into a state of existential crisis.[39]

So, trauma sets up for insecure attachments with others and with God. A world in which other people are a source of threat, rather than a source of life, is a profoundly difficult world to inhabit. But we know that for many this is a living reality. If our sense of trust and safety in the world is undermined, then flourishing in community becomes increasingly difficult. The very thing that is supposed to uphold us becomes the source of destruction and undermining. A devastating example of this is told by a participant in a sexual abuse recovery group who tells the story of her local church's attempt to "exorcise" her PTSD:

> I was in a church that demonized every problem or mishap. I finally shared with an elder's wife that I had a history of past sexual abuse, and she told me that she thought so. She said she felt a spirit of fear and seduction and that I needed to pray against these spirits. She gathered a few of her friends and prayed over me. I thought it was weird . . . I feel sick because I liked them and the church until I became their project to rid me of demons.[40]

This story is enough to make anyone cringe. Trauma is surely not a "demon" to be driven out: it is a wound to be met with free love and no presumptions. If safe love and safe boundaries are not present in the aftermath for survivors of trauma who have lost a sense of safety, we will likely end up retraumatizing the wounded in our midst.

When safe love and safe boundaries do not define our approach to trauma, a painful path is open for fracturing of safety in our relationships with others and God. If we are to understand the loss involved in the wake of horrors and trauma as they threaten basic senses of safety, we must explore how trauma creates insecure attachments with others and with God. Let us look first at the loss of safety in our relationships with others.

For survivors of trauma, the loss of safety with others feels a lot like the descriptions of insecure attachment. However, this does not mean that

39. Herman, *Trauma and Recovery*, 51.

40. Allender, *Healing the Wounded Heart*, 34–35.

all traumatized people have insecure attachments, or that all who experience insecure attachments have survived trauma. What it does mean is that because trauma confronts us with our powerlessness in the face of an overwhelming threat, and because we are often deeply ashamed of this powerlessness, trauma causes us to feel deeply insecure in our attachment with others. Trauma exposes powerlessness; powerlessness feels shameful; shame causes disconnection, i.e., insecure attachment.[41] This devastating cascade helps us to understand that a sense of threat is not the only reason why those recovering from trauma withdraw from community. Another important issue to consider is that of shame.

Shame is a natural response to the excruciating experience of powerlessness in traumatic events. "Shame is a response to helplessness, the violation of bodily integrity, and the indignity suffered in the eyes of another person."[42] Surviving trauma feels like you have experienced something so horrendous that it leaves an indelible impression that will mark you for life. It feels like your moral integrity has been so broken by violence that you are beyond hope of recovery, and your mind repeatedly tells you: "You will find out how rotten and disgusting I am and dump me as soon as you really get to know me."[43] But here, a caveat is needed. Shame is often associated with wrongdoing. Parents will relate to the image of the child hiding in the corner, refusing to show their face after taking the last piece of chocolate from the cupboard, or pushing a younger sibling over. The response: "Don't look at me!" is all too familiar for parents attempting (and sometimes failing) to toilet train their toddlers. These *shame* responses are fundamentally bound up in the belief that one ought to be rejected by others because of something we have done or something we have experienced.[44] But wrongdoing is not *always* the source of shame. In fact, as many who are recovering from trauma will attest, feelings of shame can result from experience the wrongdoing of others. It is important that we realize this, otherwise our response to those suffering shame will lack compassion; feelings of shame do not imply wrongdoing in any way, even if this captures the worry many survivors feel.

---

41. Allender, *The Wounded Heart*, 61–83.

42. Herman, *Trauma and Recovery*, 53.

43. Van der Kolk, *Body Keeps the Score*, 211.

44. This is loosely adapted from Eleonore Stump's definition of shame in *Wandering in Darkness*.

Consider the much-documented case of Malala Yousufzai, for instance:

> When the Taliban began to close schools for girls and to intimidate girls persistent in attending those few schools that were still open to them, Malala was outspoken in her defense of education for girls. And so there was a day when a Taliban gunman stopped her school bus, asked which of the girls was Malala, and shot her in the head. After multiple surgeries, she recovered; but she was left with a metal plate in her skull and an implanted device to help her hear. There is shame in the powerlessness of having been victimized in this way. . . . This is a kind of shame that does not have its source in a person's own evil acts but is still a consequence of human evil because it stems directly or indirectly from the wrongdoing of people other than the shamed person. There is a kind of diminution some people suffer that stems from the injustice inflicted on them by others.[45]

The response of shame is typical in those who have experienced abuse and who are recovering from trauma. Moreover, this understandable response of shame means that, for the survivor, "the profound disruption in basic trust, the common feelings of shame, guilt, and inferiority, and the need to avoid reminders of the trauma that might be found in social life, all foster withdrawal from close relationships."[46] Shame causes us to withdraw from others, sometimes literally hiding our faces so that we cannot encounter the other's presence. The philosopher Eleonore Stump vividly depicts this response: the "shamed person anticipates warranted rejection and abandonment on the part of real or imagined others, and consequently he is anxious about marginalization or isolation. His anxiety is directed towards a distance, an absence of union, forced on him by others with whom he himself desires some kind of closeness."[47] If relationship is key to our flourishing, then shame radically alters our capacity to flourish.

Sadly, this problem is sometimes compounded by those in the church, rather than alleviated. Jarrod Parker, in his account of undergoing therapy aimed at changing his sexual orientation as a teenager, recalls that

> I soon found myself even more depressed because I wasn't changing—and even more isolated. My church treated me like I had a

---

45. Stump, *Atonement*, 346.

46. Herman, *Trauma and Recovery*, 56.

47. Stump, "Atonement and the Problem of Shame," 113.

disease. People who had been friends stopped speaking to me. I once sat in the second row at church, but I began to feel I had to sit in the very back.[48]

Parker's response is shame; he feels as if his desires and sexual orientation provide a reason for those within the church to reject him, ostracize him, and withdraw community from him. For many, this journey from the second row to the back doesn't finish at the back but carries on out the back door. Within a church community, shame can be radically destructive, ending in people's abandonment of the church and disconnecting from community. We must lament tragedies like these and do whatever we can to stop them from happening under our own watch. In the face of the loss of safety in human relationships, the church ought to be the safest place for survivors of trauma. The church is called to be the balm for insecure attachments, and the refuge for the traumatized. Anything less than this should rightly provoke our indignation.

Losing Safety with God

Reflecting on the need for relationship for human flourishing cannot only be a psychological discussion. For we know that true flourishing is not found only in human relationship, but ultimately is found in relationship with God. The sense of flourishing relationally must be understood by seeing that fundamentally, human beings are creatures made to be images of a relational God. This is what Augustine means when he says that "our hearts are restless until they find our rest in you [God]." We were created for loving and intimate relationship not only with each other, *but with God.*

Traumatic events do not only cause painful rifts in our relationships with others. Likewise, trauma also disrupts our relationship with God. "The traumatic event challenges an ordinary person to become a theologian, a philosopher, and a jurist. The survivor is called upon to articulate the values and beliefs that she once held and that the trauma destroyed. She stands before the emptiness of evil . . . all questions are reduced to one . . . Why? . . . Why me?"[49] The question of "why" is an entirely natural and justified response in the face of horrendous evils because trauma causes us to doubt God's goodness. Even more tragically, trauma can also cause

48. Parker, "Jarrod Parker," 87.

49. Herman, *Trauma and Recovery*, 178.

us to see God as "a cruel judge" who is either powerless to help, unwilling to help, or indifferent altogether.[50] Additionally, because we know that it is often the case that "people experience God just as they experience their primary care figures," the loss of safety in trauma is only compounded by the insecure attachments we may have known from an early age.[51] While not everyone with adverse childhoods will necessarily see God exactly like their parents, there is no doubt that our relationship with God is profoundly shaped by our childhood attachments and the horrors and traumas we have encountered.

Attachment applies to our relationship with God, yet though this is a critical relationship, we may feel we have a secure or an insecure attachment to him. Experiencing a secure attachment with God gives us a feeling that God is our "safe haven" and is a source of comfort, protection, delight, and security.[52] But while many feel securely attached to God, nothing encourages insecure attachment with God more than traumatic events. Consider the story of Holocaust survivor Elie Wiesel as told by Judith Herman:

> There are people with strong and secure belief systems who can endure the ordeals of imprisonment and emerge with their faith intact or strengthened. But these are the extraordinary few. The majority of people experience the bitterness of being forsaken by God. The Holocaust survivor Wiesel gives voice to this bitterness: "Never shall I forget those flames which consumed my faith forever. Never shall I forget that nocturnal silence which deprived me, for all eternity, of the desire to live. Never shall I forget those moments which murdered my God and my soul and turned my dreams to dust. Never shall I forget those things, even if I am condemned to live as long as God Himself. Never."[53]

While stories like these are uncomfortable for many Christians to hear, it is absolutely imperative that we create space for testimonies like them that describe firsthand the effects of trauma. Trauma-safe churches are not afraid to witness such stories of trauma survivors. This is because there can be no trauma healing without telling the truth. The painful truth is that trauma often creates a feeling of insecure attachment with God.

---

50. Gostecnik et al., "Trauma and Religiousness."

51. Sartor et al., "Attachment in Spiritual Formation," 258.

52. Granqvist and Kirkpatrick, "Attachment and Religious Representations and Behavior," 919–41.

53. Herman, *Trauma and Recovery*, 94.

But here an important caveat is needed. Just as shame is not always the result of wrongdoing in our relationships with others, it is important to recognize that feeling a sense of insecurity in terms of our attachment to God is not sinful. Even Jesus felt this way. It may be helpful here to look at the cross of Christ. It is shocking to consider the fact that Jesus himself had an experience of insecure attachment with God. We can see this in one of his final cries from the cross, "My God, my God, why have you forsaken me?" (Mark 15:34). Even secular psychiatrists have counted themselves among those who see "Godforsakenness" as a particularly apt description of what trauma feels like.[54] If we are willing to recognize Jesus as a survivor of trauma (which is not difficult considering the grotesqueness of the crucifixion), we can see his cry of dereliction as an example of what insecure attachment with God looks like for humans who endure horrors. As many psychiatrists and survivors indicate, insecure attachment with God in the aftermath of trauma looks like crying out "why me?" and feeling like one who has been completely abandoned by God. This seems to be precisely what Jesus was feeling on the cross. This means that when Jesus cried out "My God, why have you forsaken me?" he was freely embracing the gambit of human emotions in the aftermath of trauma. The incredible price that it cost Christ to redeem humanity indicates that it is fair to call the experience of his passion an instance of insecure attachment with God. We can take him at his word: he actually felt forsaken by God. He felt insecurely attached.

This may seem alarming at first to say that Jesus, the eternal and perfect divine Son of God, experienced insecure (rather than secure) attachment with God. But it is Jesus' perfection that is entirely the point. The book of Hebrews tells us that "we do not have a high priest who is unable to sympathize with our weaknesses, but one who in every respect has been tempted as we are, yet without sin" (Heb 4:15). Jesus is bone of our bone and flesh of our flesh, like us in every way, yet he has never sinned. When we consider the cry of dereliction, this is incredibly good news for the traumatized. If we see insecure attachment in the cry of dereliction, and if Jesus never sinned, this means that *insecure attachment is not sinful.*[55] This means

54. Van der Kolk, *Body Keeps the Score*, 355.

55. Untangling sinfulness from normal responses to trauma is essential to posttraumatic growth: a first step for recovery must be "to *understand the response to trauma itself*: shattered beliefs about the self, others, the future. This is, I want to emphasize, the normal response to trauma; it is not a symptom of post-traumatic stress disorder, nor does it indicate a defect of character." Seligman, *Flourish*, 162. For more on posttraumatic growth, see Joseph and Hefferon, "Post-Traumatic Growth." Our work might

that when traumatized persons feel a loss of safety in their relationship with God, they are not alone. They are in the *best* of company. We will look more later in another chapter on how Jesus makes secure attachment possible in the aftermath of trauma. For now, it is enough to take up his cross as a paradigm for what insecure attachment looks like, and how it is a completely understandable experience of the loss of safety in trauma, since even God's own sinless Son knows this experience.

Seeing that insecure attachment with God is not sinful is crucial for framing our own narratives of attachment and insecure attachment with God. Consider the case of Diane, an adult survivor of childhood sexual abuse:

> My father abused me until I was four years old. He threatened to kill my mother or younger brother if I told . . . Yet my mother continued to keep us in that environment. They eventually divorced . . . After her divorce, my mother had affairs—the first one involved a priest; the other, a married man. The priest was sexually inappropriate with me . . . [He] molested me when I was eighteen . . . Growing up was also filled with constant health issues, nightmares about being chased and raped . . . I have felt alone and unprotected most of my life. I knew God was there, but his promises were not for me . . . Although I sought and served God with all of my strength, I still felt a wall and a distance between us.[56]

It is difficult to fault Diane for her sense of a lack of connection with God given the trauma she has survived. She recounts, "I was furious with God. I was also terrified of him, but longed to be close to and secure in him."[57] When sharing these conflicting desires with one of her professors in college, the response she received from the professor startled her: "How could you *not* have trust issues with him?" There was no judgment, no chastisement. Instead, the response was empathetic, validating, and freeing. Diana goes on to describe how this response freed her to take initial steps in trusting God again. Knowing that her insecure attachment was a legitimate response to trauma and was not sinful freed her to find secure attachment again.

Diane's experience shows us the importance of recognizing that insecure attachment is not sinful. Additionally, her encounter with her

---

be understood as a theological underpinning for post-traumatic growth.

56. Schmutzer, ed., *Long Journey Home*, 357–58.

57. Schmutzer, ed., *Long Journey Home*, 358.

professor shows us that our ability to relate to God is not only experienced individually but is also bound up in our ability to relate to other people. The community of the church is vital as a source of encouragement and support in the life of faith; it is in community that our understanding of God and our relationship with God is most radically shaped. There is much to be celebrated here, and we will indeed do so in good time. However, there is also a dark side to this communal dimension of our faith. The community that has such an important responsibility to shape our understanding of God and God's goodness can sometimes be a place where God's goodness and light are distorted and undermined. Consider the following case, for example:

> A young child is repeatedly and brutally beaten by her Christian parents. She is told that since God commanded the Israelites to stone their rebellious children, anything they do to her short of that is divinely approved and morally deserved. And she believes them. One night, they lock her out of the house as punishment for some misdeed. Sitting alone, bruised and bleeding, gazing at the stars, the girl has an overwhelming sense of the presence of God—a presence utterly terrifying because she perceives it to be of a being who delights in her suffering.[58]

While many of us would like to run away from such cases by placing the word "Christian" in scare quotes, to do so does not confront the reality that many survivors of trauma relate to God as a source of violence and pain, rather than life. And there is no easy fix to these problems. Even if we acknowledge that God is the source of all goodness and life, feelings of threat and shame are not always guided by rationality. As the opening story from Susan Brison highlights, these are physiological and instinctive responses to our encounters with horror. The instinctive response to God as a source of threat or rejection is sometimes hardwired into our psyches such that engaging in acts of worship or prayer can only exacerbate this distance from God.

Regaining Big Picture Safety

Finally, we must recognize that even for those who regain a sense of bodily safety and form healthy attachments through being safely loved and having safe boundaries, there can sometimes remain a residual sense of threat.

58. Panchuk, "Shattered Spiritual Self," 514.

This is because "traumatic events . . . violate the victim's faith in a natural or divine order."[59] The universe may feel like a chaotic and harmful place to be, even for those who have begun to rebuild healthy and trusting relationships with others and God. This sense of big picture safety can bubble under the surface and its undermining of flourishing can be difficult to detect. Consider an analogy: Suppose you suffer with severe cataracts on one eye, leaving you to depend on the other eye for your vision. You might never realize that the other eye is in fact shortsighted, since, in contrast, it functions very effectively. But in having cataracts removed, you might realize your "functioning" eye was less functioning than first supposed. Flourishing and functioning are relative concepts; the severity of their undermining is often seen best in contrast to "better case scenarios." Similarly, if you have spent years regaining a sense of safety in the body and are beginning to form flourishing attachment relationships with others, you might notice for the first time that there is a sense of global unease that niggles away in undetectable ways. Big picture safety is about transforming our perception of the world so that we see the damage of horrors in its true perspective, without diminishing their badness.

To illustrate the sense of big picture safety that is disrupted by trauma, consider an experiment conducted by two psychiatrists that compared the worldview of "normal" children with that of children who had endured severe abuse.[60] The experiment consisted in holding up test cards to both groups of children with innocent pictures cut out of magazines from the clinic waiting room, and then hearing the children's response to these images.

> One of our cards depicted a family scene: two kids smiling watching dad repair a car. Every child who looked at it commented on the danger to the man lying underneath the vehicle. While the control children told stories with benign endings—the car would get fixed, and maybe dad and the kids would drive to McDonald's—the traumatized kids came up with gruesome tales. One girl said that the little girl in the picture was about to smash in her father's skull with a hammer. A nine-year old boy . . . told an elaborate story about how the boy in the picture kicked away the jack, so that the car mangled his father's body . . . In card after card we saw that, despite their alertness to trouble, the children who had not been abused still trusted in an essentially benign universe

59. Herman, *Trauma and Recovery*, 51.
60. Murray et al., "Effects of Abuse on Children's Thoughts."

... [But] the responses of the clinic children were alarming ... We could only conclude that for abused children, the whole world is filled with triggers.[61]

What this experiment tragically shows is that traumatized people not only feel uncomfortable in their own skin and in attachments with others, but also tend to project a sense of insecurity onto the whole world. For me (Preston), this absence of big picture safety often manifests as a kind of "sixth sense" where people and situations are automatically classified as either safe or unsafe. I've never had to try to think of the world this way. It is just a gut reflex. But I also remember the immense relief I have felt in meeting other survivors during support groups who have also known what it feels like to lose big picture safety in this way.[62] This goes to show once more that empathy is an important aspect of restoring safety. Trauma survivors need to know that even if their loss of big picture safety doesn't fully make sense to others, the church does not condemn them for it and wants to understand these feelings.[63] Trauma-safe churches recognize the loss of big picture safety, affirm this as a fitting response, and gently offer creative ways to restore a sense of trust in the good order of God's world.

Recovering a sense of safety in all three of these dimensions (the body, relational attachments, and the big picture) is difficult and takes time. We must take seriously the profound damage inflicted by trauma for our capacity to relate to others and God. Whenever our response to such problems is glib and unsympathetic, we will not create a trauma-safe environment in the church. This will require plenty of listening, plenty of patience, and it will often require our assumptions to be radically transformed by hearing the experiences of others. That is to say, trauma-safe churches are churches who liberally witness the stories of survivors and are not threatened by their testimonies. As Shelly Rambo states, "The possibility of trauma healing lies in the capacity to witness."[64] We must hear the voices of those whose safety has been destroyed by horror and we must know that they exist in our congregations and in our wider communities. But if we are to be a place of hope as well as a place that acknowledges brokenness, we cannot stay in this place, either. While the journey to recovery may be slow, the church cannot

---

61. Van der Kolk, *Body Keeps the Score*, 106–8.

62. Schmutzer et al., *Naming Our Abuse*, 53–54.

63. "Empathy" in this case means something like the type of intersubjective openness between persons outlined in Stump, *Atonement*, 130ff.

64. Rambo, *Spirit and Trauma*, 26.

give up on the truth that God is the source of all comfort and the source of all healing. This tension must be lived out in the lives of our churches with grace and with confidence in the good news we are called to proclaim. In the next four chapters, we turn to consider how this slow recovery can be made possible through the power and love of God the Trinity and the role of the church in this process.

Part 2

The Trinity as a Source of Trauma Recovery

4

Recovering Safety
with the Father of Lights

Safety and the Trinity

Now that we have reflected on the ways in which horrors undermine a survivor's flourishing, we can think more carefully about the response of the church in the midst of this loss.

We will start by dealing with how God may heal the loss of safety that trauma survivors experience. The next few chapters reflect on the safety found in the Trinity, and for structural reasons we work through restoration by the Father, Son, and Spirit in a sequential manner, before turning to consider how the work of the Trinity is manifested in the church.

However, our starting point is with the unity of the Father, Son, and Spirit. This is because the unity of the Father, Son, and Spirit means that being safely loved by each Person of the Trinity is at the same time being loved by all of God. The breadth of God's Self—Father, Son, and Spirit—comes to make his home in each Christian. All of the Trinity makes the offer to live within us, and God does not withhold any aspect of the Godhead from this offer. Jesus promises to all Christians that "we"—the Father, Son, and Spirit—"will love them, and we will come and make our home with each of them" (John 14:23). The presence of God within us is the living opposite of both willful abuse and uncaring neglect. This recovery of security is rooted in God who says to each one of us, "I want to know you. I hear you. I believe you. I honor you." These divine intentions are matched by actions: God's love is not a theoretical one. Rather, he shows how much he treasures us and loves us by making the offer of union with himself. And because God honors our boundaries, this union will never take place without our consent.[1] Our safety is found in a spiritual bond with God that cannot be broken and is never intrusive or invasive. Secure attachment with God lasts forever.

An organic union between God and ourselves, by which God offers all of himself to us in safety, is the first step to recovery from horrors and trauma. Rediscovering our profound bonds of attachment to God the Trinity is essential to a holistic rediscovery of a sense of safety in the wake of horrors and trauma responses, because being lovingly united to God is the primary attachment that humans need. The good news is that God provides real security and safety though attachment to himself in ways that are uniquely enabled by his nature as the Trinity. As Trinity, God exists in a relationship of perfect holy love. It is as the Trinity that God unites people to himself by actually dwelling with them personally, adopting believers as his children, being a helping presence with them, offering them union with Christ who is their brother and friend, and enabling deeper intimacy with himself.

We all need a safe connection with God regardless of whether or not we are trauma survivors: each person is made for an organic union with God and to experience his love; without these a foundational part of our human orientation is missing. However, this may be a more acutely felt need by trauma survivors because if this basic attachment is missing then recovering a sense of safety will tend to be plagued by deep first-order insecurities about being loved, belonging, and having a worthwhile life.

The following chapters on rediscovering our safety with the Father, Son, and Spirit are all written with two aims in mind: that we rediscover our own sense of safety in God, and that out of this safety we are able to shepherd others. We cannot shepherd alone, and nor are we called to. We are called to love God's sheep in response to the love that is first revealed to us by the Trinity. And in doing so, we are called to testify to Christ's love (John

---

1. We do not consider this claim incommensurate with commitments to God's sovereignty over human choice, as in the intuitions of much Reformed theology. For one example, John Calvin assumed a noncompetitive view between divine and human agency by distinguishing between absolute and relative necessity, and by appealing to the Aristotelian notion of dual causality. This means that something can be ordained by God, and yet simultaneously be "not necessary in its own nature" because it operates according to its own contingency (*Institutes*, 1.16.8–9). God's sovereignty is therefore not opposed to the free operation of secondary causes but enables them. It is for this reason Calvin explicitly opposed any notion that God's sovereignty "coerces" free human action (*Institutes*, 2.3.5, 2.4.1). See Muller, *Divine Will and Human Choice*, 190–191; Vorster, *Brightest Mirror of God's Works*, 40–41.

15:27), such that the presence and holy love of the Trinity might provide the foundation and wellspring of safety for those who are wounded.

Recovering Bodily Safety

We will deal with restoring safety to the body more closely in later chapters of this book. For now, we need to make one important caveat. In considering the response of the Trinity to the crisis of horrors, one might mistakenly think that we are prioritizing a certain kind of theological response to trauma, which maintains that "God is all we need to overcome trauma," over and above a clinical response. But it is vital to see that this is not true. Our aim is not to replace or reject clinical and psychological responses to trauma recovery—these are vital for a person's ongoing recovery. In our view, the theological and clinical are not competitive. In the midst of a panic attack, controlled breathing and smelling essential oils might be an excellent way of restoring a sense of control to the body. But it might also be an opportunity to realize that at the same time the Holy Spirit is working within us through the means of breathing, essential oils, and in unseen ways in order to bring a sense of peace that passes all understanding. That's not to say that all the Holy Spirit does can be reduced to the use of essential oils, but that God works through the natural world to help us respond to trauma. God loves the world. God does not work in spite of our creatureliness but precisely in and through it.[2] The invitation of trauma recovery from a Christian perspective, therefore, is to wholeheartedly embrace creaturely means of healing with "eyes to see and ears to hear" how the triune God is at work through these means, bearing down with transcendent love in Christ, by the Spirit, and through the church in order to lead us through our horrors and trauma and into his life and peace.

Safely Loved by the Father

In the parable of the Prodigal Son we hear about God's desire to be with his children and to have them own their full status as his beloved ones. Picture the image of God our Father that is given to us by Jesus in this parable. The father in the story (who is an analogy for God) has all he needs;

2. Here we draw on the idea of a noncompetitive relationship between divine and human agency, as outlined for example in Williams, *Christ the Heart of Creation*.

he is wealthy and dignified. He is respected by his servants and eldest son. However, when the father sees his wayward son "while he was still far off," the father "was filled with compassion; he ran and put his arms around him and kissed him" (Luke 15:20). The father runs towards the son because he loves him. The father hopes for relational reconciliation with the son and hence the son's return to the status as well as role of being his son. These feelings are so keen that the father's response is undignified and uncontrollable: his love for his son literally outruns the social customs of the day. The son is loved and accepted, regardless of where he has come from and how foul he may be in his own eyes. The father does not see the son as indecent or unsuitable for a place in the family. The father is willing to give to the son a place in his home and a return to his high status. The son thinks his father's mercy is too good to be true: "Father, I have sinned against heaven and against you. I am no longer worthy to be called your son" (Luke 15:21). Despite the son's defense mechanism of self-contempt, the father's love for the son results in their reunion and the best outcome for the son. The father refuses to join in the son's invitation to call himself unworthy.

This story is important for survivors of horrors, because of the continuities and discontinuities it has with their experiences. On one hand, like the prodigal son, many survivors of trauma feel shame, but, on the other hand, unlike the prodigal son, this shame is not the result of their own wrongdoing but because they have suffered at the hands of others who have acted against their good. The most important point is that God the Father loves them unconditionally and shamelessly. God never thinks of survivors as not being his own; his enduring love is why he runs towards us with compassionate, open arms in order to celebrate the good turn of events when we are more intimately reunited to himself.

For some of us it is hard to believe that God's love would be pure and directed at our good. Perhaps we are afraid of God being a father to us; this may be because we either directly or indirectly know appalling and destructive fathers. Consider Diego's case. One of Diego's earliest memories is of trying to fend off a large man who had overpowered him. Diego remembers lying flat on his back, two arms in the air, desperately trying to catch and stop the blurry fists that sent waves of shock and pain through his body. His own father had pinned him on the bed and was beating him in the chest, stomach, and arms. "If only the bed would swallow me," Diego hoped in vain. It did not. His father was "putting him in his place." His father was not the only untrustworthy figure in his life. God appeared to be untrustworthy too: after being beaten Diego would look at the Christian poster on his wall. It depicted a bear, and the writing said, "Lord, help me to remember that today there is nothing we cannot get through together." Surely God could have helped restrain Diego's earthly father. But he had not. The next day, at primary school, Diego would try to stretch his T-shirt's sleeves all the way down his arms in order to cover the bruises on his upper arms and forearms. "I fell over," he told his friend Alejandro. But he had not, his biological father had done this. Even worse, his heavenly father was an absent father at the time when he needed him the most. From then on, Diego did not speak of his biological father, nor did he call God Father.[3]

In order to avoid unwanted associations between God and his biological father, Diego referred to God as "the Eternal One," or "the Trinity," for many years. His battle was to hold on to God, and especially to hold on to God despite God's apparent silence. As time passed, Diego developed a thirst for the natural and appropriate intimacy of the Christian use of "Our Father in heaven." There was something special in this language, but he could not draw near to God in this way. For Diego, because of God's silence, God seemed untrustworthy and hardly a source of safety. This was too much like his biological father.

Slowly, God spoke to Diego in a way that helped him begin to draw near to God with a measure of trust that God was an excellent Father; the true referent of the word, compared to which his biological father was a mere mockery or reverse version. Some important words inspired by God's Spirit helped remove some of the burden of associating God with his biological father. Diego read: "Every good and perfect gift is from above, coming down from the Father of the heavenly lights, who does not change like shifting shadows" (Jas 1:17). The distinction this passage made was vitally important for Diego: God is the "Father of heavenly lights," and does not change—an explicit and very far cry from his untrustworthy earthly father. The point is that God is a Father of a wholly different nature to human ones. God's nature is stable and unchanging. He will not fly off the handle and unexpectedly pounce upon his sons and daughters as men do. For Diego this opened the possibility to understand that God is not appalling, nor destructive. The word *Father* began to have the potential for gentle intimacy

3. For some, finding ways to relate to God as Father will mean finding new ways to pray, avoiding language that undermines the unconditional love of the Father that Jesus reveals to us. Even the acknowledgment that not everyone finds the language of fatherhood easy can bring a release from shame to some who are recovering a sense of safety with God.

with the Trinity who comes to dwell within us and treasures us as beloved children.

This did not resolve all of Diego's questions. However, he gradually began to be more trusting of God, and open to further evidence that perhaps God may be trusted and may act for the ultimate good of the world and of his children. A significant part of this evidence for God's goodness came from day-by-day trust that God was offering union with Diego in a morally pure and non-manipulative manner. The moral purity of God's nature means that from God's side, there won't be any weakness or absence of goodness in this attachment. Furthermore, our attachment to God is secured by his commitment to remain with us forever: "surely I am with you always, to the very end of the age" (Matt 28:20). At the same time, Diego's new openness to God went together with a work of undoing deep-seated assumptions about the untrustworthiness of God. By means of reassuring short prayers, Diego came to grow in trust that God's nature and commitment to us means that he will not abuse his children, nor neglect them: God will not tire of us. We will always be united to him because he will never abandon us. "My sheep listen to my voice; I know them, and they follow me. I give them eternal life, and they shall never perish; no one will snatch them out of my hand" (John 10:27–28).

The use of daily offices in the Anglican tradition is one way of reframing our sense of safety in relationship with God the Father. Morning Prayer in *The Book of Common Prayer* ends with a recognition that our safety comes from God the Father:

> O Lord, our heavenly Father, Almighty and everlasting God, who hast *safely brought us to the beginning of this day*: Defend us in the same with thy mighty power; and grant that this day we fall into no sin, neither run into any kind of danger; but that all our doings may be ordered by thy governance, to do always that which is righteous in thy sight; through Jesus Christ our Lord. Amen.[4]

The daily offices of morning prayer, evening prayer, and compline (night prayer) frame the day by joining in the prayer of the church at regular intervals. The content of these prayers changes depending on the liturgical season, but much of the structure remains the same. The repetition of these words each morning about the safety of the new day can serve as a reminder of the safety found in God, but they might also begin to reframe our understanding of the Father as our source of safety. This is not just a

4. See *Book of Common Prayer (2019)*, 23.

shift in intellectual understanding, but a reshaping of our desires and our will in important ways.[5] Consider an analogue: telling your spouse each morning that you love them seems like a good thing to do, even if you don't always feel these words. This isn't a good idea just because it's important for your spouse to know that you love them; the way you relate to your spouse changes your own perception of them. Ritual and habit have a powerful way of changing the kinds of people we are and how we relate to others. Living each day with an openness to being convinced that God is our Father who has brought us safely into a new day—even if we don't think it or feel it—can shape our sense of God as a source of safety in the long term.

The one who adopts us is a safe and trustworthy God: for this reason, we can begin to know and think of him as the excellent Father. We are not foster-cared in a short-term arrangement; adoption into God's family by grace is permanent and good news for horror and trauma survivors. We are adopted by the God of light and life, whose vital and life-renewing Word cannot be snuffed out by the powers of darkness: "in him was life, and the life was the light of men. The light shines in the darkness, and the darkness has not overcome it" (John 1:4–5). The darkness cannot overcome him, so those in union with him will not be overcome by the darkness of horror's criminality, abuse, and aftermath. Eventually, we grasp that shame is no longer the appropriate shadow under which to live; rather, God's light on the world and the moral purity of the vision he gives us may slowly open our eyes to a number of truths that free us from the inner dialogue of shame.

Being a child of God is an ongoing identity as well as a process of growing into and owning that same identity. The continual call from God reminding us that we are his children is a reality that can significantly reframe ongoing symptoms of trauma such as continual memories of violence. Our identity in God offers a larger picture in which we can come to know that horrors are horrors and not the final word. Nor are traumas the final word considered in themselves. Rather, they are the aftermath of evils through which God offers to bring incredible healing and breathtaking beauty. "No more complete victory could be imagined," because God offers this healing not *despite* our trauma response to horrors but *through* them: resurrection makes its way *through* our crucifixions.[6] For this reason, Christians can pray to God from a profound sense of safety and eventual hope, even if all earthly protection and health is waning. One practical way

5. See Smith, *You Are What You Love.*

6. Blocher, *Evil and the Cross*, 132.

that the reality of being God's child has been communicated within one mentoring group to which Scott belongs is via each member having a silver cross, with the word "Jesus" along one length of the cross, and the word "nika" (which means victory in Greek) along the other. The cross is worn by those members of the group that choose to do so as a visual and tactile reminder that God is their Father and that he has defeated evil by the victory of the cross—therefore evil will not have the final word over us, rather, God the Father speaks over us—by the Spirit and in the Son—calling us his children.

Mentoring ministries can make our adoption come fully alive within us. One of the reasons why mentoring ministries are so powerful is that a message is clearly sent to those being mentored: they are worthy of focused attention and time together. Attentive listening and care by the mentor (and other mentorees if group mentoring is the model at work) is precious and embodied evidence that God cares for his children. In the best kinds of Christian mentoring, the mentor has a heightened sensitivity to the great spiritual blessings we have received, and helps other Christians understand these. In addition, and this is especially important for helping trauma survivors recover a sense of safety, the mentor can, in a number of ways, make it clear that God can heal our wounds, including the pain of abandonment and betrayal by those who have done horrific things to us instead of pursuing good things for us. The mentor can be a channel for God's healing power: the "immeasurable greatness of his power toward us who believe" (Eph 1:19). Above all, the most powerful form of mentoring schemes for trauma recovery are those which are led by the survivors themselves. No one is more qualified to mentor the traumatized than other seasoned survivors. The willingness to let trauma survivors mentor others sends a powerful message of empowerment that the church does not think they are broken, or mere projects to be fixed. Oftentimes, offering gifts to others from one's own journey is a foundational step of healing for survivors because it exhilarates them with a renewed sense of the integrity of their own agency.[7] The empowerment of mentoring others is the opposite of the powerlessness involved in surviving trauma, and this empowerment allows survivors to embrace the truths of the Father's safe love for themselves.

Christian habits are key for owning these truths. Scott has had a long-term involvement in mentoring retreats in places as diverse as Egypt and Germany. During these times he has witnessed how God has channeled

7. Herman, *Trauma and Recovery*, 207ff.

his healing power through people involved in these retreats. Such times of healing have often involved an undoing of deep cynicism about God's care for us as his kinfolk. One instance of this healing process stands out. Following a time of sharing about doubts to do with whether or not God actually works for the good of those whose families or themselves have suffered immensely, we had a time of listening to God in prayer. God brought passages of Scripture to the mind of a number of group members, mutually assuring one another that God is for them not against them, regardless of their current afflictions. It was a moment in which it was very clear that God the Spirit had given to each person a sentence of Scripture in the service of one another. The group was like a choir, recalling the goodness of God and resisting the temptation to fall into doubts and despair. It was an instance of the children of God working together as a united family, affirming that there was hope for them all because they were safe with the "Father of lights." The group worked together to affirm that God treasures his children, accompanies us in this life, regardless of how well or how poorly we recover from horrors. The "Father of lights" does not let our infinite value be lost on one another.

Another important Christian habit that helps mentoring groups understand the Father's love for us is to invite older and wiser Christians to come in and tell their stories with God during an afternoon. Times of reflection and questions follow: what helped the visitor know God as a Father in their own local context? What symbols and signs helped bring these truths into the person's very bones: their heart, mind, and hands? After periods of reflection, the visitor can then hear the stories of group members that may still have doubts and cynicisms, and then respond with their own wisdom and prayer if appropriate.

Responding to Being Safely Loved: Growing Into Family Likeness

One of the most powerful aspects of being safely loved by God is that it is the starting point for God's grace beginning to heal our beliefs, emotions, and attitudes. These changes mean that we can grow into more wholehearted openness to God's love for us, even after being so hurt—we can even learn to trust God as a safe God. We can think of these changes in us as growing into family likeness with God, growing in trust of God, and growing in our own trustworthiness for the good of other people. God loves and transforms us into people who can positively respond to the safety he gives us. He liberates us by offering to open up our hurt selves so that we may reach out courageously and wrap our hand around his finger. For some survivors, this is very hard to do. Interpersonal trauma makes this especially difficult because of the sense of betrayal it evokes. Overwhelming violence from those we trusted makes us feel duped, and it may feel like an easy way out is to make the vow "Never again! Never again will I trust, and never again will I be betrayed."[8] Yet God helps his children grow and flourish by helping us develop family character likeness—growing up to look more and more like God the Trinity. This means growing again into the vulnerable risks of love and trusting others. This family likeness will be a great help to the survivor and to those whose lives they influence.

As we have seen, trauma may result in isolation. It may be comforting for us to know that recovery does not have to lead us to a new kind of isolation. Instead, we are born from above into God's family by the Spirit; all of us are called to a shared life of growing in Christlikeness. A good life with God and other people—which is what flourishing is—is growing into being the kind of persons that Jesus describes as "blessed." What the blessed character traits for growing in a sense of safety with God look like in practice are described by Jesus in his Beatitudes (Matt 5:3–12). Beginning with humility, and working through the virtues of humility, tender-heartedness, gentleness, justice, mercy, purity, peace-making, and courage, Jesus points out the healing influence of the love of God. The presence and works of God within us work like a medicine, mending our brokenheartedness, pain, and negative coping behaviors that we use to protect ourselves from more ache, shame, and isolation. "I can heal you, you can be good for others" are some of the most powerful words we can hear. They reverse the overwhelming feeling that a survivor's life is not worth living. On her way home from work Melanie felt a deep sense that she was no good for anyone and would only be a problem and hard work for anyone she dealt with. She tried to end her life that night. Jesus leads us in the direction of life, not death. Life with him is not just existence but slowly emerging from darkness into seeing glimpses of his goodness through the lives of others; given time and life-affirming community, we may be surprised to receive a "thanks" from someone for being either compassionate, gentle, just, or courageous. Catching ourselves in the mirror one day, we might see someone

8. See this discussed in Allender, *Wounded Heart*, 127ff.

who is growing into the treasured possession of God who is good for the world—a star in God's eyes and a beacon of light for others.

Understood in this way, virtue is not a burden: it is an invitation to an exhilarating life of flourishing as God's image. If we would like to become virtuous in this way, what do we do about it? It depends on our individual and cultural makeup, but a number of habits have been historically helpful to many people. One of these habits is visual. It is about continual reminders that we belong to a historic community that values being and becoming Christlike. Scott has a clay statue of St. Elizabeth and a photo of St. Thomas Aquinas above his desk. These saints are known for their gentle simplicity and selflessness. They are reminders that we are treasured by God, and that there is a good life that can follow on from this. We can be good for other people, and as we grow in goodness, we become evidence to ourselves (and to others) that God is working for good in the world. Living in the company of virtuous people from the past provides hope that it is likely that we too may become kind, thoughtful, self-controlled, generous, long-suffering people as we grow into deeper familiarity and intimacy with God.

The habit of reciting the Beatitudes is another daily practice to develop a deeper motivation and likelihood to become more Christlike. As one prays to welcome the day and thank God for another day of life, they may pray through the virtues as well as the hopes that accompany each one. Today, as every day, we pray for a humble disposition towards God and others, for an empathetic heart and the active habits that go with this, becoming gentle and concerned with righteousness, merciful and morally pure, a peacemaker who is willing to suffer for doing what is right in view of the kingdom of lights. We pray that we may inhabit these character traits with the right goals in mind. These are: that the justice, peace, and joy of God's kingdom of light be known on earth (Rom 14:17); that Christians may see God face-to-face and enjoy the fullness of his company (1 Cor 13:12); and finally, that we may practically be "the children of God" (Matt 5:9).

This will also involve the practice of prayer. Fortunately, Jesus gave us the ideal prayer in the Lord's Prayer. The Lord's Prayer opens a window into the heart of heaven: it shows us in the fullest way what secure attachment with God looks like in the practice of prayer. Because it is so important to our relationship with God and because it is directed to God by those who love him, we refer to it as the lover's prayer and pray it in a mood of holy love.

Attachment to God, and his life dwelling within us, is the dynamic and interpersonal context for developing healthy relationships with him, others, and ourselves. The dynamics of union with God make possible loving "the Lord your God with all your heart and with all your soul and with all your strength and with all your mind, and your neighbor as yourself" (Luke 10:27). This is because we and God can change and mold the ways that our brains process information. New ways of lovingly thinking about and relating to other people changes the pathways and connections in our brains, and over time the way we view the world is changed.[9] Human neuroplasticity means that attachment to God, and his influence upon us as whole persons, can really change us. Therefore, it is important for us to be aware of what loving God looks like in practice and how in turn this reestablishes a sense of safety. One concrete way in which our adoption into God's family makes a difference to the recovery of our own boundaries is that it enables us to relate to God in the context of earned trust. We can be responsive and communicative with God within the framework of his safe character and his work to offer attachment within secure boundaries. A positive and healthy response to his goodness towards us is to reciprocate his relational movement towards us. The most basic response is to talk to God. We call this prayer, but it is really just about being intentional in speaking with him. The Lord's Prayer is the basic Christian prayer because it was given to us by Jesus as a model for how to pray. Because it is a loving gift from Jesus and it is aimed at growing our love and trust in God, we call it the lover's prayer. We also call it the *lover's* prayer as it reminds us of our identity as people who are safely loved by God.

Many early Christians, who were under enormous pressure to find their sense of safety in the Roman Empire, prayed through the lover's prayer three times a day. Matthew 6:9–13 records the prayer for us. Jesus taught his followers to pray like this:

> Our Father in heaven,
> hallowed be your name,
> your kingdom come,
> your will be done,
>   on earth as it is in heaven.
> Give us today our daily bread.
> And forgive us our debts,
>   as we also have forgiven our debtors.

9. See Siegel, "Neuroplasticity," ch. 8 in *Pocket Guide to Interpersonal Neurobiology*. For application to trauma, see Van der Kolk, *Body Keeps the Score*, 56ff.

And lead us not into temptation,
but deliver us from the evil one.

The lover's prayer is a prayer of trust in which we who pray affirm our trust in our heavenly Father by both explicitly saying this and then by reframing the whole of our life in the context of our secure relationship with him. Importantly for survivors of trauma, we ask that God's good, just, and loving will be done on earth. In this petition, we acknowledge a willingness to explore secure attachment not just with a loving God, but with a just God. This means trusting that he can accomplish even a fuller degree of justice, reparation, repentance, and restoration from evil than we can. We also ask for what we need to survive, and for trauma survivors this includes communities of grace, medication, and therapy, as well as food. God cares about our whole person and asking him for our daily bread for the whole person is entirely appropriate for his children, to whom he gives good gifts. For trauma survivors, daily bread includes not just physical food, but all the sustenance needed to live a safe, contained, routine life that restores a sense of empowerment and agency. This is necessary for healing. Daily bread in this sense may include weekly exercise, essential oils, intentional acts of self-care, and implementing the habit of getting enough sleep each night.

In the context of being safely loved, recognizing our own contributions to our trauma and to that of others is an important and painful part of wholehearted relationships. We do not approach God in shame, but in the loving gaze of the Father of lights who in Christ has forgiven us and removed any sense of shame from our relationship with himself. Asking for forgiveness is possible because of Jesus' death for the sake of our sins, guilt, and shame. God has forgiven us, and therefore we need to ask for protection from the evil one who will tell us that we are not forgiven. Tormenting thoughts are one way by which the devil tries to imprison us within the disrupted brain pathways that develop during and after trauma. Because we are safely loved by God, we can ask God to continue to protect us and to heal us from the devastating and degrading self-talk that the devil encourages in us.

Forgiveness in trauma is a heavy and difficult topic.[10] It is important to make a number of distinctions in discussing forgiveness and trauma.[11] First, forgiveness is not the same as reconciliation. The choice to forgive is the total prerogative—"the sovereign royal right"—of the one who has been wronged and neither depends on the repentance of the wrongdoer nor means that the wrongdoer deserves to be trusted again with a new relationship.[12] Second, forgiveness is not a onetime event. It involves an ongoing process of relinquishing the desire for vengeance and ill will against the wrongdoer. Third, although it relinquishes vengeance, forgiveness is not the opposite of anger or justice, but presupposes both. Allowing for space to be angry is an important part of the forgiveness process. Similarly, forgiveness does not involve foregoing the claims of justice, but simply means foregoing the role of the judge: "Beloved, do not avenge yourselves, but leave it to the wrath of God, for it is written 'Vengeance is mine, I will repay,' says the Lord'" (Rom 12:19). Fourth and finally, forgiveness does not mean forgetting. It is by definition impossible to forget traumatic wounds such as incest or the moral injury of war. Instead, forgiveness allows one to remember traumatic betrayal in a way that no longer overwhelms the survivor with uncontrollable feelings of rage and revenge-seeking. It is important to tend to these distinctions in trauma-safe churches.

Although forgiveness feels very complex, the basic idea is simple enough, namely, that we hand over to God the justice-making that is necessary for forgiveness to occur. It is best for us to withhold the hand of vengeance at the same time as seeing the perpetrators with both boundaries and justice, mercifully leaving them to the hand of the law rather than to our own vigilantism. Seen this way, forgiveness is a divinely sanctioned challenge to God that he uphold the demands of justice. Forgiveness says something like, "God, I refuse to take your place as judge. That weight is too much for me to bear. Instead, I call on you to take up the cause of the oppressed. I do not forget the demands of justice: I demand them in full confidence by challenging you to be the only one who can set these things right." Thinking of forgiveness in this way may seem strange. But the truth is that it is more reflective of what is actually liberating and healing

10. The literature on forgiveness and trauma is vast and varied. For an introduction, see Schmutzer, ed., *Long Journey Home*, 169–85. Influential approaches to forgiveness include Bass and Davis, *Courage to Heal*; Enright, *Forgiveness Is a Choice*; and Worthington, *Just Forgiveness*.

11. These are adapted from Freedman, "'F Word' for Sexual Abuse Survivors."

12. Moltmann, "Sun of Righteousness, Arise!," 16.

for survivors. Contrary to popular opinion, most survivors do not enjoy reveling in "the revenge fantasy" but instead desperately want to be relieved of how desires for vengeance actually keep them bound and imprisoned to their perpetrators. Consider the story of Grace, an incest survivor, who explained concerns about "outing" her uncle:

> I'm wondering, if I don't expose him to church authorities, is that harbouring him? Maybe, but I just can't do it from a place of vindictiveness because that would be destructive to me. Exposing him is not just about getting him fired or punishing him. It's more about protecting the next generation. The revenge motive makes it seem like I need to lash out because I'm still bleeding, which I'm not.[13]

Grace's testimony shows that trauma survivors need safe places where anger is allowed to be part of the forgiveness process and is not taken as evidence of a simplistic desire for revenge. Such contexts can help recover a sense of safety through a process of transformation that "allows the survivor to free herself from the revenge fantasy, in which she is alone with the perpetrator."[14]

The Lord's Prayer is the liberating prayer of love between the Father and his beloved children. Reflecting on the lover's prayer continually brings out deeper and deeper possibilities for finding safe meaning and hope. For this reason, we recommend it as a daily spiritual practice in the context of communities, mealtimes, and personal prayer times. This prayer is one of the most important habits for trauma survivors because of the safe love within which we pray it.

Safe Boundaries: The Father Empowers His Children

Quite often people try to push their own agenda, and have their ways with others, sometimes violently and at other times subtly. It is hard to say "no," and maintain appropriate boundaries with others, especially when there is a power imbalance in the relationship. One of the main ways by which God helps us establish and maintain healthy and life-giving boundaries with others is by fortifying us from the inside out. Though we may feel hollowed out and worn away by trauma, Christ the King dwells in us by

---

13. Herman, "Justice from the Victim's Perspective," 591.

14. Herman, *Trauma and Recovery*, 189.

the Spirit. Jesus' spiritual presence inside us is also a living force, full of his vital energy and influence. With Jesus' life within, survivors are not alone as we try to maintain boundary and integrity with other people. We can hold off other people who want to steamroll us or use us for their purposes. We are allowed to say "No" whenever we want. We are autonomous, free, individual agents who have the right and the power to be in relationship with whoever makes us feel safe and honored. Having healthy boundaries is not only about being able to protect ourselves from predatory people. We can have healthy and life-giving boundaries that are not only good for us, but good for other people too. This is because Jesus, the most righteous person who has ever lived, shares his thoughts with us. His insights about people and situations may be shared with us so that situations may be resolved well. In addition, by the power of the Holy Spirit, we receive the Father's supernatural strength to deal rightly with complex and potentially overwhelming relationships and situations. With the Father's support, we have the courage to respond in "love, joy, peace, forbearance, kindness, goodness, faithfulness, gentleness and self-control" (Gal 5:22–23). When these qualities shape our boundaries with other people, we will have a good influence on both them and ourselves. Both parties will change slightly as a result of each interaction. Virtues rather than vices may result from such relationships as both parties habitually enable safety through healthy boundaries with one another.[15]

To illustrate this, consider the story of Andrew, a male survivor of childhood sexual abuse. Andrew describes how anger functioned as a "shotgun" that helped him feel safe from threats in social situations, while also realizing this is a dysfunctional response:

> I did sixty push-ups every morning. My body was ready to be "called up" for service at any moment, or so I thought. I had physical strength. I had some anger too . . . *For abuse survivors, anger functions like yellow police tape. It cordons off the crime scene, identifies the culprit, and lets none inside but the most trustworthy* . . . One of the most devastating conversations I ever had with my therapist was when he pointed out my anger to me. He called it my "shotgun." His observation felt incredibly unfair. There was a reason for my anger, and he explained why I had clung to it. He said I

---

15. Although some might think "habits" refer only to negative patterns of behavior, this is not always the case. Habits can involve positive, purposeful behaviors whose regular practice develops virtues such as humility, meekness, peacemaking, righteousness, and so forth. See Johnson, *Human Rites,* and Smith, *You Are What You Love.*

learned to cope by always being "on duty." It's called *hypervigilance* . . . I'm still learning to put my shotgun down. It's not easy. My wife helps me . . . I'm determined not to take my anger out on my kids. When my hands are finally crossed, may my children respect the calloused hands that put the shotgun away in order to learn a new skill—holding my kids even tighter. *Lord, teach us to play.*[16]

As we can see, the Holy Spirit enables us to do more than respond to people (whom we may have misunderstood!) with a fight-or-flight response. In the workplace, for example, under inappropriate pressure from our managers, we can be assertive but not aggressive because Jesus helps us pursue righteousness rather than rage. The fruit of the Holy Spirit in persons and communities is one of the keys to restoring and maintaining a sense of safe boundaries in the wake of trauma.

When we misunderstand the intentions of others and respond with hypervigilance this often inhibits rather than creates healthy boundaries, because it emotionally entangles us with the perceived threat. Yet this does not mean that survivors are completely off base when feeling overprotective. Oftentimes, survivors have a keener sense than most of whether or not social situations bear the manipulative dynamics involved in overt abuse. In these situations, our response toward survivors experiencing this kind of hyperarousal must involve a posture of empathy, kindness, and curiosity. This involves learning to bless our hyperarousal and avoidance responses for the ways these have allowed us to survive in the past, while seeking more healthy and integrative ways of relating in the present. For me (Preston), this has been a long process of learning how to build bridges with safe people rather than burning bridges over anything that makes me uncomfortable. Despite what trauma triggers indicate, not everything and everyone is a threat. That is important to recognize for trauma recovery, but it is easier said than done. It is a long and difficult process to unlearn what past harm has taught us. If you have not experienced this kind of post-traumatic stress it is imperative to take incredible care not to blame the survivor for their desire to have strong boundaries. At the end of the day, we have to honor these strong boundaries no matter how inconvenient they seem to us. It is an important part of the healing process for survivors to regain a sense of agency and empowerment necessary for recovering safety. In time and with patient care, these strong boundaries can become more

16. Schmutzer et al., *Naming Our Abuse*, 53–54.

flexible as those in recovery learn that it is possible to have genuine safety with others in the world.

Each person's boundaries are their own prerogative. Above all, we must be more concerned with the safety of boundaries than the inconvenience of hypervigilance. A trauma-safe church cares more about safety *for* trauma survivors than safety *from* them. Andrew (from the story above) puts the point this way: "Later in my journey, I realized that those who called me out for my anger issues were confusing hostility with anger. They objected to my anger without ever pausing to ask why it was there—and when they did find out, it was the shotgun that offended them, not my abuse!"[17] We must be committed to prioritizing the safety of trauma survivors over our own convenience or moral superiority. Careful listening and empathy are the first step in prioritizing others over ourselves in these situations. We need to be willing to ask good questions of care and concern even when it feels inconvenient or risky. In this way, we can join survivors as they learn to foster healthy boundaries on their own terms that enable rather than diminish secure connection with others.

Big Picture Safety in the Father's Love

God the Father of lights also helps us rediscover and live in the light of a larger sense of safety. The heavenly Father provides a sense of safety in the world. Recovering a sense of big picture safety is about shifting our perspective on the global state of the universe and our place in it—even when we have to face the questions of suffering and death. The shift in perspective firstly comes by way of recognizing our status as children of God, and in time developing the beliefs, behaviors, and emotions that reflect this status. As we have seen previously, relating to God as the loving Father revealed in Jesus can be an important step in recovering our sense of being safely loved, and a starting point for post-traumatic growth. Being safely loved positively alters our sense of identity and gives us a larger story within which to understand our place, meaning, and roles in the world as it is now and as it will be after our resurrection. The big idea is that because of our adoption as God's children and our union with him by the Holy Spirit, nothing can separate us from his love and the perfect future he has for us.

Knowing this status as children changes our sense of safety in the world. Consider the story of Daniel, a university professor. Daniel's life has

17. Schmutzer et al., *Naming Our Abuse*, 53.

not always been easy, particularly as he wrestled with his own sexuality and the ostracization from the church he had felt coming out as gay in a very conservative culture. This eventually culminated in Daniel walking away from faith and the church for many years, describing himself as an atheist in light of the lack of safety and love he felt both in the church and in relationship with God. He returned to the church later in his life and was eventually ordained as an Anglican priest, rediscovering his identity as one who was safely loved by the Father. This profoundly shaped Daniel's approach to teaching. Although Daniel taught philosophy in a public university, he approached this as a child of God. One tangible symbol of this was the icon of the good shepherd which hung on the wall of his office. He once described its role as reminding him of the infinite value and worth of each student he encountered. Each one was a child loved by God. The sense of safety he had found in encountering God's love was shared with all that he met.

The big picture sense of safety that is offered in being adopted as children of God should not be mistaken for a sense that all is well in the world. Children of God may feel securely attached to God, but this does not mean they are blind to the atrocities in the world. Our sense of safety is located in the broader narrative of God's creation. As Paul puts it in Romans, "We know that the whole creation has been groaning in labor pains until now; and not only the creation, but we ourselves, who have the first fruits of the Spirit, groan inwardly while we wait for adoption, the redemption of our bodies" (Rom 8:22–23). Thus, we *know* that the creation is groaning in expectation, we know that the world is not as it should be. Being adopted as children doesn't mean a guarantee of safety in the here and now, and it doesn't mean that we will not suffer future blows or that horror and trauma have no impact on us. This sense of realism is crucial for recovering a sense of safety that speaks to our lives now and our lives as they will be. In the present we are safe in the sense that we are God's children, yet we are not invulnerable to future horrors. This is painful to name. Safety with God is true safety, but it is only partially experienced in the present. This can be a key area of tension for trauma survivors: our identity and future are safe with God despite trauma and death, yet while living in a fallen world we are still vulnerable to horrors. This does not mean we cannot create trauma-safe churches, only that trauma-safe churches do not mean that we live in a trauma-safe world. The church may be a trauma-safe environment though the world is not. The world is not the eschatologically safe community that the church is. And although Christians are not of the world, we do live in the world and all the vulnerabilities to horror and trauma this entails.[18] While this may seem terrifying and paralyzing at first, we know from trauma survivors not only the devastation of life, but also our profound resiliency. Recovering a sense of big picture safety means learning to gather the courage to face the ways we are still vulnerable to horrors and trauma without being paralyzed by this feeling.

Given that Christian security with God our Father takes place in a context in which we may be harmed still, rediscovering and recovering big picture safety is a hopeful expression of trust by survivors. Big picture safety relies on God in the "here and now," in the hope that the renewed and healed "then and future" is guaranteed for us by God himself. For our safety is bound up in our adoption as children in this often dark and unpredictable world, but it also looks forward to a time when injustice will be eradicated. As Paul continues his discussion of creation's groaning in Romans 8, he writes, "creation itself will be set free from its bondage to decay and will obtain the freedom of the glory of the children of God. . . . For in hope we were saved. Now hope that is seen is not hope. For who hopes for what is seen? But if we hope for what we do not see, we wait for it with patience" (Rom 8:22, 24–25). Big picture safety is not only about gaining a physical sense of safety, but also about a temporal sense of safety. Put simply, the Christian hope is that darkness will not have the final say; the dawn of Easter Sunday has already broken into our universe and the rising sun will one day light up the whole sky. The decay caused by sin and death has been halted by Good Friday and the one who rises on Easter Sunday offers us the beginnings of life to the full until all emptiness is filled and we flourish with God.[19] Paul concludes his reflection on creation's bondage with these words:

> What then are we to say about these things? If God is for us, who is against us? He who did not withhold his own Son, but gave him up for all of us, will he not with him also give us everything else? Who will bring any charge against God's elect? It is God who justifies. Who is to condemn? It is Christ Jesus, who died, yes, who was raised, who is at the right hand of God, who indeed intercedes for us. Who will separate us from the love of Christ? Will hardship, or distress, or persecution, or famine, or nakedness, or peril, or sword? As it is written,

18. Adams, "Coherence of Christology."
19. Harrower, *God of All Comfort*, 7–24, 169–75.

> "For your sake we are being killed all day long;
> we are accounted as sheep to be slaughtered."
>
> No, in all these things we are more than conquerors through
> him who loved us. For I am convinced that neither death, nor life,
> nor angels, nor rulers, nor things present, nor things to come, nor
> powers, nor height, nor depth, nor anything else in all creation,
> will be able to separate us from the love of God in Christ Jesus our
> Lord. (Rom 8:31–39)

Nothing can separate Christians from the love of God; neither can anything separate us from being alive in reconciled union with God. Because Christians are baptized into Jesus' death and resurrection, "just as Christ was raised from the dead through the glory of the Father, we too may live a new life" (Rom 6:3). This new life starts the day we are baptized, regardless of whether this was before or after the traumas we suffer: "we have been brought from death to life" (Rom 6:13), and it will be an eternal new life: "For if we have been united with him in a death like his, we will certainly also be united with him in a resurrection like his" (Rom 6:3). In baptism, God our Father joyfully and warmly receives us fully home to himself. Robed in Jesus' righteousness and given the signet ring of adoption, we are embraced by God as he comes to dwell in us and we are given a quality of life that is eternal.

As immortal children of God, we will always be alive, yet realists about biological death's inevitability in this present life, as well as death's many faces in experiences of trauma. We can be realists about biological death, however it is not the final fact of our lives. We can face it full on, lament over it, and recognize it for the evil that it is in the present. At the same time, though, we can see through it to the resurrection of all believers in the Father's heaven. More than that we can see through to the time when we will see God face-to-face: "For now we see only a reflection as in a mirror; then we shall see face to face. Now I know in part; then I shall know fully, even as I am fully known" (1 Cor 12:13). The basis for this hope is that we are known by God now, known as his children, reconciled children, who are loved with an unbreakable and faithful love: "Love always protects, it never fails" (1 Cor 12:7–8). In this life, God protects the core of our identity as we wait for perfection and wholeness in our guaranteed future. God protects this core of our identity no matter how disfigured, malformed, or beyond hope of recovery we may feel in this life. In the next life he will reunite us to glorified bodies and make us fully alive for the place, relationships, and time when "completeness comes" (1 Cor 13:10). In the life of the world to come, God the Trinity promises to take all of ourselves—even the inestimable depths of the wounds of trauma—and make them means of unending communion with himself.

To close this chapter, consider the story of Daniel, a male survivor of sexual abuse. "The man who groomed, molested and repeatedly raped me was a Roman Catholic priest. I placed my trust in him and he violated me time and again. He bore the title, 'Father'... Where was God? That God allowed these crimes to occur—even as He bears titles like Shield, Defender, Fortress, Deliverer, Shepherd, and Savior—challenges the survivor's view of God's potency or willingness to save ... Did God think we were not worthy of saving from *this* hell?"[20] After asking these painful questions, Daniel shares a breathtaking letter which he wrote to his younger abused self as an imaginative exercise of healing. In the letter to his little boy self, Daniel thanks his younger self for helping him recover safety to call God "Father" once again:

> Dear Danny ... I am so grateful for the last three years of reconnecting after thirty-five years of forced and forgotten silence ... I am also so glad that you have invited me into this painful past, Danny. And you have allowed me to feel. Anger. Grief. Mourning. Terror. Depression. Isolation. Anguish. And freedom. Freedom to discover, to be awed, to receive, to weep, to be silent, to play. And freedom to embrace our heavenly Father as a Daddy who was there and who really understands ... You were a believer long before I understood this gospel. Thank you for persevering and speaking still.[21]

---

20. Schmutzer et al., *Naming Our Abuse*, 64.

21. Schmutzer et al., *Naming Our Abuse*, 150.

5

Safely Accompanied
by Jesus Our Friend

Surviving trauma is a profoundly isolating experience. Because healing must always occur where the wound has occurred, recovery from
trauma has to account for the way trauma isolates us from friendships. This
raises a very important question for our journey with God in recovering
safety. How does God the Trinity accompany us in trauma recovery to
counter our isolation with friendship? In Jesus, we can be sure that God
himself knows what it is like to be human in a traumatic world and that
he desires to be our friend in this world. Abiding with Jesus provides a
profoundly intimate route to trauma recovery by allowing us to experience
the balm of connection with God in a very personal way. In Jesus, we are
accompanied by God as our safe friend after trauma.

Consider the story of Natalie, a survivor of spousal abuse and rape.
Natalie tells how her connection with Jesus made a profound difference in
her own journey of trauma recovery:

> I was born in the north of England into 1980s evangelical Christi-
> anity . . . I had internalized implicit evangelical messages that my
> virginity marked my "set apartness" for Jesus . . . I was 17 when a
> mutual friend introduced me to Craig, who had recently become
> a Christian. What more did I need to know? He was washed in
> Jesus' blood, ticking the only box that mattered. And so began the
> worst years of my life. I told him I was committed to sexual absti-
> nence; within 12 days, he had coerced me into sex . . . Nobody had
> told me about consent, so I attributed my intense anxiety at being
> sexually abused to having betrayed Jesus. Within six months, I was
> pregnant . . . Craig isolated, humiliated and controlled me, lied to
> me and cheated on me. I was pregnant and working three jobs. I

> believed my love, forgiveness and compliance would enable Jesus to save Craig. Then everything would be wonderful. But it wasn't . . .
>
> Within a year, Craig had been convicted of sex offenses against a teenage girl . . . In 2005, I was 21 and six months pregnant . . . Craig raped me and, a week later, my son was born three months premature . . .
>
> After a month of sitting beside my tiny son's incubator, watching him unable to breathe without a ventilator, I reported Craig to the police for raping me. He was charged . . . This is where I would say that I met Jesus for real . . . I was totally alone, highly traumatized, with two children dependent on me. At the end of everything, I believed I found the God Who Is . . . In a hospital with no hope, I chose the God who hadn't offered any hope other than his own presence.[1]

Natalie goes on to note that although her early Christian community instilled values early on that left her vulnerable to trauma, she still found that "Christian communities have much to commend themselves to traumatized people" because they "provided key elements of trauma therapy: places of testimony and being witnessed to, safe touch, belonging, meaningful relationships, and the facility to re-story life with the continuing presence of Jesus' love, rhythm and song, meditation and more."[2] Abiding in Jesus allows us to experience being safely loved by God in the context of an intimate, personal, and healing relationship.

As Jesus tells us in John 15, we access the love of God as Father by abiding in him. The sense of being safely loved we find through the person of Jesus is not that of a far away and inaccessible God, but of God incarnate as a human being "who in every respect has been tested as we are, yet without sin" (Heb 4:15). In other words, the love we find by abiding in Jesus is one of complete empathy but lacking in the limitations caused by sin in every other human being. We can perhaps forget that in the suffering of death and dereliction, Jesus endured the force of human horror in ways we cannot easily fathom. Yet, Jesus' measureless suffering was matched by his incessant trust in the goodness and love of his Father. For those recovering a sense of being safely loved, there can be great comfort in knowing that we approach God through the humanity of Jesus Christ, the traumatized one, who knows the pain and force of horror from the inside, as well as

1. Collins, "Broken or Superpowered?," 196–97.
2. Collins, "Broken or Superpowered?," 212.

the struggle and reward of finding secure attachment with God again after trauma.

Jesus welcomes his people, and he says: "I want to know you. I hear you. I believe you." He says these things to us because he is our friend who laid down his life for us: he said, "I call you friends." Understanding our friendship with Jesus is one of the most important aspects of how the Trinity makes a difference to recovery from trauma, and it has many practical aspects to it. One of these is ongoing conversation with Jesus. This is important because a friendship with Jesus is an ongoing, active friendship with a real person. It is a friendship that may grow in intensity and deepen over the years. Friendship with Jesus is about living life with Jesus as he lovingly offers to dwell within us, alongside us, and to be a person who is working for our good. This friendship draws on a deep familiarity with him as he is revealed in the Gospels in particular but goes far beyond merely reading about his works and words in the past. Recovering a sense of being loved by God means knowing Jesus and experiencing his love for ourselves in the present. Jesus is the historical man who lived and died, but also the living Lord "who is at the right hand of God, who indeed intercedes for us" (Rom 8:34). The ascended Jesus is alive and continues to work on our behalf today.

Reading about Jesus in Scripture or works of theology is not the same as cultivating a friendship with him in the present. Christian growth begins with being taught by Jesus himself, and growing in familiarity with him today. "You heard about him and were taught by him, as the truth is in Jesus, to take off your former way of life, the old self that is corrupted by deceitful desires, to be renewed in the spirit of your minds, and to put on the new self, the one created according to God's likeness in righteousness and purity of the truth" (Eph 4:21–24). Verse 21 literally reads: "you learn him," in the sense of learning who someone is and what they are like, as two people get to know one another. Survivors can be learners of the person of Jesus; we can grow in our knowledge of him in the context of his company. In the context of a safe and gentle relationship with Jesus we can learn to trust others with a greater sense of freedom, less hypervigilance, and with less suspicion that everyone will betray us. We can become capable of healthier and safer relationships with other people; we can grow according to the glorious design that God has for us: towards recovering healthy desires, healthy perspectives on others, and so more fully be trusting and true images of God's faithfulness and purity. No matter how deep the betrayal of trauma or how prickly survivors feel in broken relationships, there is real hope for renewing trust in others in the aftermath of trauma. "The air that we breathe is so polluted by mistrust that it almost chokes us. But where we have broken through the layer of mistrust, we have been able to discover a confidence hitherto undreamed of."[3]

How can we break through the layer of mistrust in relationship with others and in relationship with Jesus after trauma? Most of us would like to deepen in our relationship with Jesus, especially in the aftermath of horrors and trauma. However, how to be a friend of Jesus in practice, and what this might look like, remains mysterious to most of us. In what follows we outline the ways in which our five senses can be mediums of his communication with us through hearing, sight, touch, taste, and smell, and then we describe the kind of friendship we can expect from Jesus, the unique nature of communication that we might have with him.

Bodily Safety in Christ

Trying to connect with God can feel very abstract. God is immortal, invisible, and infinite. We, on the other hand, are finite. We get tired, hungry, and cold. When threatened, we feel fear in our bodies much like animals being backed into a corner. But when loved, we feel pleasure in our bodies of rich connection with others. Our bodies play a central role in our lives and relationships. For embodied creatures like us it can feel difficult to relate to an infinite God.

One of the stunning affirmations of the Christian faith is that God has a body, and this body belongs to Jesus Christ. In the incarnation, God came among humanity as a genuine member of the human race in order to share in our experience so that our connection with God might be restored. "Since, therefore, the children share in flesh and blood, he himself likewise shared the same things, so that through death he might destroy the one who has the power of death" (Heb 2:14). As Calvin puts it, "God's natural Son fashioned for himself a body from our body, flesh from our flesh, bones from our bones, that he might be one with us."[4] The good news of Jesus is that God has chosen to be with us in the very bodily ways most natural to us. We are free to enjoy the safety of connection with God in our bodily senses because in Jesus God has entered into these senses completely.

3. Bonhoeffer, *Letters and Papers from Prison*, 11–12.

4. Calvin, *Institutes* 2.12.2.

Touching

Jesus may mediate his touch and its effects upon people by various means. By his touch Jesus may say "I love you, you are safe with me." What kinds of things may be mediums of Jesus' touch, or mediums through which we touch Jesus? The following ways are listed in terms of their significance and power. The primary one is the Lord's Supper, because Jesus sanctified this as a means of grace for us during his lifetime. In this ritual, believers get to touch the bread that is also at once this Christ's body. In touching the bread and drinking the wine, the believer experiences a form of physicality from Christ to them. It is not the touch of a loving friend's hand in the same way we experience the touch of other human persons, but it is a touch that is specially associated with Jesus and salvation: it is a baked and liquid touch like no other. This touch is particularly intimate as Jesus is taken in the hand then consumed: Jesus is as near to us in the bread and wine as we are to our own stomach. In bread and wine, Jesus intimately offers us a close connection of touch with himself. This is a powerful tactile reminder that by the Spirit Jesus truly is within us without qualification; as the bread and wine are within us, so is the Spirit of Christ within us. In the Eucharist we touch Jesus and he touches us in a mediated manner. For survivors of trauma, the sacramental touch between Jesus and ourselves is a special connection because Jesus meets our broken bodies with his own broken body. In the mutual meeting of our broken bodies, Jesus offers us a safe connection that is deeper than what words can express. Like a hug between two suffering people, the Lord's Supper offers survivors a table to feast with the suffering Savior that anyone can join, no matter how full of doubt or despair. "What my mind doubts, my mouth tastes of the Lord's goodness. When my faith falters, my fingers can touch the truth."[5]

While Jesus offers us his own touch, other people may also offer safe touch as the followers of Jesus. A person who is a human just as Jesus is may strongly mediate Jesus' touch from one human being to another. A long-lasting tradition within Christianity has argued that godly people may be God's "hands and feet in the world." When appropriate and with permission, a hand on the shoulder of a person for whom one is praying may be sensed as the loving and steadying hand of Jesus. Such laying on of hands has proven very meaningful for trauma survivors within liturgies

---

5 Vander Zee, *Christ, Baptism, and the Lord's Supper*, 25.

of healing.[6] This is because the structure of embodied practice in liturgies offers a powerful antidote to survivors who have come to expect chaos and unpredictable violence in their exhausted and hypervigilant bodies. I (Preston) have experienced this kind of healing during regular Anglican healing liturgies with anointing of oil for the sick, which includes mental ailments. In Scotland, my Anglican pastor frequently offered a gentle touch of prayer for healing during such services. I felt safe and cared for by the very presence of Jesus, and I often imagined that it was Christ himself before me to touch with gentle and honoring care. The combination of risk (kneeling in front of a towering priest) and safety (being met with a gentle and consenting touch) was a remarkable balm to my PTSD. It never felt condescending but was a dignifying act of restoring honor and structure to my body fractured by trauma. In fact, it is the reason I am currently being ordained as an Anglican priest, so I can offer trauma-safe care to others.

The presence and touch of loving animals such as pet dogs are also a sign of Christ's safe nearness to us.[7] As living beings who remember and care for those they love and protect, dogs in particular may have a role communicating Jesus' safe love to their owners. Not all animals can do this, but animals such as dogs and horses have a degree of care towards their owners that may, though remotely, be signs that point to Jesus' loving presence with the believer. The role of pet dogs and horses is well known in trauma recovery circles for good reason. This is because humans share the same emotional center of the brain with mammals that is responsible for our capacity for rich social life but is also the wordless, visceral, emotional place where trauma wreaks havoc in survivors. This means that "when adults or children are too skittish or shut down to derive comfort from human beings, relationships with other mammals can help. Dogs and horses and even dolphins offer less complicated companionship while providing the necessary sense of safety."[8] Consider for example the story of Jennifer and her horse:

> Some people don't remember anybody they felt safe with. For them, engaging with horses or dogs may be much safer than dealing with human beings . . . Jennifer, a member of the first graduating class

6. See Gould, "Healing the Wounded Heart." See also Schmutzer, "Spiritual Formation and Sexual Abuse," 77–81.

7. See this elaborated in Harrower, *God of All Comfort*, 203–5; Root, *Grace of Dogs*, 114.

8. Van der Kolk, *Body Keeps the Score*, 80.

of the Van der Kolk Center, who had come to the program as an out-of-control, mute fourteen-year-old, said during her graduation ceremony that having been entrusted with the responsibility of caring for a horse was the critical first step for her. Her growing bond with her horse helped her feel safe enough to begin to relate to the staff of the center and then to focus on her classes, take her SATs, and be accepted to college.[9]

Another survivor of sexual violence, Marcia, sheds light from her own experience on what it is like to benefit from an embodied connection with animals after trauma. For Marcia, the therapeutic experience of caring for her horses provided a sense of safety not only in terms of a loving relationship but also as a lesson in the empowerment of a healthy form of vigilance:

> Even though they are the biggest of the animals I care for, my horses are the most fearful of these creatures . . . Connecting with a horse is about building trust and cultivating confidence in these huge creatures that they are able to trust you, they are able to trust the space, they are able to trust this moment . . . Horses are intuitive enough to learn how to simultaneously trust and remain vigilant . . . They are prey animals, so they watch, literally out of the corner of their eyes. Horses' eyes are physiologically situated for this kind of vigilance. My horse embodies an honesty I need. They show me everyday how lack of safety and life-giving trust can coexist. And cultivating trust is an embodied practice constructed from breath, body language, and a deep connection that horses intrinsically have with everything around it.[10]

Because Christians recognize that God created and sustains all things through his Word Jesus Christ, there is no threat in affirming that even the animal kingdom is a means that God uses to communicate his healing presence to survivors of trauma. Animals have long held a special place in the Christian self-understanding. As C. S. Lewis puts, it "Even now more animals than you might expect are ready to adore man if they are given a reasonable opportunity: for man was made to be the priest and even, in one sense, the Christ, of the animals."[11] Surviving trauma is a superb example of a reasonable opportunity to allow animals to adore humans who are plagued by the effects of horrors.

---

9. Van der Kolk, *Body Keeps the Score*, 213.

10. Shoop, "Body-Wise," 244–45.

11. Lewis, *Problem of Pain*, 66.

Smelling

The sense of smell is also important for reassuring Christians that Christ is present and caring towards us. Incense is used in Christian churches to symbolize Christ's availability to us for receiving our prayers. As we light incense we pray: "O LORD, I call upon You; hasten to me! Give ear to my voice when I call to You! May my prayer be counted as incense before You" (Ps 141:1–2). These prayers are intended to renew the person who prays in the context of a safe relationship with God; they are prayers that are fundamentally good for the one who prays: "Set a guard, O LORD, over my mouth; Keep watch over the door of my lips. Do not incline my heart to any evil thing, to practice deeds of wickedness with men who do iniquity; And do not let me eat of their delicacies" (Ps 141:3–4). The psalm is prayed with a deep reassurance of safety with God: "For my eyes are toward You, O GOD, the Lord; In You I take refuge; do not leave me defenseless" (Ps 141:8).

Furthermore, as incense rises to Christ, we are reminded that Christ, as our high priest, prays for us and guides our worship to God (Heb 2:12). Being in a safe relationship with Jesus involves communication, as we have noted. Incense, however, reminds us that Jesus does, in fact, gladly receive those prayers from us. Jesus also receives our prayers in their best form: incense has the sense of purification attached to it, thereby communicating that our prayers are received in their purest form despite our mumbling and often mixed motives for making certain requests.[12] Smelling incense reminds us that Jesus is our perfect high priest who takes our broken prayers fractured by trauma to his own lips, makes them his own, sanctifies them, and offers them in perfection to the Father. In return, he places his own perfect prayer to God on our lips, that we may know that God is our Father and that he receives us as beloved children. "This is the 'wonderful exchange' by which Christ takes what is ours (our broken lives and unworthy prayers), sanctifies them, offers them without spot or wrinkle to the Father, and gives them back to us, that we might 'feed' upon him in thanksgiving."[13] Incense is a powerful smell to symbolize this wonderful exchange and assure us that even traumatized prayers are perfect to God through Jesus.

Frankincense may be used in private or public contexts as a reminder of Jesus' death for the sake of dealing with the guilt of sin. This symbolic

---

12. Bernard of Clairvaux, *On the Love of God*, 72.

13. Torrance, *Worship, Community and the Triune God of Grace*, 15.

use of a spice reminds us that we are clean in God's eyes and that he loves us without reserve, that there is no condemnation for those who are forgiven and united to Christ. Because of this, we may approach Jesus as a friend and Lord without fear. Such a reminder of Christ's work on the cross reminds us that we can be open to Christ, not defensively avoidant of him.

Speaking

Scott's German uncle Roland and his spiritual practices in the context of mentoring retreats are examples of Jesus speaking in a polyphonic way through his "vocal cords." For example, some years ago, in the context of prayer and openness to God, as group members shared key concerns about our lives and offered reflective words of wisdom and scriptural insights to one another, it became clear that some members were feeling deeply unsafe and at the same time God was saying to us "I am with you and I will never leave you." God did this during the course of a five-day retreat through the regular services at the monastery in which we stayed, the baroque artwork to do with God's history with people, the ongoing commitment of the mentoring group members to one another's welfare (going on fifteen years now), songs to do with the ongoing presence of the Spirit with God's people, the example of Nicolaus Zinzendorf's life, the German tradition of using advent candles, and an emphasis on Psalms that emphasized God's promises to his people. All of these were the vocal cords of God, saying "I am with you and will never leave you" to the group at a time when it was most needed.[14] In other contexts, God may use other means for speaking—such as the spoken words of liturgies—to reassure us of his safety and love by hearing the voice of Jesus. An example of this can be taken from any number of the "Words of Comfort" in the Anglican prayer book, which deals even with those difficult times in which we may not perceive God's comfort because we have failed or sinned against others. It can often feel impossible to untangle our shame from our guilt. Through the living voice of Jesus in the liturgy, there is comfort yet. "Hear the Word of God to all who truly turn to him. Come to me, all who labor and are heavy laden, and I will give you rest. Matt. 11:28."[15]

14. At other times, God has used other means such as the fellowship and input of the brothers at the Kloster Triefenstein monastery, as well as the use of their smaller chapel for dedicated healing services.

15. *Book of Common Prayer (2019)*, 130.

Kierkegaard reflects on the power of these words of comfort in the context of receiving communion. What makes these words of comfort meaningful is that Jesus is the one actually speaking them:

> It must be his voice you hear when he says, "come here all you who labor and are heavy laden," therefore it is his voice that invites you. And it must be his voice you hear when he says, "this is my body." For at the altar there is no speaking about him; there he himself is personally present, it is he who speaks—if not, then you are not at the altar. In a physical sense one can just point to the altar and say, "there it is"; but spiritually understood it is still really only there if you hear his voice there.[16]

Ultimately in the context of liturgy only Christ can speak these words of comfort. When Christ speaks these words they are unlike any merely human words of comfort because they are spoken by God, the one who is reconciling the world to himself in Christ. In light of this we can rest assured that we are safely loved by Christ who draws near to us and draws us near to himself.

Safely Loved: Abiding in Jesus

We are safely loved by Jesus. Jesus' love for us is the love of a long-term friend and companion, whose presence takes on a more focused and special importance in the wake of horrors and trauma. Jesus accompanies us in daily life during the process of recovery. Accompaniment is a special form of friendship that Jesus has for us, and it involves a unique response. Because it is different than most kinds of friendship we may experience, such as shorter-term friendships centered on mutual interests and professional benefits, it is worth describing carefully with a close analogy. This analogy is the kind of South American friendship in which people *acompañan*—accompany—one another.

Scott grew up in Argentina and experienced *acompañan* in practice with adult friendships with Beto, Hector, and Kate. Living on the edge of a slum and working in far-flung hospitals put a spotlight on friendships that are mostly there for the sake of the person, not the benefits of such a relationship. Living with very little, both physically and in terms of hope for change, means that often all we have is the presence of other people, and

---

16. Kierkegaard, *Discourses at the Communion on Fridays*, 24.

their capacity to be symbols of what good things God has given us at that moment. Accompaniment friendship is realistic. It does not offer unrealistic hopes or immediate resolutions to problems; there is little need to worry about tomorrow, because all we really have to deal with is "today with God and with one another." Though it is not always the case, a long-lasting, loyal, and loving kind of friendship may flourish in otherwise bleak situations, the kind of friendship in which people can *acompañar*—accompany—one another. It is one of the most powerful symbols of being safely loved in difficult times and places, when we seemingly have little to offer to other people other than our moral commitment to be a safe and loving friend back to them. In practice, to accompany one another refers to the kind of friendship in which people are friends for one another in hard places, in places where it is often best to sit with one another and merely be there, making the best of—and rejoicing in—the fact that we are the gift of a person to one another, in solidarity at this moment in time. This kind of friendship is seen most clearly when life is bleak—for example, when sitting in the darkness that follows power failure or sitting on the floor at a friend's bedside when they suffer food poisoning. The keys to accompaniment friendships are presence, consideration, conversation, and encouragement.

Focused presence to one another is a symbol of recognizing our collective and individual dignity; I remain with you and you remain with me because we recognize that we are worthy of someone's interest and presence. This kind of presence is a sort of direct parallel to the experience of "being safely loved," which we explored earlier in relation to attachment theory. It requires the ability to be with another, to track with their emotions, and to desire to share in the experience of another regardless of the quality of that experience. As we have seen, this experience of being intimately with others is what human beings were made by God for. We were made for secure attachment, for sharing in others, for presence with others. Part of the uniqueness of human being lies in the fact that we are made for experiencing the glory of other people, and of God, which means that being alone is fundamentally unnatural and painful. Pain of the lonely kind is mostly overcome by the presence of other people. The presence of someone who sees us as valuable enough to be present and interested in us is a visible sign that we are worth remembering and being given attention, that we have real worth in God's attentive eyes. Accompanying one another is the way in which images of God may mirror God's kindness, holiness, and long-suffering love for human beings. Friendly presence is considerate of the other; it is willing to sit on the floor or make time in a busy schedule. It takes the friend into account and regards them highly, not as an imposition but as someone who is beloved by God and worthy of being loved by people too. Considerate friendship is one of the main channels by which God's empathy and benevolence may be known during this life.[17]

Accompanying one another involves observing the world together and talking it through. Sharing and clarifying a shared vantage point from which to see what is going on around us helps us feel safe and sane. I (Scott) remember looking out at packs of familiar yet strange street dogs at night, observing them and talking them over with Kate. This helped me come to grips with their presence and also with the ways in which we could coexist with them. Encouragement is hard to muster up for oneself. But each encounter of presence, consideration, and conversation with a friend encourages us to at least hold on to our humanity. Friendship stops us from giving up on our bodies, minds, and souls; friendship shows us that we have something left of the creative, relational, and moral capacities that make us unique amongst creatures. Accompaniment friendship is therefore at least an encouragement to continue living though there is very little of a visible horizon beyond today and tonight. Accompaniment by other people shows us the value of our own lives. As a consequence, we can sit together in friendship, and then in time respond beyond this to those others who may need accompaniment from us.

There are many ways in which Jesus' friendship with us is a form of safe accompaniment. For example, Jesus promised to "abide" in us (John 15:4). Forms of safe accompaniment patterned after this kind of "abiding" with Jesus help us to experience secure attachment to him and (therefore!) to God. He calls us his friends in the context of knowing God and his renewing and reconciling works: "I have called you friends, for everything that I learned from my Father I have made known to you" (John 15:15). Jesus' commitment to us is long term and is a safe one. It is long term because he is with us "until the end of the age" in a real sense: he is livingly present within every Christian (Matt 28:19–20). Friendship with Jesus is safe because of his nature. He is the holy and loving God who became incarnate as the only perfectly faithful person there has ever been—Jesus is utterly trustworthy. He can therefore love us in a safe way. Not only can he, but he will because friendship with Jesus is friendship in the kingdom of God, which is righteousness, peace, and joy in the Holy Spirit (Rom 14:17).

17. For a detailed description of this kind of presence, see Stump, *Atonement*, 129ff.

For this reason, righteousness, peace, and joy in the Spirit will be important features and goals for the friendship.

For example, righteousness in this relationship means that Jesus will treat us rightly according to his relational obligations towards us. He will treat us according to our dignity as images of God as God's children: he will relate to us mindful of the obligations and boundaries that our identity places on his actions towards us. Because the friendship is ordered by the peace (or shalom) of the kingdom, Jesus will challenge us to become safer people for the sake of others. As the righteous one who acts rightly, he will also help us by the Spirit to become more virtuous, leaving behind vices that war against our souls and against friendship with him. Through the process of dwelling within us, walking alongside us, and being conversationally interested in us, by his Spirit he will also help *us* to become safe people as we grow in "love, joy, peace, patience, kindness, goodness, faithfulness, gentleness, self-control" (Gal 5:22–23). Jesus will applaud these changes with joy, because in his kingdom, joy is the response to those things that are worthy of celebration: such as becoming a friend who is more patient, kind, good, faithful, gentle, and self-controlled. In other words, Jesus is a safe friend for us because of his nature and because our friendship with him takes place within the kingdom of God. Being safely loved by Jesus and our response to his accompaniment has tremendous consequences for us in the wake of horrors and trauma.

Responding to Being Safely Loved by Jesus

But what does being safely loved and accompanied by Jesus look like in practice? Essentially, being safely loved by Jesus is very much like being loved by another person. This is because Jesus is a real person who really loves us. A big part of this relates to Jesus' ongoing presence with us and companionship in the context of our daily lives. The difficulty, though, is that usually we cannot see him directly or immediately, neither do we hear or touch him directly. However, we do see, hear, touch, and taste him—albeit indirectly and over the medium term. This relationship therefore requires careful discernment and takes some getting used to—just like any other relationship. Though this often feels slower, or partial, compared to other relationships, it more than makes up for it in terms of its impact and outcomes for us.

The impact and outcomes of this friendship are unique because of Jesus' perfect divine and human natures, the kingdom of God as the context for the relationship, and union with God as its goal. These mean that being safely loved and accompanied by Jesus will be directed by him to the end of having a good impact on us in terms of growth in righteousness, peace which is growth in personal and relational wholesomeness, and joy in terms of celebrating that which is good. Jesus will guide and lead us to celebrate growth in these qualities in terms of our relational, moral, and creative capacities in the context of a relationship with himself and those whom he brings across our path. One of the most potent ways of fostering post-traumatic growth in our relationship with Jesus is through various spiritual disciplines. In what follows we outline spiritual disciplines that reinforce the reality that Jesus is our safe, trustworthy, and loving companion who walks with us and renews us in the wake of horrors and trauma.

Two pieces of art in particular point to the vital presence of Jesus in our lives. The first is a copy of the well-known icon of Menas. In this icon Jesus has his arm around Menas as a sign of friendship and protection. Jesus has savior written around him, assuring the viewer that not only does Jesus care for us, but also he is the rescuer, who will keep us safe with himself. Whereas some icons are full of action, such as Jesus dragging people up and away from the power of death, this one is of two figures who stand side by side comfortably. This image communicates the idea that Jesus is the guarantor of our safety from the devil and our own sinfulness, and in addition he is our safe companion through this life.

The second important image is icon-like with a Greco-like use of black and reds; a large canvas of Jesus painted amidst the two thieves and the sun and the moon. This dramatic image is deliberately hung at an angle so that it leans into the viewer, with Jesus' eyes fixed on the person who looks at the painting. The effect is that one feels like they really are in the scene beside Jesus.[18] Not only that, but they are also known by him, as made clear by the emphasis on his humanity in the work. The layered painting technique creates a stained glass and translucent effect to Jesus and the panels around him, giving the impression of seeing through Jesus, just as he sees through the viewer. Taken together, these two images, both of which are in a prayer room, make the point that Jesus is with us always, and he has his arm around us—regardless of what we or others make of our situation at any given point of recovery.

18. This painting is a personal piece created by one of the authors, Scott Harrower.

A lit candle is another spiritual practice that Scott has used for decades to signify the presence of Christ. Lighting candles has also been a liturgical indication of the presence of Christ in church services for generations. Jesus is the light of the world who shines in the darkness of recovery, whose illuminating and life-giving presence cannot be snuffed out, even though the darkness tries to overwhelm us as it tried to overwhelm him in Jerusalem two thousand years ago. Scott's candle sits in a pottery bowl, reminding us of our shared earthy nature with Jesus: the one who is present with us is the one who understands us because he too shares our humanity. Having experienced the deep trials that a human can, he is present as the empathetic friend, whose safe love is deeply informed by what it is like to be you or me. His presence is also the presence of someone who knows our past, present, and future. He delighted in making us (Prov 8:30–31), delights in us now, and intends a perfect future for us with him. This means he is a friend who knows all of us, even though we may believe we have been irreparably broken into a thousand pieces by life's griefs.

One of the most important aspects of a safe and ongoing relation with Jesus is to know how to tune in to conversations with him. In most cases, talking with Jesus seems to be mostly one way *at the time*. We may pray to him, or pray the Lord's Prayer, and not particularly hear back or converse with himself in a back-and-forth manner. The most important point to understand is that this is not the end of the conversation. Conversations with Jesus are long and ranging ones. We may talk with him about an issue and a topic, and he will answer, but it won't usually be immediate and direct in the form of an audible voice. The usual course is that Jesus will speak back to us through a range of mediums and channels over time. So, we need to be attentive to what kinds of ways he might use to speak to us, and then we also need to practice the art of tuning into him and being aware that he might continue our conversations at any time because he is always with us.

For example, Scott makes a spiritual practice out of going for a walk in the mornings. He begins the walk with prayers of thankfulness, then moves to a point of conversation. The conversation may be an attempt to "digest" and work though a recent experience, such as a workplace win or loss; or it may have to do with a family or health issue. Basically, the conversation involves laying out the situation before Jesus, thanking him for the clearly good parts of it, and then asking questions, or asking for help for ways forward or making sense of those aspects Scott cannot understand yet. Jesus may respond at the time in a direct manner such as with an impression that comes to mind, or a closely related idea, or with a reminder of an event or person to do with the situation. The great news is that, because Christ lives in us by the Spirit, and God literally upholds all things through Christ, we are absolutely free to trust our senses and impressions of the world around us as keys to how Jesus may be speaking to us in that moment. The key is to be mindful that Jesus, unlike most friends, can continue the conversation beyond the point in time when we are thinking about it. Over the next day, or week, or month, Jesus will resource our ruminations and discernment to do with the issues at hand. He picks up today right where we left off yesterday. For example, he may bring Scriptures to mind, involve us in a church service, or make our paths cross with people who are insightful or lead us to read a biography of a virtuous Christian to help us. These are all instruments of Jesus' long and rangy conversations with us. We can discern which are genuinely from Jesus by testing them according to whether or not they lead to righteousness, peace, and joy.

Scott thinks of Jesus' conversational instruments with the analogy of his "vocal cords." Because Jesus is the Logos through whom and for whom all things have been made, he has such a close relationship to all things that he may employ any of them in order to speak in just the right way to anyone at any time. Jesus can employ anything from a biblical text, to a Gregorian chant, to a sunset, to an angel in order to speak to us according to our temperament, degrees of openness and needs. This has been long recognized: for example, Augustine wrote: "Heaven and earth and all that they contain tell me to love You."[19] Christians have believed for a long time that those who have seen God as he has revealed himself in Jesus are free to see God everywhere else he has revealed himself in creation. Indeed, "the world is charged with the grandeur of God."[20]

Hearing God speak in all of creation is especially refreshing to survivors for recovering a big picture sense of safety. Because of the hyperarousal and overstimulation of an internal threat response, survivors often find it hard to trust their bodily senses as they move in the world. Being traumatized feels like having your own senses betray you daily. Instead of feeling refreshed by the world around them, survivors often feel exhausted and on edge from anticipating threats. For me (Preston), a significant step in my journey of trauma recovery has been learning to trust again in my God-given ability to rest in my body and to enjoy a sense of my place in creation

19. Augustine, *Confessions* 10:6.
20. Hopkins, "God's Grandeur," 66.

as a means of feeling the care of Jesus. I can trust my body to respond to the daily care of Jesus, whether in the endorphins of a morning jog or the warmth of an evening bath. In addition to feeling safe, it is also exhilarating to be open to hearing from Jesus in the mundane, day-to-day rhythms of life. Where trauma takes away agency, being open to God in one's senses restores a sense of dignity. That is a holy rush for survivors. There is one particular Christian hymn that captures this experience for me:

> This is my Father's world
> He shines in all that's fair
> In the rustling grass I hear him pass
> He speaks to me everywhere.[21]

The implication of this is an openness to hearing from Jesus through a wide range of means that point us towards deeper righteous, peaceful, and joyful intimacy with the Trinity, who is the safe and loving reference point of our lives.

Recovering Safe Boundaries: Christ Lives in Me

In friendship with Jesus, survivors not only have the offer of being safely loved but are empowered to establish safe boundaries. As we have seen, this is an absolutely imperative aspect of trauma recovery and the re-creation of secure attachments. Recovering safe boundaries is the rebuilding work that needs to occur in the wake of trauma: it will resist all forms of intrusion and violation. Recovering safe boundaries requires an unapologetic and upright stance that says, "I am united to God and his treasured child, I have infinite dignity and am worthy of respect. I am my own person in communion with God and his church. All people need to observe healthy boundaries in relationship to me and all Christians."

Establishing boundaries is in many ways the opposite of trauma. Trauma creates a sense of utter powerlessness and incapacity; it hollows out the agency of the survivor and manifests a sense of futility that results from a freeze response to past threats. The goal of recovery is to "resolve" where traumatic memory has gotten stuck in this way. This happens by allowing survivors to experience a fight-or-flight response for the first time in the present that the trauma had made impossible in the past. Where trauma involves the total surrender and domination of the survivor, recovering safe

---

21. "This Is My Father's World," 209.

boundaries involves "learning to fight" in a way that was not possible for the survivor the first time around, during the original traumatic event.

Recovering safe boundaries with others means learning to be an active participant in our own stories of recovery by being progressively able to distinguish between the trauma of the past and the triggers of the present. Consider the story of Stephanie, who developed a PTSD response after being viciously attacked by insects:

> At 42, Stephanie was terrified to sit in her backyard. It was beautifully landscaped and her gardener kept it in great shape. But she could not make use of it herself . . . When she was 11, Stephanie was attacked by a swarm of angry wasps. Her father doused her with water and pulled her to safety but could not calm her panic. Even at the hospital she kept crying, "I can't get away! Get me away! I can't get away!" The emergency room doctor treated her many stings and prescribed a sedative to calm her hysteria. Nonetheless, for the next 30-plus years, Stephanie avoided lawns, trees, and flowers—anything that could attract a bee or a wasp—at all costs.[22]

In a carefully devised plan with her therapist, Stephanie slowly exposed herself to her fear by visiting a local park. Stephanie's therapist describes the process of helping her realize that her fear in the present was different from the pain of the past, because despite her PTSD response she was actually completely safe on that day of being in the park:

> A single bee, not even a wasp, flew quickly past our heads . . . In the same way she had described to me, she instantly fell to the ground, covered her head, and started screaming, "I can't get away!" For a few seconds I held back, evaluating her situation. Then I knelt down beside her and said in a firm voice, "Stephanie, you *did* get away!" . . . Still panicked, she looked at me. I repeated, "You got away. You did get away!" I could see in her eyes she was trying to make sense of where she was and what I was saying. . . . "You're sure?" she asked in a small, slightly skeptical voice. "Quite sure. Absolutely sure." By this time we were sitting facing each other on the grass. "Would you like me to tell you how I am so sure . . . or can you figure it out?" Stephanie thought for a moment. She looked around. Then realization dawned. Her eyes wide, she looked like a little kid who had figured out the test answer after a

---

22. Rothschild, *8 Keys to Safe Trauma Recovery*, 29–30.

long struggle. "Oh! I must have gotten away. I'm here. Is that what you mean?"[23]

Stephanie's therapist responded with an eager affirmation to her question. Stephanie was not a young child being swarmed with bees: she was an adult woman who was safe in a park with her therapist. Being able to distinguish her past trauma from her present triggers helped Stephanie not feel frozen and stuck in the trauma memories. Instead of feeling dissociated, Stephanie felt alive, free, and energized. She felt the thrill of restored agency. Through a careful approach to her hypervigilant fear and avoidance response, Stephanie and her therapist were able to help her recognize that her trauma was in the past. Instead of being subject to ongoing terror, Stephanie was able to find a new way forward in how she approached her trauma response.

Stephanie was able to recover safety by being empowered to respond differently to a commonplace horror of nature (swarming wasps). However, this same principle applies to interpersonal forms of trauma as well. Being empowered helps survivors to recover safety by restoring the kind of agency and autonomy that is necessary for healthy boundaries with the world around them. Being empowered in this way helps recovery because it is the opposite of trauma. Trauma involves a destruction of agency during an event of violence. During an interpersonal trauma like sexual abuse, survivors are traumatized by having their personal boundaries ignored and degraded by a perpetrator. By violating the survivor's boundary, the perpetrator has communicated to the survivor that they do not appreciate or honor the autonomy, wishes, desires, or personal agency of the survivor. Recovery involves coming alongside survivors to communicate the opposite. This will involve restoring proper boundaries to survivors by communicating that we honor their personal choices and we want to empower them to establish the boundaries that they feel comfortable with.

In the aftermath of having their boundaries violated and agency degraded by a perpetrator, many survivors go on to implicitly distrust even the most sensitive caretakers during recovery. It can feel difficult to know where to begin to promote healthy boundaries and empowerment for survivors we love. Oftentimes, in an attempt to feel safe, survivors will set impossible standards for loved ones so that these standards cannot be met. Then they are confirmed in their suspicion and their commitment to not trust. Maybe you are trying to get too close, so I shut you out because you aren't honoring my autonomy. Or maybe you aren't coming close enough,

23. Rothschild, *8 Keys to Safe Trauma Recovery*, 32–33.

so I shut you out because you don't care enough to try to understand me. Either way, by setting up pseudo-boundaries the survivor ensures that no real healing can take place. To be clear, this is not a conscious choice. It is a sophisticated defense mechanism that is remarkable in its ability to keep out future perpetrators. Tragically, these impossible standards also shut out allies for healing.

What is needed for recovery is a "therapeutic alliance" between survivors and their friends.[24] A therapeutic alliance recovers safe boundaries by countering these defenses with an invitation to a real relationship. We must replace pseudo-boundaries that are self-sabotaging and self-protective with real boundaries that honor the dignity of all parties and invite genuine connection through realistic expectations. This will often feel scary for survivors because establishing real boundaries invites the risk and the promise of real healing. However, the risk is well worth the reward. In this context, the wise therapist and friend will offer to join the survivor in a shared endeavor of recovery that is much richer than shutting off relationship.

Jesus is the perfect model of a friend who joins survivors in a therapeutic alliance. In our journey of coming to accept that the trauma is in the past in order to risk trusting people again in real relationships in the present, these people will sometimes fail us. But Jesus never will. He is the perfect friend who knows how to perfectly honor our boundaries and to help us establish safety by learning healthy ways of relating to others as we risk being truly vulnerable. Like Stephanie's therapist, Christ is a friend who journeys with us into our fear responses and reminds us that "that was then, and this is now." An important part of making the distinction between past and present is learning to relate differently to our trauma in the present than we did in the past. This means recovering a sense of autonomy that was not possible when the trauma occurred. In the context of healthy relationships and newly formed secure attachments, this means establishing new ways of learning boundaries with others. For some, this will be as simple as going to a self-defense class and feeling the thrill of a structured danger encounter in our bodies. For others, it will mean constructing a carefully planned confrontation with our family of origin.[25] No matter the specific way we learn to create new boundaries in the present with the world around us, the goal is always the same: recovering agency, autonomy, and restoring honor to ourselves in relation to others. We do not owe others

---

24. See Herman, *Trauma and Recovery*, 133–54.
25. Herman, *Trauma and Recovery*, 196–202.

anything except what we consent. Jesus is a friend who will never violate our boundaries but instead of this will always invite us to safe relationship with himself in a way that honors our autonomy in friendship with him.

However, Jesus is not just an external friend who relates to us with safe boundaries. He is also an internal friend who is always near to help us establish safe boundaries with others around us. Throughout the New Testament, Paul uses a variation of the phrase "Christ in you" some 164 times.[26] Union with Christ represents a major theme of Paul's theology and the New Testament in general. The idea of this theme is simple and profound: through faith, Christ actually dwells in believers by a personal, organic, and living union.[27] Christ dwells in us, and we dwell in him. As the Gospel of John puts it, we "abide" in Christ in order that we may receive from Jesus the same divine love that Jesus receives from the Father (John 15:9; 17:21).

In John's Gospel, Jesus tells us that sharing in his love from the Father by a living union with him allows us to "take heart" (*tharseo*), which means to be of good cheer, to be emboldened, to be daring. Jesus gives this command in another key New Testament passage where he heals a paralytic and a bleeding woman (Matt 9:2, 22). In another passage, Jesus' disciples join in this pattern by telling a blind man to "take heart" and rise up to meet Jesus' call (Mark 10:49). In these passages, the command to "take heart" is immediately followed by the activity and agency of the sick person. When they are called by Jesus, their damaged bodies are able to "get moving" and get unstuck from the rut of their sickness.

A similar pattern is key for trauma recovery. Traumatized persons feel "stuck" and in some cases are literally paralyzed by the terror of the past threat they have endured. Their bodies are keeping the score of a past terror. Recovery involves helping such survivors to "get moving" again by resolving this freeze response with new ways of promoting personal agency and autonomy.[28] As Jesus puts it, trauma recovery involves "taking heart" and being bold to move again after trauma. This is only possible when Jesus personally calls us to "rise and walk." But Jesus did not just make this call to the sick of his day. He longs to personally indwell all who come to him in faith. "I ask not only on behalf of these, but on behalf of those who will believe in me through their word" (John 17:20).

26. Reid, *Our Life in Christ*, 12.

27. For an excellent treatment of this theme, see Johnson, *One with Christ*.

28. Rothschild, *8 Keys to Safe Trauma Recovery*, 115ff.

To be trauma-safe churches, we must be willing to follow Jesus in inviting survivors to "take heart" and to restore safe boundaries through the exhilaration of recovering personal agency and autonomy. Trauma-safe places and people have no reservations in honoring the autonomy of the individual over their own healing. In Herman's words, "Trauma robs the victim of a sense of power and control; the guiding principle of recovery is to restore power and control to the survivor."[29] Safety cannot occur without knowing that you are the arbiter of your own body, story, and healing journey. Recovering safe boundaries means letting survivors of horrors and trauma know that their story is not too much for us to handle. We can hold your story. In fact, we want to hold your story and to know your horrors, on your terms. This is our calling as the people of God, and this is how we stand alongside the traumatized in our midst. Practically, this means strict policies of confidentiality, determined first by the wishes of each individual for sharing their story, as well as clear well-defined procedures in our institutions and designated people who are easily accessible and qualified to walk with survivors and advocate for them within each organization. Trauma-safe churches have systems and people in place who are available and willing at any time to witness a survivor's story told on their terms.

However, it is important to remember that boundaries are always a two-way street. Empowering trauma survivors to recovery safe boundaries does not mean that pastors or caretakers are at the beck and call of the survivor's prerogative, day or night. This would be the opposite of safe boundaries because it would involve a codependent arrangement that assumes the church's attention is completely continuous with the survivor's demands. In this state of affairs, the demands of the survivor are actually not very different from the demands of the original perpetrator because in both cases the pseudo-boundary has been set unilaterally: it has been dictated by the terms of one party. Instead, what is needed is a healthy and safe boundary that is set bilaterally in a process of reciprocal negotiation between two parties that care for one another. This involves a mutual stance of honor and delight where trauma-safe church members can say to one another, "I recognize your needs and I have my own needs, and we can form a mutually healthy alliance to fulfill both." These are not unilaterally set pseudo-boundaries: these are real boundaries that have been set bilaterally. Rather than dishonoring the survivor, such a stance is profoundly dignifying because it approaches survivors as human beings who have moral and

29. Herman, *Trauma and Recovery*, 159.

creative agency to engage in healthy relationships. It is patronizing to treat survivors as if we could possibly offer undying attention at all times. We are not God. We are the trauma-safe church. This means that empowering safe boundaries requires that we create real boundaries that honor all persons rather than a unilateral pseudo-boundary that is dictated by one person alone. This process of negotiating safe boundaries is part of healthy life in community and restoring secure attachments after trauma.

Regaining Big Picture Safety through Jesus the Light

Recovering big picture safety is about perceiving the world differently because of the friendship we have found in Christ. We have already gestured to the way big picture safety is recovered through having our eyes open to the friendship of Jesus all around us in God's world. It is now worth elaborating on how this big picture safety manifests in our day-to-day sensations and bodily practice. Through friendship with Jesus, we will experience the world differently through our sight, touch, taste, hearing, and smelling.

For example, Christ may be seen through the life and works of fellow Christians. The life of a Christian is like a stained-glass window through which a too-bright light may be seen more directly. The loving and holy power of Jesus is too bright for us to see directly, therefore he shows us this through the actions and words and presence of those who are united to himself by the Spirit. For good reason the body of Christ is described as having eyes and ears, and feet. The body of Christ has the gift of mercy, which means that one person may be mercifully present for another Christian as a sign of Jesus' loving care. For example, consider Scott's grandmother Enid and her neighbor Ella. Because Jesus indwells both people in this situation, he knows how to share his concern for one person (Ella) with the other (Enid), and thereby motivate Enid to care for the Ella in a way approved by God and according to his love. In this way, Jesus shares his friendship with others in a way that allows us to participate in his care for his friends. Ella will see God's care for her in action as she witnesses Enid's care for her. Scott's grandmother Enid cared for her neighbors throughout her life, despite the challenges of being a single mother with three children. At her funeral, there were many stories of God's kindness being made known through her actions, from taking into care extra children to driving people to church on Sundays.

The reason that good works are such sure signs of Christ and his kingdom at work in people's lives is that they are works of righteousness that aim to bring wholeness to others and therefore are worth celebrating with joy; this is the kingdom of God on earth: righteousness, peace, and joy in the Spirit.

Memorial places and dedicated spaces also remind us of Christ's loving care for us. Enid is now dead. It is now her turn to more clearly rest in Christ's safe presence. When Scott visits the memorial garden at St. Silas Church, where her ashes were spread, Scott can ruminate on her life and example. She pointed others to the fact that Jesus was alive and working for the good in the wake of terrible trauma she herself had suffered at the hands of her ex-husband. Memorial places serve to give us pause and consider God's goodness to us, together with the promise of safe eternal rest in fellowship with himself, the church, and his angels. Taking the time to visit and remain for a time in Christian memorial places is a key spiritual practice, a reminder that the world is graced with God's presence through his people in particular.

Building memorial walls, or photo walls of remembrance, is another useful spiritual practice that reminds us of God's extraordinary care. If one uses stones, such as the stone memorial Scott has in his front yard, then the names of places, events, or special people may be inscribed on them as reminders for today of God's past care as well as of the fact that he is caring for us today—even if this is largely or totally unseen. Some of the names we have include "Kohler" and "Winnetka," special people and a special church through which we grew to know and experience Jesus' care in new ways. Photo boards may play a similar role. Looking into the eyes of those people who cared for us reminds us that Jesus was caring for us through them.

Though less common, Jesus may at times give waking visions to his people. This involves a form of seeing that transcends sight to do with visible things. It is a vision of perception, aside from the empirical world, in which one is awake and able to see something that Jesus directly gives to the person to see. These visions often have the role of confirming a truth that will become, or which is, especially pertinent to the person in question. These visions are rare, and not a sign of superior spirituality, but signs of Jesus' love for that person according to need, temperament, and gifts.[30]

30. For a rich discussion of such forms of mystical prayer, see Mascall, *Christ, the Christian, and the Church*, 201–27.

Conclusion

To conclude, we have been given the gift of a long-lasting friendship with Jesus. He is our friend in many ways that parallel friendship with other people, however, the communicative aspect of the friendship takes place over longer times and through various channels. As corresponds to being human and a friend to human beings, Jesus communicates with us through our five senses, in ways that most people can receive his care. Jesus meets us right where our wounds have occurred. Recovery from trauma and horrors involves growing accustomed to how Jesus may communicate with us, and how we may reciprocate this communication with him. Because Jesus is the best of friends, his friendship with us will never be manipulative or abusive, but will lead to growth in righteousness, peace, and joy in the Spirit.

Jesus is our friend after trauma. He safely loves us, empowers us for the creation of safe boundaries with himself and others, and restores our big picture sense of safety. All of this means that Jesus is God's offer to be our unfailing friend in the context of a healing relationship that aids safe trauma recovery. To see this, consider army chaplain Adam Tietje, who tells the story of how friendship with Jesus during his experience of war trauma helped him survive and aided his process of recovery in the aftermath. He describes what it was like watching his friends die gruesome deaths and how this caused him to fear how he could survive and make it back home:

> That day—July 12, 2010—was the first of many that increasingly led me to wonder if I—if we—would ever make it home. Even if we did, how could we ever be the same, physically, psychologically, or spiritually? Two days later, a sniper shot one of our soldiers in the head while he was standing guard in one of the towers . . . The bullet went through his helmet, his skull, his brain, and lodged itself on the other side of the helmet. I'll never forget the way his body bounced on the litter as they took him toward the gate or the mess of blood, bone, and brain that resulted from the devastating force of the bullet's impact . . .
>
> July 30th was the next devastating milestone for our battalion . . . two more soldiers were killed, another had his foot amputated, and many others were wounded. Those who stayed could no longer keep their hands from shaking. The combat and traumatic stress were overwhelming . . .
>
> I am not sure I truly knew fear until I knew it that day and the next . . . When the dust settled that day and I finally laid my head on my sleeping bag, the flashbacks kept coming as my body

involuntarily recoiled at the reliving of each shock. I am not sure how I ever made it to sleep that night.[31]

After a much needed leave from the horrors of his deployment, the first stop Adam made was to a chapel. Adam recalls the experience he had in this chapel of picking up a journal filled with the letters of Mother Teresa as she described her own struggle with a feeling of God's absence. One quote stuck out to Adam: "I have come to love the darkness for I believe now that it is a part, a very, very, small part of Jesus's darkness and pain on earth." Adam recalls the significance of these words on the friendship of Jesus for his trauma:

> As I read those words, I laid down my burden and wept. In this quote I found the hope I needed to keep going. In my experience of God-abandonment, in the midst of great suffering and evil, I found strength in knowing that Christ, too, suffered pain and darkness such that now all suffering is bound and contained by his own and through which his love can be known.[32]

31. Tietje, *Pastoral Theology of Holy Saturday*, 2–6.

32. Tietje, *Pastoral Theology of Holy Saturday*, 7.

6

The Spirit of Comfort and Safety Within

> Terrors overwhelm me;
> > my dignity is driven away as by the wind,
> > my safety vanishes like a cloud.
> > > (Job 30:15)
>
> In peace I will lie down and sleep,
> > for you alone, LORD,
> > make me dwell in safety.
> > > (Psalm 4:8)

The Holy Spirit: The Safe Healing Presence of God

Trauma is like a series of tattoos that punch wounds into our body, soul, and mind; its deep marks are reminders of the threat that people may once again harm and hurt us. Survivors of trauma have very strong personal memories that continually whisper: "this world and its people are not safe." Consider Luc. He has not felt safe in the company of other people for as long as he can remember his father's violence and his mother's neglect. Luc yearns to feel safe and at peace. He only gains glimpses of that when he sits in a local park—all alone and only at nighttime—when no one can see him. On a nighttime walk, he will often take time to sit in the middle of a dark cluster of trees, for a time he feels sheltered and hidden. If only he could rest there and fall into a peaceful sleep.

Eventually he must return to the world of people and be, as he puts it, "on the move from one vaguely nontoxic relationship to another." The outcomes of Luc's "vaguely nontoxic relationships," are not so vague: he feels taken advantage of most of the time. As a result of this Luc lives in a self-protective and defensive manner. He keeps people at bay with his cynicism and short temper, and sadly feels like he is doomed to be alone. Against his deepest longings, Luc's defensiveness and cynicism unintentionally hurt (often *really* hurt) the few people who care about him. Alone and despondent, he lives without joy, with no reason to think his life might work out somehow, let alone make a good difference to anyone else.

In the context of Luc's life, and against a background of neglect and bleak hopes, Jesus' promise to be with his followers as Lord, friend, and source of safety seems too good to be true. Only untrustworthy people make such big promises. Though we might want to believe that Jesus is nontoxic and non-manipulative, many of us have simply not experienced safe medium- or long-term relationships before. For many, pain in the stomach and anxiety in the chest start spreading as soon as we think that Jesus may want anything long-term or even mid-term with us. Confronted with Jesus' promise to be with his followers and to be a source of safety for them, Luc's first response is to scoff; after all, hasn't Jesus just taken off? Doesn't he just go away, just like everyone else does?

Jesus knew that his first few followers did not want him to ascend to the right hand of the Father for the sake of continuing his ministry from there. As his friends and followers, the tight-knit group of disciples did not want to feel the pain of absence. Peter had replied to Jesus' question about their commitment to one another with "To whom shall we go?" (John 6:68). The disciples did not want Jesus to leave them, and Jesus promised that he would not leave his followers alone. By his own Spirit and after his ascension, Jesus would be present with his disciples once again, promising: "I will not leave you as orphans—I will come to you" (John 14:8). He promises to be with every disciple in every place and at every time. He promises that he will be with each of his disciples by the presence of his Spirit until that time that he powerfully returns to Earth to renew and reorder all things around himself in holy love. Jesus sent his Spirit to his first disciples and sends his Spirit to believers today: he said, "I tell you the truth, it is to your advantage that I go away; for if I do not go away, the Helper will not come to you; but if I go, I will send Him to you" (John 16:7). Jesus' promise has been fulfilled —this is why the Holy Spirit is called the "Spirit of promise" (Eph 1:13).

Jesus has done as he has promised, and by the presence of his Spirit he is with Luc as Lord, friend, and as a source of safety.

"By this we know that we abide in Him and He in us, because He has given us of His Spirit" (1 John 4:13). Our prayer is that, in faith and over a period of time with the help of others, Luc may know that Jesus lives in him and that he lives in union with God. Luc is not alone, because the Holy "nontoxic" Spirit lives in him and unites him to God. The remainder of this chapter will discuss the presence of the Spirit in the lives of followers of Jesus, the consequences that this has for recovering a sense of safety in the world, and how the Spirit works to enable people and groups to appreciate and actualize their new safety in the Spirit. We will explore the vital presence and works of the Spirit for the survivors recovering a sense of safety as well as the agency to develop safety in the wake of trauma.

Safely Loved: Discovering Safe Union with God by the Spirit

Across time, and through the presence and ministries of the Holy Spirit, Jesus is with his disciples because he loves them—he loved his first followers, and he loves us now. His good pleasure and will is to unite people to himself by his Spirit, forming an organic and unbreakable bond with us. This is not the temporary, breakable bond of glue or a staple or a drunken kiss at the pub: the bond is a person of the Trinity, and because the Trinity will never end and grants us everlasting life in union with God, our bond with the Trinity will never end. The presence of the Spirit within us is a truly secure attachment with God the Trinity.

For one of our friends, Paola, a deep and permanent connection with anyone, especially God, was something she never even thought was possible. "I lived my life passing through what I thought were faceless crowds. I assumed no one deep down cared for anyone else, especially when the chips are down. Once, I walked past a lady having an asthma attack, and I just kept on going without helping her. I felt like a ghost. Like there is little substance to me: I was so disconnected from others and even my own body that I felt like I could almost walk through people. I was utterly disconnected and irrelevant to pretty much everybody. I used to repeat a mantra to myself: I'm just passing through."

The Spirit provides a *deposit* or a *pledge* of the full inheritance of eternal life that we are promised as children of God (Eph 1:4). This eternal life has a quality that begins now: a relationship with the triune God orients us towards healthy, live-giving relationships across the breadth of our lives today. God makes his own presence possible in our lives, and we are also spiritually connected to other people who are likewise filled with the Spirit. These connections are the new living sinews that hold us together as Christian people and help us move meaningfully in the world once again.

God slowly heals us from the weight, shame, and confusion that stem from deep experiences of pain. We don't have to force ourselves to break these shackles and afflictions; rather, God the Holy Spirit helps us to grow in new ways, even after trauma. This begins with helping us distinguish between what is true and what are the fears that horrors have taught us to live by. God the Trinity has loving and good purposes for us, for example life-giving relationships, a renewed character, and the freedom to serve others in love. Each of these involves healing as well as flourishing in the relational, moral, and creative aspects of being humans made in God's image.

To help us appreciate this, God gives us of a "Spirit of wisdom and of revelation in the knowledge of him" (Eph 2:17). And what does this wisdom and knowledge show us? God reveals that our lives are generated by the overflow of his grace, love, and good pleasure. God takes pleasure and interest in us; we are defined by God's loving interest. In fact, our lives are the overflow of the love of the Father, Son, and Holy Spirit. Our lives are not merely the polluted overflow of human damage and shame. God declares a loving "yes!" over our lives, and a "no!" that liberates us from living under other powers. Growing into the knowledge of God's "Yes!" is a blessing because it enables us to trust his goodness and trust that he has come near to us in mercy. He has come near and he is staying near: we are God's own inheritance (Eph 2:18). Because we are his precious legacy, he will never let us go. When we know that he will never let us go, we can accept his help to heal in full confidence that he will not cut us off during the long up-and-down process of recovery. God gives us a free and unending embrace for all we are today, trauma history included.

The importance of the Holy Spirit being the Spirit of truth comes to the fore at the starting point for our healing from trauma and its ongoing wounds. Jesus promised the Spirit of truth as helper for those who love him, because he wants our new life in his kingdom to succeed. Jesus said, "I will ask the Father, and he will give you another Helper to help you and be with you forever—the Spirit of truth" (John 14:16–17). Yes, Jesus delights in us and takes pleasure directing and celebrating renewal in our lives. He may be the only person who truly "has our back" and wants things to work out for us—but he is that person. The Spirit comes to those who love God in order to lead people to the truth that sets them free from the devil, from patterns of self-protective and generally sinful ways of life. We are led into a new life by the Spirit's works as "the Counselor" (John 16:7), and the "convicter" of wrongdoers (John 16:8). Importantly, we can trust the Spirit's counsel and support because he will never confuse trauma with moral culpability: God neither condemns nor convicts us of surviving trauma. Instead, through the Spirit he invites us to repent when self-protection has led to sinful actions toward others in response to our trauma. We are invited to such repentance because God dignifies us as morally creative agents, no matter the trauma we have survived. But God the Spirit will never ask repentance for the wound of trauma itself as we are never morally culpable for surviving atrocity.[1]

This Helper Spirit speaks on behalf of divine love for us. Confirming the powerful loving work of the Father and the Son involves the Spirit pointing out what God has done for those he loves in the past, what he is doing now, and what he will do in the future. Perhaps the first work the Spirit does is to confirm the fact that we are safe with him, and for this reason he is called the Spirit of comfort. The Spirit is the Comforter, who continually assures us of God's truths about ourselves, despite what our night terrors suggest. Jesus promised that when the Comforter comes to live within a person, "he will teach you all things and bring to your remembrance all that I have said to you" (John 14:26). The voice of the Spirit mediates the words of Jesus to us. He comforts us when we are gripped by anxiety and shame, for example, and feel unstable and unworthy to be God's children.

The Spirit within Us: Responding to Being Safely Loved

The Spirit Helps Us Appreciate and Own a Safe Life with God

The insights we receive from Jesus by his Spirit mean that we can healthily work through the downs and ups of living with the consequences of trauma such as complex PTSD. Safety in a permanent relationship with a loving and trustworthy God provides us with a starting point for listening

---

1. For a helpful treatment of repentance in trauma recovery, see Allender, *Wounded Heart*, 197ff.

to Jesus through the Spirit. The Spirit may speak to us in a mind-to-mind way that humans communicate; however, instead of vocal cords, he will mostly use Scriptures, trusted Christian friendships, church liturgies such as the Lord's Supper, and the use of the charismatic gifts such as prophecy in the church. Over time the Spirit's perspective and truths shape our understanding and how we live, so that as we become new people that live in new ways, we may in time transcend some of the pain and disruption that trauma has brought. As these wounds are healed, the basic relational attachment and health which we may receive in the Spirit may result in that we can accept and pray the following psalm as our own: "You will not fear the terror of night" (Psalm 91:5, NIV).

We can see, then, that the Spirit's presence is a healing presence. The Spirit comes to us so that we may become more holy and loving people; he renews our character and concerns so that we may become living reflections of God's own holy love for others. Such renewal enables us to have quality relationships with other people and further the kingdom of God on earth. Healing begins with the safety of being brought near to God and to other believers, and the restoration God brings to us occurs as we Christians grow together into a holy temple, "a dwelling of God in the Spirit" (Eph 2:22).

Return to Paola's story. For Paola, a bond with the loving and holy God is the foundation for her safety in what is still a strange and alienating world. Her outlook and lifestyle has changed because she trusts that God will not harm her and is trustworthy—even if she still finds him surprising and "weirdly nice." Paola and her local prayer group appreciate the fact that the safety of a promise fulfilled (the promise of the Spirit) means that we can be confident in the safety found in the reality of union with Jesus (he is loving and trustworthy).[2] Deeply thankful that God has "set his seal of ownership on us, and put his Spirit in our hearts as a deposit, guaranteeing what is to come" (2 Cor 1:22), they usually begin their meetings with thanksgiving. In the context of prayer, a stable relationship with God often involves illustrations of this safety with God. For example, he is the foundation upon which we build a life, or the home from which we venture out into the world. For Paola, Psalm 144:2 brings together God's love for us and the safety we find in him: "my rock and my fortress, my stronghold and my deliverer, my shield, in whom I take refuge, who subdues the peoples under

---

2. Note that we don't intend to commit to a certain view on the Trinity. Our account is compatible with both Latin and social understandings of the Trinitarian relations.

me" (Ps 144:2). Before trying to sleep, Paola often recites: "In peace I will lie down and sleep, for you alone, LORD, make me dwell in safety" (Ps 4:8). We can trust that the God who raised Jesus from the dead has the power to hold on to us, to prevent us from falling away from him into utter desolation—the desolation expressed by Marco as "I am like a leaf randomly falling into a puddle, drifting down into murky water, until I sink in one way or another. We all sink in the end." The idea of an end to life and to our own being is appealing because it includes the end of pain.

For Christians, however, the end of pain and aching begins in part today as we experience glimpses of the Spirit's presence within and his healing work within us. Resting in God is the starting point for settling down our restless hearts and minds; as Saint Augustine famously prayed: "you move us to delight in praising you, because you have made us for yourself and so our hearts are restless until they find their rest in you."[3] The end that we hope for is not a full stop, but a goal. It is an interpersonal goal: rest in the stable love of God.[4] One day we will see God face-to-face in the context of understanding God more fully within the new heavens and the new earth: "then we shall see face to face. Now I know in part; then I shall know fully, even as I am fully known" (1 Cor 13:12). We are fully known right now in the sense that the Spirit who made us knows how life is going for us and how we are developing as people, because the Spirit lives inside us and understands us entirely. Surprisingly he does not run away from us or leave us out in the cold. He remains with us, as near as we are to ourselves, until we reach the place of eternal safety and rest. In the meantime, he does not sit passively alongside us but helps us to heal, to grow, to become Christlike and therefore someone who can be good for other people. This is particularly welcome news for trauma survivors who live with a stigmatized identity as though they are only capable of shameful relationships.[5] Through the presence of the Spirit, survivors may know that they have a wealth of good to offer others.

The safety we have and may sense in our communion with God by the Spirit can give us the courage to explore and participate in therapies that may help us recover from trauma. Importantly, this Spirit-led recovery process of healing may take unconventional forms that are adapted to the unique demands of trauma care and this process may reveal unique ways that

3. Augustine, *Confessions* 1.1.3.

4. Durand, *Les Émotions De Dieu*.

5. Herman, *Trauma and Recovery*, 194.

survivors can experience communion with God even amid chronic diagnoses.[6] Whatever shape this process takes, we can turn to consider how the Spirit helps us be safely open to participating in, and joining forces with, therapies that may enable our healing.

A Spirit-Led Healing Process

How does the Spirit safely bring healing to the effects of horrors and trauma and thereby allow us to regain our sense of autonomy? One thing the Spirit may do is to help us to gradually set aside dysfunctional coping mechanisms that have been fundamentally shaped by surviving trauma. Defensive survival techniques and patterns of life are sometimes helpful short term, yet medium term lead to ways of living that are unrelentingly dominated by pain and brokenness across our being. Take dissociation for example. Although adaptive in the moments of trauma to help us survive, ongoing patterns of dissociation are highly maladaptive for our present relationships with others.[7] Dissociation is therefore a "tragic adaptation" for survivors because "in an effort to shut off terrifying sensations, they also deadened their capacity to feel fully alive."[8] A new way is possible: within the safety of a loving and holy relationship with himself, the Spirit works with our biological processes to slowly rewire our minds and bodies with the aim of renewing us so that we may flourish once again as relational, moral, and creative beings. In fact, the Spirit may work in us to end a majority portion of our trauma responses so that we mostly recover from particular horrors, and in addition we become Christlike people who are God's good channels of his holy love for other people.

Empirical studies in psychological science are suggestive for how this might take place within our bodies and minds. Human brains are constantly being shaped and molded by our environments as well as our own internal and bodily processing of what we experience. Therefore, our view of the world, our character, and our responses to everything that goes on is constantly shaped and redirected according to patterns of thinking. For example, numerous psychological science studies show that the more a person is grateful for the good things they experience, the more grateful they become over time. So habits to do with thinking and using our bodies

6. For more on this, see Swinton, *Finding Jesus in the Storm*.

7. Herman, *Trauma and Recovery*, 45.

8. Van der Kolk, *Body Keeps the Score*, 92.

reinforce those patterns into who we are (and are becoming). It is no surprise therefore that Paul prays that believers may be strengthened in their "inner being" as they constantly grow in their thankfulness and appreciation for God's love for them: "I pray that you, being rooted and established in love, may have power, together with all the Lord's people, to grasp how wide and long and high and deep is the love of Christ, and to know this love that surpasses knowledge" (Eph 3:17–18). Constant appreciation for God's love will shape us into people who have a deep default sense of security in union with God by the presence of the Spirit. Thankfulness leads to progressive assurance that God loves us, regardless of what we believe about ourselves. In sum, thankfulness for God's grace towards us is vital for healing in the aftermath of trauma. Being thankful will slowly assure us of God's unbreakable bond with us and the new start to life that he gives us. The safety we have within this relationship is the starting point for new patterns of life, quality relationships, and creative action—all with God's help and in the company of fellow Christians. The Spirit can work in our lives so that we no longer feel overwhelmingly unsafe and disconnected, but rather gradually safer and connected to other people. The Spirit will usually work through the input and work of therapists and friends, because God values human beings as his images and is committed to human agency as a primary way by which he works in the world. The Spirit can lead us to find the truth about, and be open to participate in, best practices through which therapists and friends may help our recovery process.

Therapists and friends are vital in the process of aiding post-traumatic healing for survivors who feel disconnected from other people and unsafe. Babette Rothschild is a respected and authoritative trauma therapist who recounts her story working with Janet, molested by her father, who had a hard time being close to people, physically and otherwise, and felt hopeless because of it, because although she longed for connection, she felt viscerally unsafe to engage closely with others. For example, she would dissociate when people hugged her. So, Rothschild invited Janet to bring a friend to therapy. They then went through a mindfulness exercise, where Janet would closely listen to her body for signals of distress, and attempt to engage in small increments of physical contact with her friend. They went for a hug and Janet dissociated and felt panic. After listening to her body and contemplating a more doable action point, Janet smiled and invited her friend to simply put a hand on her shoulder. She could handle it, and she enjoyed the warm touch of her friend. Although she also felt sad because she longed to be closer than her traumatized body and psyche could handle, she also appreciated the small measure of connection that was possible. They were able to accomplish this by giving Janet space to be mindful of her body and how distressed it was during normal human connections.[9]

Therapists and friends are invaluable, and so are mindfulness techniques such as the one described above.[10] One challenge to the effectiveness of these therapies and their helpfulness in our process of recovery, is that survivors need to actively and courageously participate in the best therapies. Engaging with life-changing therapy is very hard work. It is draining emotionally, confronting, and requires being vulnerable to new feelings and ways of seeing. It is also physically painful at times. For these reasons, participation in therapy after trauma may be short lived, and the implementation of recovery techniques may also be short lived. In this context a key way in which the Spirit helps us is by giving us both the foundational security to explore and engage in therapy, and also the empowerment to participate and persevere with it. Of course, this is not to say that only Christians have the moral fortitude necessary for trauma therapy or that Spirit-empowerment is a prerequisite for ongoing interventions in recovery. However, the presence of the comforting and abiding Spirit can be a significant spiritual resource for the long haul of trauma recovery. We can draw on Paul's language of walking with the Spirit to reflect on the presence and enablement of the Spirit for the survivor in their journey of recovery.

Recovering Safe Boundaries: The Spirit of Protection

"Since we live by the Spirit, let us keep in step with the Spirit" (Gal 5:25). The Spirit enlivens us to God and draws us into a dynamic process of actively responding to his life-giving power. The processes involved in healing are many, and they involve our response to the Spirit's works through friends, therapists, the ministries of the church, and our own Christian spiritual practices.

---

9. Rothschild, *8 Keys to Safe Trauma Recovery*, 11–18. Herman writes, "Recovery still begins, always, with safety . . . Safety always begins with the body." Herman, *Trauma and Recovery*, 269.

10. It is vital to note that mindfulness has a very strong empirical foundation and is a proven PTSD soothing technique, because it engages the medial prefrontal cortex, and helps people to be self-aware of their bodies in a way that runs counter to dissociation. See Van der Kolk, *Body Keeps the Score*, 90, 209.

An illustration of the Spirit's invisible yet energetic work is seen in the way that the breeze seemingly stirs sad-looking willow trees into a dancing flurry of branches and leaves. By the wind's power and influence the trees come alive and seem to spin and stir and wave their branches in surprising and beautiful ways. When we think of our lives, we know that when God's Spirit moves in us, we may also be in tune with the new song and new dance that the Spirit enlivens within us. We may respond, and he invites us to. We can respond positively, joining in harmony with the Spirit—moving in a new way as we join in with the Spirit's work in our communities and persons, characterized by the expressions of "love, joy, peace, forbearance, kindness, goodness, faithfulness, gentleness and self-control" (Gal 5:22–23). Imagine a forest of willow trees moving in rhythm with the mighty wind. When God comes and speaks new life into existence in our communities we will "go out in joy and be led forth in peace; the mountains and hills will burst into song before you, and all the trees of the field will clap their hands" (Isa 55:12). Over the course of time, new life in the Spirit begins to look different, it feels different, in contrast to a life lived in the wake of suffering, guilt, and undeserved shame. Luc's life changed after becoming a Christian and taking part in therapy groups as he was enabled to do so by the Spirit and his friends who drove him to weekly meetings. A new life in the Spirit is called being "born again" for good reason. It means being born into God's reign of life, love, and light (John 3:5), and he empowers us to participate in both those secular and sacred channels of healing that yield life, light, and love.

To illustrate this, consider again the story mentioned earlier of Andrew's ongoing response and commitment to healing from trauma. He is a male survivor of childhood sexual abuse. Andrew describes how anger functioned as a "shotgun" that helped him feel safe from threats in social situations, yet he realized that this was a dysfunctional response and then with God's help bravely learnt to choose the way of love, light, and life instead:

> I did sixty push-ups every morning. My body was ready to be "called up" for service at any moment, or so I thought. I had physical strength. I had some anger too . . . *For abuse survivors, anger functions like yellow police tape. It cordons off the crime scene, identifies the culprit, and lets none inside but the most trustworthy . . .*
>
> One of the most devastating conversations I ever had with my therapist was when he pointed out my anger to me. He called it my "shotgun." His observation felt incredibly unfair. There was

a reason for my anger, and he explained why I had clung to it. He said I learned to cope by always being "on duty." It's called *hypervigilance* . . .

I'm still learning to put my shotgun down. It's not easy. My wife helps me . . . I'm determined not to take my anger out on my kids. When my hands are finally crossed, may my children respect the calloused hands that put the shotgun away in order to learn a new skill—holding my kids even tighter. *Lord, teach us to play.*[11]

With God's help Andrew courageously committed to replacing defensiveness with loving openness to his children and to others. His life is a vivid symbol of the powerful Spirit whose work may heal our wounds. Walking in a way that follows the lead of the Spirit opens us to new potential for love and holiness with others. This is rewarding yet often involves difficult changes such as going to counseling, taking medication, and even learning to relate to our bodies in new ways such as becoming accustomed to receiving a caring hug without freezing up in hypervigilance and possibly reacting with anger.

Learning to love in new ways is courageous and hard work. Yet we can cooperate with God by responding to those instrument of healing that he gives us, such as the gift of good counseling. He can help us to move beyond responding to our loved ones with a fight-or-flight response. He can also help us move beyond a paralyzed freeze response. We may become gentle, fair, and merciful people as Jesus wants us to be.[12] Instead of feeling bound to fighting, fleeing, and freezing, we are invited to be peacemakers, to mourn, and to hunger and thirst for justice. When we get in the habit of being this kind of person, we will find that we become increasingly gentle, fair, and merciful. Each time we act virtuously we become healthier as a person and as a community member, thus more likely to contribute to other people's good and to do the good works God has prepared for us to do.

Medium term, as a result of this, healthier persons and communities may emerge as a result of walking with the Spirit. Yet, this positive change is not for our own sake but rather in order to be living symbols of God's life-giving love. As a symbol, we embody the invisible reality that God is present with us and working to heal us at the same time as to draw people to himself. In other words, we are healed so that we may shine amongst the

---

11. Schmutzer et al., *Naming Our Abuse*, 53–54.

12. "Blessed are the meek . . . blessed are those who hunger and thirst for righteousness . . . blessed are the merciful" (Matt 5:5–7).

peoples of the Earth as "stars in the sky," pointing the way to God (Phil 2:5). In addition to being symbols of grace in the present, we may also have such an impact for good in the lives of others that we may leave legacies of God's healing for the next generation. Our prayer is that in the same way that the sunflowers rotate throughout the day in order to follow the sun's journey across the sky, so may we can learn to see the Spirit's good works in the world around us. Following the signs of his work, may we follow his lead in order to find opportunities for healing for our communities and ourselves so that, ultimately, we may be channels of praise to God and channels of the Spirit's healing in others' lives.

Being moved by the Spirit, relating to others in fresh ways, discovering new ways of being in the world after trauma and imagining the hopeful possibilities—these all involve recovering safe boundaries. If being safely loved involves feeling the Holy Spirit as the Comforter and pledge of God's love, then recovering safe boundaries involves allowing the Spirit to inspire new possibilities of dignity and self-care.

We have seen in an earlier chapter how safe boundaries are important for secure attachments with others and with God. While being safely loved allows us to be connected to others, the recovery of safe boundaries allows us to honor this connection without confusion and in sustainable ways. Boundaries allow us to dignify the agency and autonomy of those with whom we are in relationship by identifying our desires, preferences, expectations, limits, and so forth, and then understanding and respecting that these vary from person to person. Your wishes are not always my wishes, and my wishes are not always the same as yours. That is okay because we are different, we are not the same person.[13]

The Holy Spirit helps us recover safe boundaries after trauma in that we are protected from ongoing traumatization by setting clear expectations for how we are to be treated and then making this clear to others. For those in situations of domestic violence this means gathering the courage to break off from those who are mistreating us and creating space between ourselves and abusive relationships. Sometimes this may even mean restricting our interaction with toxic family members or friends and finding healthier relationships. Through the Spirit we can remember that we are not people who deserve abuse, but "heirs according to the hope of eternal life" because

13. "Boundaries define us. They define what is me and what is not me. A boundary shows me where I end and someone else begins, leading me to a sense of ownership. Knowing what I am to own and take responsibility for gives me freedom." Cloud and Townsend, *Boundaries*, 31.

"God our Savior appeared, he saved us . . . the Spirit he poured out on us richly through Jesus Christ our Savior" (Titus 3:4–7). The Spirit lives in us and we are worthy of safety from trauma.

However, we must note that safe boundaries are not only about protection from ongoing traumatization and unsafe people. They apply also even to people who make us feel safely loved. This is because no amount of being safely loved will ever be enough or annul the need for our ownership of ourselves. To understand this think about a loving and healthy family gathering during a holiday. If your family is safe you will likely look forward to the decorations, the home-cooked meals, the hugs and kisses from loved ones, the smells of home, and the traditional games. But if these went on forever you would burn out. At the end of the day you look forward to having the chance to be alone. You need to breathe and to recharge. This doesn't mean you don't love your family or don't enjoy being safely loved by them. It just means that being safely loved needs safe boundaries to flourish.

For trauma survivors setting these boundaries may involve helping others learn when we need relational space. For example, it may be helpful to inform our loved ones that certain interactions or forms of physical contact make us uncomfortable or are triggering. These conversations can be awkward but with the Spirit's help it is worth the risk. The Spirit empowers us to speak on our own behalf and he will give us the words to speak (Luke 12:12). When we need to consider what actions to take in our relationships for our flourishing the Holy Spirit will "guide you into all truth" (John 16:13). But the Spirit also will help us to let go of our unrealistic expectations of others. Complex trauma such as prolonged childhood abuse can leave dysfunctional styles of relating in us because that is what we learned. Walking with the Spirit will involve learning to find new ways of relating that honor the boundaries of others. For example, rather than anxiously clinging to our closest friends or our spouse and demanding tokens of love we can learn to accept that everyone is human and no one can fulfill us in the way that God intends for his own presence in our lives. Rather than demanding the world of others we can honor their limitations and their boundaries and turn to the Spirit in us who is the unfailing sign that God loves us and is never leaving us. "The Spirit of truth . . . you know him, because he abides with you, and he will be in you. I will not leave you orphaned; I am coming to you" (John 14:18).

For ourselves and for others safe boundaries are a way of honoring our limitations as finite humans who cannot love others perfectly, only safely, and we need to own nobody else but ourselves:

> I accept, to some degree, my own limits as a human, finite, sinful person. Consequently, I establish boundaries to better serve those with whom I am in relationship. A boundary like the number of hours I sleep at night is seldom violated because I am able to function better when I get seven hours of rest. I seldom interrupt my time with my children to talk over the phone because I am not owned by the phone. I am not required nor indebted to talk to everyone who might want to talk with me. Boundaries are an acknowledgment of my finiteness and a gift of mercy to my soul.[14]

Recovering safe boundaries in ways such as this allows us to properly relate to others regardless of whether they are trauma-safe or not. We cannot control others but only ourselves and we are also only responsible for ourselves. A prayer that captures the importance of safe boundaries in larger perspective is the "Serenity Prayer" often repeated among Alcoholics Anonymous: "God grant me the serenity to accept the things I cannot change, courage to change things I can, and wisdom to know the difference."[15]

Learning to Say "No"

While recovering safe boundaries involves our broader relationships, it also has specific application to protecting us from unsafe people and relationships. In the work above we considered how we may say "Yes" to the healing works of Spirit in tandem with secular and sacred therapies and friends. In addition to helping us say "Yes," the Spirit also helps us say "Not now," "Please wait," or "No" as appropriate. The Spirit is the Spirit of truth, the Advocate and Counselor, who helps us establish and maintain healthy boundaries with other people. In the context of trauma therapy and recovery, the Spirit comes alongside survivors and empowers them to discern what is best for their own unique journey of recovery. Trauma recovery is like snowflakes in that no two paths are exactly alike and the Spirit knows this and welcomes the uniqueness of each survivor's journey. This will involve setting boundaries with others that are particular to each survivor's

14. Allender, *Wounded Heart*, 178.

15. A. A. Grapevine, "The Serenity Prayer."

own story, pace, and desires for healing. Establishing and maintaining these is vital to recovery, to flourishing once again and to helping others. Quite often people try to push their own agenda, and have their ways with others, sometimes violently and sometimes in more subtle ways. It is hard to say "no" and maintain appropriate boundaries with others, especially when there is a power imbalance in the relationship. One of the main ways by which God helps us establish and maintain healthy and life-giving boundaries with others is by fortifying us from the inside out. Though we may feel hollowed out and worn away by trauma, Christ the king dwells in us by the Spirit. Jesus' spiritual presence inside us brings with himself his living force, full of his vital energy and influence. With Jesus' life within, survivors are not alone as we try to maintain boundaries and integrity with other people. We can hold off other people who want to steamroll us, or use us for their purposes. We are allowed to say "Yes," "Not now," "Please wait," or "No" as appropriate. Here we can take our lead from what Paul says about Christian boundaries in light of the Spirit's work within the person and the Christian community. Firstly, we will see how he appeals to the work of the Spirit to resist religious abuse by people with selfish motivations, and secondly how he sees the Spirit at work in maintaining healthy boundaries between well-meaning Christians.

One of the main reasons that St. Paul wrote his epistle to the house churches in Galatia was out of concern that the Christians are being coerced by people who "are zealous to win you over, but for no good" (Gal 4:17). The pressure to become passionate followers of a quasi-Christian sect and to conform to a rule-based (not grace-based) lifestyle was very strong. St. Paul could see that this was confusing and detrimental for Christian faith. Those who wanted to take advantage of believers were refocusing these Christians on themselves—a "zeal for them" and rule keeping—which are forms of slavery (Gal 5:1, 10). These pressures were "no good" because they tricked Christians in having to justify themselves by association with the right leadership and with a certain guideline for life.

But these kinds of pressures from leadership are also no good because they come from leaders who are fundamentally abusive: they treat "you as an object they are willing to harm for their own benefit."[16] This abuse is often clothed in the behaviors and language we associate with religious life, and though it looks life-giving it is toxic. In such situations, Christians were not regarded as persons with high dignity but only as a means to popularity

16. Mullen, *Something's Not Right*, 2.

and control. Religious abuse is a form of horrors that degrades the agency, relationality and creativity, and lively faith of everyday Christians. It cumulatively uses abusive tactics to target and undermine others so that they are easily controllable by pseudo-Christian false leaders. In the early church, as today, the motivation that drove the sect leaders to pressure Christians was "no good" because it was concerned with these toxic leaders, instead of the Father who sends the Spirit of the Son into our lives, as the central reference point for faith. Becoming the center of their follower's attention was the abusive leaders' goal; it is fundamentally disordering because the horror-making leaders started a movement that was self-focused rather than God and other-person focused (Gal 4:17). Religious abuse and toxic religion were a relatively common problem in early Christianity; it is a common problem today.[17]

Paul rejected and stood up to this to abusive and passionately coercive pattern of sub-Christian leadership. The Holy Spirit enabled Paul to write: "That kind of persuasion does not come from the one who calls you" (Gal 5:8). Strength accompanied Paul's insight that someone is trying to take advantage of us for their own gain and at our own cost. The Holy Spirit gives us the strength to stand up to horror-makers and those who would undermine Christian safety: "for the Spirit God gave us does not make us timid, but gives us power, love and self-discipline" (2 Tim 1:7).

The Spirit not only gives us our initial safety with God but maintains it, giving us an ongoing sense of safety in the aftermath of abuse. He also helps us maintain our safety by giving individuals and groups the power, love, and self-discipline to work towards healthy churches. Such strength comes via the Holy Spirit, in tandem with the faith of the community and the individual strength to withstand the misdirected pressure and passion of dangerous leadership in the church. The Spirit reassures us that our righteousness in God's eyes is given to us by faith in Christ, adoption into God's family by the Spirit: "because we are God's children now, God sent the Spirit of his Son into our hearts, the Spirit who calls out 'Abba, Father.' So, you are no longer slaves, but God's children" (Gal 4:6–7). Because our foundational dependence is on the Spirit and not particular people, the power of the Spirit will see us through our pilgrimage to heaven.[18]

17. DeGroat, *When Narcissism Comes to Church.*

18. "By faith we eagerly await through the Spirit the righteousness for which we hope" (Gal 5:5).

Healthy Boundaries between Well-Meaning Christians

Many Christians are well meaning, and they are not the predatory self-focused leaders described in the epistle to the Galatians, nor those we see in contemporary churches. Yet we do need to maintain healthy boundaries with one another in order to be safe for one another and in order that we flourish as relational, moral, and creative images of God together. Boundaries are not just needed for unhealthy people. Healthy boundaries are a necessary component of safe, secure attachments with loving people as well. When we flourish safely together, we are more able to cooperate with the Spirit's work of building up the body of Christ into maturity.

How does the Spirit help us maintain healthy boundaries with other Christians? The first step is to take ownership of our daily responsibilities so that we are not tempted to turn them into inappropriate burdens that we expect others to bear. With the help of the Spirit "each of you should carry your own load" (Gal 6:5) in the context of family life and generosity in the kingdom of God. In this context, load means "'cargo,' or 'the burden of daily toil.'"[19] Load therefore refers to "the everyday things we all need to do. These loads are like knapsacks. Knapsacks are possible to carry. We are expected to carry our own. We are expected to deal with our own feelings, attitudes, and behaviors, as well as the responsibilities God has given to each one of us, even though it takes effort."[20]

These daily responsibilities can be carried when we are well within ourselves and our context does not pressure us beyond our own capacities. In such a context, we flourish by carrying our own loads and not being obliged to carry another person's responsibilities as long as they are able to do so. If they try to manipulate or coerce us into carrying these, they are being abusive, as they are treating you as an instrument to do what they want, regardless of the cost to you and those for whom you bear your own daily duties, such as your children. When a person is relating with this pattern toward us, we are in the throes of a "codependent" relationship. Codependency is "an emotional, psychological, and behavioral condition that develops as a result of an individual's prolonged exposure to, and practice of, a set of oppressive rules—rules which prevent the open expression of feeling as well as the direct discussion of personal and interpersonal problems," which results in "a diminished capacity to initiative or to participate

---

19. Cloud and Townsend, *Boundaries*, 33.
20. Cloud and Townsend, *Boundaries*, 33.

in loving relationships."[21] Codependency is a form of insecure attachment between two persons that lacks safe boundaries. The antidote to codependency is to practice "detachment," which "is not detaching from the person we care about, but from the agony of involvement." Detachment is not "a cold, hostile withdrawal" but is instead "releasing, or detaching from, a person or problem *in love*."[22] When we practice detaching ourselves from a codependent relationship, we calmly choose to forego unrealistic expectations from others. We set safe boundaries for ourselves and those trying to use us to meet their own emotional needs.

The Spirit empowers us to detach from codependent relationships that do not reflect the safe boundaries of life in God. The Spirit gives us the power and wisdom to draw boundaries when people overstep what they want to take from, or get out of, other people. One of Paul's prayers was that his fellow Christians would receive "the wisdom and understanding that the Spirit gives" so that they may do what is best in any given situation (Col 1:9). In this way we can, in "whatever [we] do, whether in word or deed, do it all in the name of the Lord Jesus, giving thanks to God the Father through him" (Col 3:17). Our words and deeds can serve God without inappropriate interference by other people when the Spirit gives us the knowledge we need, as individuals or as workplace teams or churches, so that we may carry out the good works that God has for us to do. Therefore, the Spirit protects us so that we might do God's will by helping us preserve boundaries against those who would have us inappropriately do their menial daily duties for them.

By the power of the Holy Spirit, we can be given the internal emotional, cognitive, and spiritual capacity to carry our own loads and resist being co-opted into inappropriate relationships of abusive servitude with those who are too slothful to carry their own. The Holy Spirit may give the quality of holiness to the ways in which supernatural strength, discipline, and love are brought to bear on potentially toxic situations. Holy intentions and goals enable us to more clearly deal justly as well as virtuously with complex and potentially overwhelming relationships and situations. There is an emotional as well as a cognitive aspect to having strong boundaries with the strength that Jesus provides by the Holy Spirit. The Holy Spirit is morally pure, therefore his life and influence within us frees us from merely reacting to others out of our feelings of fear. We have the new possibilities of

21. Beattie, *Codependent No More*, 30.

22. Beattie, *Codependent No More*, 55ff.

responding with active "love, joy, peace, forbearance, kindness, goodness, faithfulness, gentleness and self-control" (Gal 5:22–23). When these qualities shape our boundaries with other people we will have a good influence on both them and ourselves. Both parties will change slightly as a result of each interaction. We must remember that we can never control others, only our own responses to them. But our responses may gradually have a positive impact on the habits of those around us. Virtues rather than vices may be the results of such relationships as both parties habitually enable safety through healthy boundaries.

In the workplace, for example, under inappropriate pressure from our managers, we can be assertive but not aggressive, because Jesus helps us pursue righteousness rather than rage. The fruit of the Holy Spirit in persons and communities is one of the keys to restoring and maintaining a sense of safe boundaries.

Daily duties are different from burdens. While duties are bearable, burdens are weighty problems that simply cannot be carried alone: "burdens are like boulders. They can crush us. We shouldn't be expected to carry a boulder by ourselves! It would break our backs. We need help with the boulders—those times of crisis and tragedy in our lives."[23]

Paul recognized that when it comes to life's burdens, we need each other and can rightly call upon each other for help. He writes: "Carry each other's burdens, and in this way you will fulfill the law of Christ" (Gal 6:2). Though it is important to set healthy boundaries that protect us from one another, there is another sense in which an awareness of boundaries gives us the room to grow in capacity so that at the right time we can step in and help others. The difference between codependency and healthy burden-bearing is in the sense of *obligation* we feel in the relationship. If you feel like you *have to* bear someone else's burden, chances are there is some detaching that needs to happen. However, if you do not feel obligated but *freely desire* in the context of a *mutually attentive* relationship to help the other person, this may be a case of healthy burden-bearing. This healthy form is the kind of burden-bearing we find in Scripture. Galatians 6:2 is about helping one another at those times when we simply cannot, and aren't meant to, carry an overwhelming weight alone: "This verse shows our responsibility to one another. Many times, others have 'burdens' that are too big to bear. They do not have enough strength, resources, or knowledge to carry the load, and

23. Cloud and Townsend, *Boundaries*, 33.

they need help. Denying ourselves to do for others what they cannot do for themselves is showing the sacrificial love of Christ."[24]

In the wake of trauma and past absuse, it is often hard to serve others in love because we fear being taken advantage of once again. We may misunderstand the intentions of others and respond to them with forms of hypervigilance. However, this often inhibits rather than creates healthy boundaries and service for one another. This does not mean that survivors are completely off base when feeling overprotective of themselves and others. Oftentimes, survivors have a keener sense than most for whether or not manipulative dynamics are at play in given situations.[25] Still, the perception of these dynamics may take on an exaggerated form within the post-traumatic frame of a hyper-aroused mind and body. Starting with empathy, kindness, and curiosity, we can learn to slowly trust again, and hence to serve again, only where and when this is appropriate. This is part of being given the freedom for service; we are "called to be free. But do not use your freedom to indulge the flesh; rather, serve one another humbly in love" (Gal 5:13). Spirit-given freedom from the after-effects of trauma means that we can be freed to care for people in new ways. Thus, another way that we find safety in the Spirit is that he gives us the safety to serve others by setting us free from many of the dynamics that would hold us back from loving others to the extent of what is required in a given situation. This is great news for survivors of trauma who often want to make the world a better place.

We have to learn to thank our hypervigilance for how it has protected us in the past, while seeking new ways forward where healthy boundaries can be placed without burning bridges. For me (Preston), this means choosing not to "torch anthills," as my friend once told me. Not everything and everyone is a threat. But this also means those of us who are on the outside of trauma need to take incredible care not to blame the survivor for their desire to have strong boundaries. Ultimately, we have to honor these requests as it is part of the process for survivors to regain a sense of agency and empowerment necessary for recovering safety. To understand this, think about the analogy of driving a car and swerving to avoid an oncoming pedestrian. If you swerve the car to the right and you are driving fast, chances are that after missing the pedestrian you will "overcorrect" by swerving too far to the left. You are correcting yourself, but you have

---

24. Cloud and Townsend, *Boundaries*, 32.

25. On modes of knowing in the aftermath of horrors and trauma, see Rambo, *Spirit and Trauma*, 26–37, 40, 81–110. Here Rambo draws on Caruth, ed., *Trauma*, 6–7.

to overcorrect in order to get back on track. The same is true for trauma survivors. Because trauma is surviving an event of powerlessness, many survivors are unfamiliar with what it feels like to exert their own agency or autonomy. When they first learn, it is thrilling, but it is also subject to overcorrection, which can look like burning bridges in relationships and overreacting to the slightest threat. It may be an overcorrection, but it is an important part of the process, and we must give survivors the space they need to learn their own autonomy again to create safe boundaries. It is a skill being relearned. In that sense, even overcorrections are to be blessed as steps in the process of trauma recovery.

At the end of the day, each person's boundaries are their own prerogative. Above all, we must be more concerned with the safety of boundaries than the inconvenience of hypervigilance. A trauma-safe church cares more about safety *for* trauma survivors than safety *from* them. Andrew (story above) puts the point this way: "Later in my journey, I realized that those who called me out for my anger issues were confusing hostility with anger. They objected to my anger without ever pausing to ask why it was there—and when they did find out, it was the shotgun that offended them, not my abuse!"[26] We must be committed to prioritizing the safety of trauma survivors over our own convenience or moral superiority. In this way, we can join survivors as they learn to foster healthy boundaries on their own terms that enable rather than diminish secure connection with others.

Regaining Big Picture Safety: The Spirit's Help for the Prayer-less

The Spirit ensures the safety of our intimacy with God. He does so by keeping our channels of communication open with God even when we cannot even utter a word with God. This slowly helps to rebuild our sense of safety in the universe. The Spirit prays on behalf of the prayer-less. We may fear that those times when we cannot pray as a result of trauma are offensive to God. We might think, "If I can't at least pray to God, he might just turn his back on me." This feels very unsafe and like our relationship with God may be scuttled by our own fragility. But not only will God never abandon us due to our union with him by the Spirit, he also keeps the channels of communication between us and him open. Because he is holy and loving, as well as the bond of love between the Father and the Son, the Spirit therefore

26. Schmutzer et al., *Naming Our Abuse*, 53.

is ready to be the communicative and vital bond between us and God. Because he is the vital bond, "the Spirit helps us in our weakness. We do not know what we ought to pray for, but the Spirit himself intercedes for us through wordless groans. And he who searches our hearts knows the mind of the Spirit, because the Spirit intercedes for God's people in accordance with the will of God" (Rom 8:26–27).

When we cannot pray, at those moments when we can't even bring ourselves to utter the Lord's Prayer, the Spirit takes our groanings and pains to God in the form of prayers for relief. The Spirit works for our good and on our behalf when we are exhausted and withered by the ongoing storm of trauma and its open wounds. He asks our good Father in heaven for good things, not evil things for us: "how much more will your Father in heaven give good gifts to those who ask him!" (Matt 7:11).

In addition to actively praying for us when we can't pray words of our own, the Spirit also has gifted us a range of prayers for us to pray, with prayers to suit any situation or life stage. The Spirit-breathed Scriptures are the Spirit's own way to build us up and develop our communicative agency in the context of our developing relationship and intimacy with God. For example, his words enable us to mourn well, as he gives us words for vocalizing our losses, yet doing so in the context of a sure hope of seeing God face-to-face one day:

> My soul thirsts for God,
> for the living God.
> When shall I come and behold
> the face of God?
> My tears have been my food
> day and night. (Ps 42:2–3, NRSV)

Looking Back and Looking Forwards with the Spirit

This has been a long chapter because of the many important ways by which we are given various forms of safety by the Spirit in the context of trauma and its aftermath. The Spirit provides our foundational safety in life by uniting us to God in a vital and communicative union with himself. Because our bond with God is his own Spirit, this bond cannot be broken. The Spirit of truth also helps us to feel safe with God existentially as we come to understand, appreciate, and be thankful for the union he has with us, and which unites us to other believers. As the healer, the Spirit safely transforms our will, mind, and passions so that we may once again flourish as God's images; the Spirit even helps us cooperate with this healing process by giving us the very virtues that we need to walk with him in new ways of light, life, and love. Though this process has its hills and valleys, there is a safe direction to this whole process, which is towards face-to-face relationship with God in the safe haven for humanity. The Spirit helps us develop the agency to live safely amidst the complexity of human relationships; he does this by helping us develop and maintain healthy boundaries with both healthy as well as toxic people and organizations. The Spirit gives us the safety of knowing that he will preserve our prayer life with God even when we cannot; he also gives us his own inspired words in the Bible through which we can pray. We can see how vital the presence and works of the Holy Spirit are for recovering a sense of safety and the agency for being safe in the wake of trauma.

It seems fitting to round out this chapter with a prayer for trauma survivors and their caregivers.

> A prayer for caregivers and survivors
>
> "For this reason I kneel before the Father, from whom every family in heaven and on earth derives its name. I pray that out of his glorious riches he may strengthen you with power through his Spirit in your inner being, so that Christ may dwell in your hearts through faith. And I pray that you, being rooted and established in love, may have power, together with all the Lord's holy people, to grasp how wide and long and high and deep is the love of Christ, and to know this love that surpasses knowledge—that you may be filled to the measure of all the fullness of God." (Eph 3:14–19)
>
> Amen.

7

The Church
as a Community of Safety

The Double Witness of the Church

We have already seen that one of the horrors of trauma is the disruption of our God-given flourishing in community. Recovering from trauma includes finding ways of reconnecting to the life of community and the flourishing that this life affords.[1] The reason why community life and flourishing are connected to one another is that people are created by God for the purpose of morally sound interpersonal relationships. When we have healthy relationships with other people, we are experiencing our human nature as it was intended by God to be enjoyed, which means we are more fully alive than when we are alone. The book of Genesis describes our relational constitution as we are the image of God together (Gen 1:26–27).

The open and empathetic welcome of a holy and loving community can make a profound difference in the lives of those recovering from trauma. If the church is to act as a source of hope in the world it must to do so by proclaiming a double witness: witnessing the stories of survivors—which involves recognizing and affirming the atrocities of those afflicted by trauma, welcoming survivors with kindness and curiosity—and also witnessing to the power of God's Trinitarian works and the hope that these bring. Through a double witness, trauma-safe churches not only listen to trauma but also offer the hope of healing. In allowing God to work through the church its members are able to serve as counter-evidence to horrors and trauma. Whereas the horrors of this world might suggest to some that God is either nonexistent, dismissive, or not present in the lives of his creation,

---

1. Herman, *Trauma and Recovery*, 196ff.

the church offers a healing witness in a new direction. *The church stands as evidence of God's presence and activity for the good and renewal of the world by being responsive to the will of the Spirit and conformed to the person of Christ.* Where trauma instills a sense of meaninglessness and hopelessness in the world, God the Trinity provides a foundation for the recovery of safety through the church.

But we know that these can be difficult paragraphs to read for those who have experienced trauma in and through the church. Consider again the following case already mentioned from Michelle Panchuk's work on religious trauma:

> A young boy is raped by a clergy member in his church and sworn to secrecy in the name of God. The clergy member tells him that disclosing the abuse to anyone will hurt the reputation of the church and undermine the work of God in the world. Whatever this child may come to believe about the church, the sight of a priest or even a church building continues to make him physically ill.[2]

For those who suffer at the hands of the church, the idea that God works through the church may be a repulsive thought. We need to welcome this repulsion and affirm it. Great harm has been inflicted on many in the name of God through the advocates of God's church. We need to proceed with caution when thinking about how the church might play a role in the recovery of safety. In particular, we must avoid a triumphalist view of the church by seeing that the church is not a "pure body" but is rather a "mixed body" of both saints and sinners.[3] While the church is one body that is sanctified in union with Christ, the church still lives east of Eden in a fallen world and this sinfulness is still manifest in the body. When the church sins and traumatizes its members, it is acting out of sync with who the church really is in Christ. While the church is destined for perfect purity through its living union with Christ, we must recognize that this purity is not only far from complete but is contradicted by sinful members in the present.

This being the case we must recognize that for some, recovery from trauma cannot mean rejoining the same community that was a source of harm and destruction. This is completely legitimate. But as we will see in this chapter, leaving a particular church community is not the same as leaving *the church*. One can leave one's community without leaving the larger

2. Panchuk, "Shattered Spiritual Self," 514.
3. McGrath, *Theology*, 157.

church united to Christ. And thus, while we hope that there are communities that can counter and transform the perceptions of those damaged by the church, efforts to rejoin local church communities cannot be forced or rushed. The pressure on survivors to do so is tempered by the fact that God is the agent of transformation and healing and not the church institutions or local congregations. In other words, what we most need is to root our practices of recovery in response to the ministries of the Trinity.

Before we consider more carefully the work of the Trinity in the church, an important clarification is needed: the church is a place where bodily safety is crucial. Judith Herman's words are worth recalling again: "Recovery still begins, always, with safety . . . Safety always begins with the body."[4] In our experiences both personally and as carers, trauma always manifests itself most acutely in the body, and one of the most effective routes for healing trauma begins at the somatic level.[5] This connects to the fact that formative attachments in infancy are registered (like trauma) at the somatic, kinesthetic, preverbal level. Secure attachment happens in the body before it happens in words. The same is true of insecure attachment and trauma recovery. Safety is always visceral and emotional before it is cognitive. One of the principal reasons safety never gets off the ground for people or survivors who are suffering in silence is because of a lack of basic safety at this level of the body. Therefore, before anything else, trauma-safe churches must create spaces to bless the bodies of survivors and honor their personal boundaries. Without this, no trauma recovery can take place. Trauma-safe people and places create an environment where the rule is "always ask before touching." Not presuming to hug or touch may seem so simple, but many survivors have grown up in environments where they did not have autonomy over their own bodies. Restoring control of the individual to their own body is a powerful and easy first step to recovering safety. We will discuss this vital point further in our final chapters on creating trauma-safe churches, but for now, we turn to the role of the church as a channel for God's life, love, and light in the lives of survivors and carers.

---

4. Herman, *Trauma and Recovery*, 269.

5. By "carers" we don't mean only a professional role. Rather, we intend this as an inclusive category covering anyone who offers care to survivors, including friends, family, peers, and the survivor themselves in the case of self-care.

The Trinitarian Foundation of the Church

The church and its members have a unique opportunity to stand as witnesses and to be symbols of the new safety that God offers to people. The New Testament talks of the community of the church not merely as a loving community of people, but as the place in which the persons of the Trinity dwell and work. In terms of the focused presence of the Trinity on Earth, it is God's people: Paul assures the Corinthian house churches that "you yourselves are God's temple and that God's Spirit dwells in your midst" (1 Cor 3:16). The church is also the primary channel through which God the Trinity ministers to the world. Consider Paul's words in 1 Corinthians:

> For just as the body is one and has many members, and all the members of the body, though many, are one body, so it is with Christ. For in the one Spirit we were all baptized into one body— Jews or Greeks, slaves or free—and we were all made to drink of one Spirit. (1 Cor 12:12–13)

If we are to reflect on the role of the church in positively contributing to a person or community's recovery from trauma, the first thing to acknowledge is that it is not *our* church, but God's—it was not instituted by us, we do not sustain it, build it, and it will last beyond our own best attempts to rescue it. The church is God's church. Yes, the church is united as one community, but it is not united by our best attempts at enforcing this unity. It is instituted by the work of the Spirit and united in Christ to serve the will of God in the world.[6] In other words, the church is one because God is one.

This emphasis on the oneness of God being the source of the church's unity was also taught by Jesus. Some of the final teachings of Jesus before his ascension focus on the unity of God's church in and through the work of the Trinity. Recall Jesus' words in John 17:

> As you, Father, are in me and I am in you, may they also be in us, so that the world may believe that you have sent me. The glory that you have given me I have given them, so that they may be one, as we are one, I in them and you in me, that they may become

6. The words of the Jewish Shema prayer ("Hear, O Israel: the LORD our God, the LORD is one," Deut 6:4) would be more than familiar to most Hebrew readers of Paul's epistles. The prayer served as a framing liturgy for daily life, much as the words of the Lord's Prayer do for many Christians. Paul's use of oneness language in 1 Corinthians affirms that the church is one because God is one. First Corinthians 12 provides an "ecclesial application of the [Jewish] Shema," and its emphasis on the oneness of God." See Byers, "One Body of the Shema in 1 Corinthians," 532.

completely one, so that the world may know that you have sent me and have loved them even as you have loved me. Father, I desire that those also, whom you have given me, may be with me where I am, to see my glory, which you have given me because you loved me before the foundation of the world. (John 17:21–24)

The community of the church is, at its most basic level, the union between people and God by his Spirit through the holy and loving means of the Trinity's work in our midst. In terms of our own personal perspective and experience of it, becoming part of this community occurs when we by faith join in the loving and holy unity that exists between the Father, the Son, and the Spirit. This involves entering into a knowing relationship with God by perceiving God's greatness and goodness through such means as the virtues of holy people, God's speech to us in Scripture, and the promises of God's love in the liturgy. Through knowing the Trinity's presence and love by such means believers join together in worshipping and serving him: "*the glory that you have given me I have given them, so that they may be one, as we are one*" (John 17:22). Embracing the love of the Trinity as this is offered in the church, we become one by sharing in the glory of God's love. As the church, we participate in the glory of the Trinity.

So, the unity of the church does not start with the church but with God the Trinity. From its inception, the community of the church is not something initiated by human hands, even if it has significant implications for human living. The church is not like our local Rotary club, because the church is something significantly more than a local gathering of like-minded individuals. The church is more than the sum of its parts. As the church, we are not constituted primarily by our efforts at gathering. Instead, we are gathered up by God and constituted as the living body of Christ by the actual work of the Trinity in our midst. Being a trauma-safe church starts with this recognition that it is only by the work of the Trinity that we can offer anything of hope to a broken world.

But what is the practical relevance of such a claim for the church grappling in the midst of a crisis of horrors? Put simply, realizing that the church is God's church, and it is most fully united when it glories in God's love shifts the perspective when we come to think about the church's role in healing those recovering from trauma. A community in which *we* enforce unity by insisting that the traumatized sit through services and participate by "pushing through the pain" to get to a place of healing emphasizes human hands and wills as the primary agents of healing. That puts a lot of pressure on pastors, parishioners, and survivors. This is not just bad pastoral ministry but bad theology, period. For if the church is to be a community of safety, then this is because it is a community through which the perfect love of the persons of Trinity can minister. And this is only made possible when we realize that healing is primarily God's work and ours *via participation* in it alone. In fact, we need to go a step further and realize that God even ministers through community *in spite of* the horrors inflicted in the name of the church. There is a profound grace in seeing that God continues to provide hope even when human hands have repeatedly defiled the body of Christ by traumatizing its members.

When we gain this Trinitarian perspective on the role of the church in recovering from trauma, the first thing that we should see is that the boundaries of community we create in our churches and denominations are not synonymous with the boundaries of the church as a work of the Spirit and the body of Christ. While survivors can leave a gathered community of the church, because they are held by Christ in the Spirit, we cannot think of these people as having left the church. The church is a community of safety united to Christ by the Spirit, which means that survivors are always members of the universal church even if they no longer attend local church services. There is a great release that comes from recognizing that leaving a congregation, denomination, or community is not the same as leaving the church. It is the presence and works of the Trinity that define who is inside and outside of the church, not people and their buildings. There is solace here for the lonely worshipper who is recovering from the immense damage done by trauma. The survivor is not separated from the church because he or she is not separated from God. In fact, Christ lives in the survivor; he or she may be visibly lonely but is not utterly lonely. The survivor is invisibly united to all Christians across all time and places, which means that the great cloud of deceased Christians who are in the intermediate state with Christ look on the survivor's life with love and hope. The survivor is also surrounded by God's ministering angels. For the period of time that this survivor worships and serves God in visible solitude, he or she may grow into a deeper intensity of relationship with him. This experience of long-lasting safety with God may form a strong attachment to him that in time allows the survivor to engage with a Christian community.

Realizing that many have difficulty feeling safe in church communities and that belonging to the church does not depend on being present in corporate worship every Sunday is a helpful point of reflection for those who seek to be good shepherds. Church ministers today may find it difficult at first to recognize the forms that survivor's spiritual practices may take either because they are unfamiliar with the dynamics of trauma, or else because they may mistrust what God can do in the life of a solitary Christian. As ministers in the church, it is important to see that pastoral care is not dependent on attendance at corporate worship. God may care for his sheep in ways that exceed a local church's weekly routines. Welcoming God's surprising ways of care for his sheep and the surprising ways in which survivors may nurture their faith is key to being helpful to those who have lost a sense of safety and seek welcome in the gathered church community. We need to trust that God can care for people in irregular as well as in regular ways. For non-traumatized people who see trauma as an "irregular" experience of other people, it should hardly be surprising if the spirituality of survivors takes "irregular" forms. To the extent that ministers and lay leaders fail to acknowledge the deep disturbances that trauma may generate in a person's spiritual life, and therefore the unique shape that healing must take, they perpetuate the survivor's sense of alienation and isolation. There is no "one-size-fits-all" formula for trauma, recovery, or pastoral care. We must care for each trauma in the special way it manifests. Failing to provide attentive care for God's people is a grievous shortcoming because of the problems that it compounds within survivors, such as helplessness and hopelessness.

Demanding conformity to an external norm such as unfailing weekly church attendance, and shaming parishioner failure to meet this standard can actually reinforce the hypervigilance of PTSD. This is counterproductive to trauma recovery. Instead, as members of trauma-safe churches we need to be willing and eager to meet survivors exactly where they are. If we care about what each sheep *needs*, then we must find ways of understanding that particular person. Trauma is completely idiosyncratic, and so is the path to recovery.[7] Our pastoral care should reflect these idiosyncrasies and accommodate to each survivor. A failure to do this will perpetuate the harmful and counterproductive idea that there is any kind of "one-size-fits-all" approach to trauma recovery. For example, a seemingly innocuous public message noticing that someone was missing from a service for the third week in a row might only compound feelings of shame associated with withdrawing from community. We must find ways of seeing the individual

7. See this forcefully underlined in Rothschild, *8 Keys to Safe Trauma Recovery*.

for who they are, finding ways to of reassuring them that above all else, they are loved by God.

As a trauma survivor with PTSD, I (Preston) recall a relevant experience in which I was triggered during a Sunday morning sermon by a pastor's description of domestic violence. My whole body froze, my perception narrowed, and I felt dissociated inside and very nauseous. I felt like the congregation had put a spotlight on me. It was embarrassing for me to have to get up during a sermon and retreat to the bathroom, just so I could splash cold water on my face, catch my breath, and try to return my body to a state of normal relaxation. Rather than shaming me for this response or treating me awkwardly, my friends who knew my trauma history checked in with me to make sure I was okay, affirmed my retreat to the bathroom (even telling me how proud they were of me), and encouraged me to do this as much as I needed in the future. This response from my local church members made a huge difference for my trauma recovery in a church setting. It is ministry practices like this that emerge from seeing every Christian through Christ's gaze and perspective; it requires ministering out of a union with Christ that is so intimate that we begin to develop "the mind of Christ" for the sake of the other person's good (1 Cor 2:16).

For the survivor recovering this sense of being safely loved, there are many tools, stretching back over the history of the church, that might help recover this sense of being safely loved within the church. Belonging to the church as a community of safety means that regardless of where survivors go to church on Sunday, they remain in spiritual communion with the universal church across the ages. Our communion extends to include saints from the past and luminaries from the present, though they do not see each other face-to-face. The encouragement we receive from the stories of virtuous Christians from the past (by looking at the lives of saints) or from those present, or from Christian music from the past and present, assures us that we belong to a long story in which God has been faithful to his people. For example, one might draw great comfort by considering the lives of past saints such as Perpetua and Felicity, who perceived God was present with them and communicated directly to them even while they were under house arrest, in prison, and in the arena to be devoured by wild beasts as martyrs. The prayers, lives, stories, and biblical commentaries of past and present members of the body of Christ are very helpful tools through which God may work in carers and survivors to grow in confidence that we do belong to God regardless of church attendance patterns. This often goes alongside encouraging growth in Christlikeness as we try to live our daily lives emulating the qualities that Jesus' disciples have historically valued, such as humility, mourning over evil, gentleness, being just, merciful, pure-hearted, peacemaking, and perseverant in doing good (Matt 5:3–10).

For those not currently participating in a particular Christian community, the spirituality of Christian monastic hermits has a lot to offer, and one of the authors of this book (Scott) currently lives by their wisdom and example. These practices include a regular pattern of prayer, spiritual accountability and confession to a qualified person, Bible reading, creating sacred spaces, purposeful work, and participating in the Lord's Supper.

These and other practices have long been honored in the church. However, for some of us this vocation of mostly spiritual solitude has been thrust on us through suffering. Though unusual today, it is not historically unusual, as many Christian saints have lived in near solitude across the centuries. When trauma survivors experience isolation there may be deep comfort in knowing that solitude is one form that secure attachment with God can take in the lives of Christians. Solitude with God should not be stigmatized but is a welcome gift in trauma-safe churches. Although trauma is isolating, it is comforting to know that this isolation can be offered to God and transformed into the gift of solitude. Importantly, by encouraging church members, survivors and otherwise, to exercise the gift of solitude, this does not mean further isolation because in solitude one encounters the spiritual grace of communion with God and all Christians in union with God.[8] The spiritual discipline of solitude is a valid vocation that God offers to church members, survivors and otherwise, and it is an honorable vocation, not a shameful one or a second best when it is received as an extraordinary gift akin to the gift of celibacy.

Whether we are active participants in local Christian congregations or not, the life of God the Trinity provides the organic foundation and energy for healing us and helping us slowly become deeper lovers of God and of our fellow human beings.

The Church as a Community of Holy Difference

For anyone on the margins of the church, those on the inside can appear so unlike us that even imagining being part of such a community can disrupt

8. For an excellent introduction to solitude as a Christian practice, see Nouwen, *Way of the Heart*.

our sense of identity. Our lives are not neat enough, our appearance not perfect enough, our faith not strong enough. For trauma survivors in particular, just making eye contact with other church members on Sunday morning may be hard work. This sense of being outside and feeling disconnected can manifest itself as a strange combination of judgment and ostracization; of seeing people unlike me but also recoiling at the possibility of being like them. This outsider phenomena might occur for many reasons, not least because we cannot know just how much like us those who appear shiny and perfect really are. In fact, these people are probably much more insecure, broken, faithless, and unstable than they might appear. They are also probably more traumatized than they are able to admit.

But it's possible this phenomenon has a deeper root; that there is an expectation that "Christian people" or "churchgoing folk" fit a certain mold. This is very easily projected—if the people who are placed in positions of authority or visibility are of one kind, then very easily that *kind* can become the norm not only for belonging to that particular community, but also for dictating the expectations of Christian discipleship. In the same way that a church in which those preaching sermons are never those confessing sins is a church in which there is no room to admit to mistakes, a church in which the preachers never deal with mental health challenges is a church in which the issues with which many people wrestle are essentially ignored.[9]

A church in which being psychologically typical is a prerequisite for effectively preaching the gospel is a church in which those recovering from trauma will never be accepted. Worse still, such recovery will not be meaningfully and intentionally supported because even if recovery is permissible, it will likely be faked in order to conform to group expectations: "Feeling that one has to mimic one's spiritual life in order to fit in with what other human beings think is the norm can only be destructive."[10]

The reality is that the church, the true church of Jesus Christ, has always been and will always be a community of radical diversity and

---

9. "The absence of preaching on mental health issues leads to a gap in the spiritual lives of a congregation in which the power of the gospel is not brought to bear on a fundamentally important issue in many people's lives. The word of God needs to be preached into all areas of human experience . . . Similarly, Bible study and preaching that do not take lamentation seriously deprive people of a powerful biblical resource—the psalms of lament—that has the potential to bring about the holy articulation of pain and sadness, which leads to a sense of shared experience of belonging in the midst of brokenness." Swinton, *Finding Jesus in the Storm*, 210.

10. Swinton, *Finding Jesus in the Storm*, 86.

difference in terms of its local cultural expressions. In addition, the degree of healing that various members in the church will have experienced will also vary. Every Christian needs God's healing works and balms in their lives. Pretending this is not the case obscures the fact that Christian salvation is about being healed in terms of our relationships with God, each other, within ourselves, and with nature. Though it may be more comfortable to spend time with those who appear to be healthier, that is not the call of the church as a people group. Every member of God's family matters. Moreover, every member of God's family needs healing of one kind or another because every member knows something of the trauma of living in a fallen world. To become trauma-safe churches, we must learn to normalize trauma instead of stigmatizing it. This means we must embrace the diversity of our group in its beauty and brokenness.

It is important to make a distinction here about difference in the body of the church. While diversity may be beautiful, it may also stem from brokenness. Sometimes as with trauma the diversity is caused by brokenness such as the survivor who is psychologically atypical due to PTSD. Other times, as with race, the diversity is not caused by brokenness, rather brokenness is caused by diversity when this is viewed through the violent lens of racism. Some forms of diversity are created by tragedy while others are just a part of the diverse fabric of humanity. Making this distinction helps to clarify that by celebrating difference and diversity trauma-safe churches are not celebrating the violence of trauma. Rather the point is to embrace the diversity of all people as they are both whole and broken with "unconditional positive regard."[11]

Whenever particular local manifestations of the church choose to ignore the diversity of its members both whole and broken, they fail to participate as fully as they might in the community of beautiful difference that the Holy Spirit is instigating in the world. The depiction of the Day of Pentecost in Acts 2 describes the Holy Spirit's initiation of the church as "sudden" and unexpected (Acts 2:1). The power that comes as people see God's work in the community of faith is a work that brings about a huge diversity; the disciples speaking in foreign tongues in the power of the Spirit is a mark of the inclusivity and difference of the church from its inception. But it is only by the Spirit that such difference can fully be embraced. Consider the implications of Paul's claim that the church is *one body* in Christ through the baptism of the Spirit:

11. Rogers, *On Becoming a Person*, 62.

> The members of the body that seem to be weaker are indispens-
> able, and those members of the body that we think less honorable
> we clothe with greater honor, and our less respectable members
> are treated with greater respect; whereas our more respectable
> members do not need this. But God has so arranged the body,
> giving the greater honor to the inferior member there may be no
> dissension within the body, but the members may have the same
> care for one another. If one member suffers, all suffer together with
> it; if one member is honored, all rejoice together with it. (1 Cor
> 12:14–26)

By Paul's way of thinking, the least of these in our midst are really the first
among us, meaning that the traumatized in the church who have been silenced, shamed, and overlooked are now to be empowered, honored, and
lifted up. Paul's image of the body is one in which those most disrespected
by culture or society of our time are those who have pride of place in the
church. Thus, those who have been traumatized, or have felt ostracized by
the community of the church, or who feel that their shame is too great to
participate, may actually be amongst the most honorable and important
parts of the community of the church. The implication is that if the church
wishes to reflect this reality it must find ways not only of including those
who are seen as inferior by society, but of honoring these people. At the very
least, this involves hearing their stories, recognizing their pain, acknowledging their existence—in other words, not pretending that the church is
a community only for the healthy and spiritually enlivened. A great place
to acknowledge such difference in the community is to include voices from
within our tradition that speak to the horror of human existence; to not shy
away from engaging with passages of Scripture that speak of lament. It also
includes interceding for those suffering abuse, such as domestic or sexual
abuse, in our regular cycles of corporate prayer; to use examples in our
preaching of those who reflect the difference that exists in the community
of church as the body of Christ.[12] These are all tangible and simple ways in
which the voices of the ostracized might be given recognition in the narrative of our liturgies.

We can draw something even stronger than this from Paul's words in
1 Corinthians 12. Not only are outsiders and those deemed as inferior to be
honored, but we *need* these members in our communities. The body will not
function without difference. So, the inclusion, recognition, and honoring of

---

12. For an introduction to trauma-informed preaching, see Travis, *Unspeakable*.

those recovering from trauma is not only for the sake of recovery. It is not the healthy leaning over to minister to the broken. Rather, those who are not suffering because of trauma need, and benefit from, the inclusion of the traumatized in the community of faith. This shift of emphasis is crucial, for it turns the issue away from a question of pity and caring for the vulnerable to recognize that without finding ways of including all of God's children in the church, the church fails to represent Christ's body.

The church community that reflects its true identity is one in which the suffering of one member is bound up in the suffering of all and the honoring of one is bound up in the rejoicing of all. There are different ways of interpreting this recognition of common pain. First, we must see it is a reality. Even in the community in which the pain of trauma is not recognized or felt as common pain, objectively speaking, the wounds inflicted on the members of the church are wounds inflicted on us all. Martin Luther makes the point well by concluding, "Therefore, when we feel pain, when we suffer, when we die, let us turn to this, firmly believing and certain that it is not we alone, but Christ and the Church who are in pain and are suffering and are dying with us."[13] This realization can only lead to further lament when we see that in cases in which the wounds of trauma are inflicted by the church, there is a kind of self-harm involved. The destruction and violation of victims of trauma is a destruction and violation of Christ's very body.

Consider the case of how the African Methodist Episcopal denomination (AME) was formed. One of the founders was Richard Allen, who was born a slave in 1760 and earned his freedom in 1786 after converting to Methodism. He began preaching and was invited to preach regularly at an interracial church called St. George's, where Black worshippers were treated as second-class citizens. One day Allen and his fellow Black minister Rev. Absalom Jones accidentally knelt to pray in a spot reserved for white members and one of the church's white trustees objected:

> We had not been long upon our knees before I heard a considerable scuffing and low talking. I raised my head up and saw one of the trustees, H–M–, having hold of the Rev. Absalom Jones, pulling him up off his knees, and saying, "You must get up—you must not kneel here." Mr. Jones replied, "wait until prayer is over." Mr. H–M– said, "no, you must get up now." Mr. Jones said, "wait until prayer is over, and I will get up and trouble you no more."[14]

13. Luther, *Luther's Works*, 42:163.
14. This story is cited in Tisby, *Color of Compromise*, 53–54.

After the fallout from this incident, Allen and many like him became part of the tragic and inexcusable trend of a culturally forced exodus of Black Christians from white churches in the United States. The theological truth about this trauma needs to be clearly stated. In cases like this the church has traded its theological identity for cultural violence. By denying the diversity that makes up its actual unity, the church has torn itself apart because it has denied Christ and those who belong to him. By depriving its members, the church dismembered itself. The history of racism in America is a testament to this truth. When we traumatize or retraumatize the members of Christ's body we are traumatizing Christ himself and those who belong to him, because the objective reality is that we are one body in him. What one member suffers we all suffer. Where trauma has fragmented the one body, our unity must be remembered.

Second, however, we know that regardless of the objective status of the body, this level of unity and identification does not come easily or quickly in its outward forms. We're told in Acts 2 that the result of the Spirit's unifying work was that "All who believed were together and had all things in common; they would sell their possessions and goods and distribute the proceeds to all, as any had need. Day by day, as they spent much time together in the temple, they broke bread at home and ate their food with glad and generous hearts, praising God and having the goodwill of all the people" (Acts 2:45–47). We cannot straightforwardly go back to the church of the first century, but that doesn't mean that we cannot seek to learn from it and strive to embody its ethos and practices. Making room not only to worship God, but to sit and eat together is vital for the church that wants to express outwardly the truth that their pain and joy is bound together. Trauma-safe churches outwardly express that the life of its members is life together where joys and sorrows are shared. Sharing our joys and sorrows together within the body of Christ means that we need to be healthily open to one another during the appalling as well as the uplifting seasons of life, as a way to serve the body and survive together—even in the wake of trauma. "When our brother or sister in Jesus struggles to hold onto the great joy of Jesus, other brothers and sisters hold it for him or her."[15] Importantly, adopting Jesus' teaching on the virtues of humility, meekness, mercy, mourning, and righteousness shape how we do this. We can come alongside one another, and for those experiencing a loss of the presence and hope in Jesus, express hard-won hope:

15. Swinton, *Finding Jesus in the Storm*, 87.

142

OK, for now it feels like Jesus has abandoned you . . . At this moment you don't feel the way I feel, but I desperately want to help you hold on to the possibility that God exists, and the possibility that God loves you, and the possibility that joy might be closer than you think. I know that's not how you feel, but it remains a possibility, and I want to hold that for you.[16]

Scott remembers a difficult time when his German uncle, Roland, came alongside him in prayer and merely said the words *"ich bin bei dir"*—"I am with you." Roland's presence, his words, and the virtuous mode of life within which they were spoken, assured Scott of both God's and the Christian community's presence with him despite not sensing this at the time. Roland essentially said, "I want to sit with you in this darkness (as best I can), and I want to say to you that I love you and that God loves you and that we can wait together. The storm will pass. Let me hold joy for you for a little while."[17]

Finally, an acknowledgment that the church surpasses the limits and boundaries we attempt to place on human community leads to the recognition that the church extends beyond even our sense of denomination and tradition. For those who are unable to return to gathered worship—because this is too painful or detrimental to trauma recovery—even their acts of private devotion can be seen as part of the church's worship. There is something freeing that comes in seeing that the life of the church is not limited by our structures. The simple words of the Lord's Prayer, which we explored more carefully in chapter 4, might serve as a simple way of joining our prayer to the ongoing worship of the community of the church, stretching across cultures and across history. One very tangible manifestation of this corporate participation is the use of Daily Offices—morning prayer, evening prayer, and compline. These are not mere acts of private devotion, but simple, structured forms of prayer which allow us to join in the prayer of the whole church. The Daily Offices can be points of stability for those in ordained ministry, allowing them to participate in the prayer life of the church and lead the congregation in prayer in a way that does not depend on their own ebbing and flowing in relationship with God. The Anglican theologian Evelyn Underhill puts it like this:

What we all need then, and the priest I suppose needs very specially, is some link between our own fluctuating communion with

16. Swinton, *Finding Jesus in the Storm*, 87.

17. Swinton, *Finding Jesus in the Storm*, 87.

> God and the great continuous action of the Church; a devotional
> pattern, a reminder of the vast life of prayer coming out of the
> past, stretching forward to the future, into which our small prayer
> is woven; something which shall steady us, transcend our chang-
> ing feelings, and keep our minds in tune with the Mind of the
> Church.[18]

Underhill's comments are aimed at those in licensed ministry, but we might think that they have some import for the prayer life of those in the midst of trauma recovery. As the psychiatrist Bessel van der Kolk observes, "all trauma is preverbal . . . trauma victims themselves become literally speech-less—when the language area of the brain shuts down."[19] Van der Kolk is describing the phenomenon that during traumatic events the Broca's area of the brain—the part of the neocortex responsible for regulating lan-guage—is severely compromised for trauma survivors, such that PTSD has debilitating effects similar to the speech impairments of strokes.[20] This is why survivors frequently find it exceedingly difficult to find adequate language for speaking about the atrocities they have endured. The simple liturgies of the Daily Office provide a predictable and constant source of words, even for those who find themselves wordless. The bar for partici-pation in such liturgies is very low—one need not even step foot inside a church building to join the ongoing prayer of the church. This is good news for trauma survivors and an important reminder for trauma-safe churches.

The Eucharist as a Source of Medicinal Unity

We conclude this chapter by thinking about the role of the Eucharist (or Holy Communion, or the Lord's Supper) in uniting the church as one body in Christ. It is a long-standing claim of Christian theology that the Eu-charist is a source of unity in the church; by participating in the body and blood of Christ (however we think this claim should be interpreted), we are participating in Christ's body, the church. As the theologian J. B. Torrance puts it, "We are never more truly human than at the Lord's Table, when Christ draws us into his life of communion with the Father and into com-munion with one another."[21]

18. Underhill, *Collected Papers*, 149–50.

19. Van der Kolk, *Body Keeps the Score*, 43, 244.

20. Van der Kolk, *Body Keeps the Score*, 43.

21. Torrance, *Worship, Community and the Triune God of Grace*, 39.

The Eucharist is both a sign and a means of unity in the church—but it is so because it allows us to participate in the life of the one God of Israel through the sacrifice of Christ, the one Lord.[22] Again, as with the discussion of common pain, there is both a universal and local manifestation of this truth. We know that as a community when we share in the bread and wine that we are never more fully united, however fragmented our local group may be. For this reason, it is crucial for a local community that wishes to embody and participate in the unity of the church to celebrate the Eucharist together, in whatever form this takes. Indeed, the practice of taking the celebration of the community out to the housebound and sick may be one such way that those recovering from trauma can be included, even if they cannot yet gather. The traumatized are no less worthy of home-delivered communion than the other sick in our midst. Taking bread and wine to our survivors outside the weekly gathering can be a powerful, tangible sign that we see and value their wounds.

There are also important connections between trauma and Eucharist that can emphasize the trauma at the heart of the Christian gospel. In the Eucharist we are constantly remembering the traumatic event of Christ's body broken *for us,* and indeed of his full life offered as a sacrifice for us. We can rightly say that "bodies and memories come together in the celebration of the Eucharist . . . [T]he Eucharist becomes the ideal place to search for the somatic memory at the heart of the Christian faith."[23] As we have seen, surviving trauma leaves behind terrifying memories and intolerable sensations in the bodies of survivors. Recovery therefore involves soothing these terrors in embodied ways that speak deeper than words. It is significant in this respect that the church has central spiritual practices that can profoundly minister to trauma survivors. We can think of this ministry in terms of the double witness introduced in this chapter. For some the Eucharist provides a witness to the laments and losses of trauma. In the Eucharist, the crucified Christ ministers to our memories of terror when he meets our brokenness with his own broken body. In a cathartic embrace of Christ and survivor, practices like the Eucharist offer a safe space where all church members can see their pain "mirrored" and transformed in Christ

22. Indeed, it is no accident that in writing on the appropriate practice of the Eucharist in 1 Corinthians 10 that Paul again evokes the oneness language of the Shema: "the cup of blessing that we bless, is it not a sharing in the blood of Christ? The bread that we break, is it not a sharing in the body of Christ? Because there is one bread, we who are many are one body, for we all partake of the one bread" (1 Cor 10:16–17).

23. See O'Donnell, *Broken Bodies.*

and in one another.[24] For others the Eucharist provides a witness to God's Trinitarian works of healing by offering a symbol of God's life and love as this is reassured by the corporate witness to it. In this sense, the risen and ascended Christ ministers his resurrection wholeness and healing to his church as one who has been through trauma himself but now rests perfectly in the love of God.[25] As a double witness to both the losses and healing of trauma, the Eucharist offers a safe space in trauma-sensitive churches for survivor care. If we wish to recognize and affirm the place of trauma in our community, we might look no further than this bodily memory of Christ's self-sacrificial trauma.

We return to Preston's story. In the same church community where pastors and friends welcomed my trauma responses, they also encouraged me by communicating that my trauma triggers were not a threat to their communal identity. This helped me to regain a sense of safety. But that was not all. To this day the strongest memories I retain from my experience in that community was the emphasis placed on the Lord's Supper. I knew what to expect every week. It was a ritual I craved. After the music and the sermon, the pastor would invite us with unscripted, heartfelt words to come, "taste and see" that God was good and that he was giving himself to us in the broken body and blood of his Son. Music would play and as desired groups of friends would meander to the front to huddle around small tables where a single celebrant would mutter very intimate words of institution under the cover of the music. It was a personal experience for us all. Loaves of bread were torn and dipped in large bowls of wine. It was a sensory experience that viscerally invited my whole body, traumatized as it was, to the broken body of Christ. And around me were people who loved me enough to enter my brokenness with me. My brokenness was met by Christ's broken body in the Eucharist and the larger body of the corporate church. And through it all, I was the one who chose when to get up and approach the table. It was the perfect mix of restored agency, embodiment, and accompaniment to meet me in my trauma with a healing witness.

As we can see, the Eucharist can be a powerful healing ritual in trauma-safe churches because in it the traumatized Christ offers himself to his traumatized people in an intimate way as his body meets the body. Because

24. On the mirroring between Christ and survivors, see Jones, *Trauma and Grace*, 75–83.

25. For the importance of Christ's ascension for atonement, see Moffitt, *Atonement and the Logic of Resurrection*.

of the vulnerability of such practices, it is very important that we never force anyone to take the Eucharist or coerce them in any way. An experience as vulnerable as tasting and swallowing needs to be the free decision of each individual member of the church. Remember, trauma is the experience of powerlessness; the first principle of trauma recovery is restoring agency and empowering survivors. Personal empowerment also applies to our Eucharistic practices. We must take care in trauma-safe churches to practice ministries of embodiment while also safeguarding the structure and order of such vulnerable experiences.

Preston's story shows how we might also see that the act of participating in the Eucharist playing a medicinal role in our lives. To make this point, consider how eating bread and wine might play a similar role in trauma recovery to that of eating for those who are recovering from eating disorders. In the case of anorexia, for instance, "rational persuasion, therapy and . . . pharmaceuticals tend not to help, at least not on their own . . . [T]he road to recovery lies in getting them to eat."[26] In this example, recovery from eating disorders is not primarily about persuading people to change their mind but retraining the body and the mind to relate to food differently; it requires a shift in perception. Eating and drinking slowly reshape the mind and the body such that the perception of these practices is transformed, even when there is resistance on a purely cognitive level. Perhaps we can imagine that something similar happens in the practice of the Eucharist.[27] Just as eating food might transform the perception of the world for those suffering from eating disorders, perhaps eating and drinking the bread and wine in the Eucharist can transform our perception of ourselves and our world. We might extend this account to also include a shift of perception of one another as fellow members in the body of Christ. In these cases, the Eucharist is a ritual that helps us change perception. "In their best uses, rituals teach us how to see more truly, and for us to do that, our bodies must be involved."[28]

26. Cuneo, *Ritualized Faith*, 194.

27. Cuneo writes that "important elements that contribute to the loosening of the grip of the disorder do not consist in the presentation or acceptance of propositions about God or God's activity or experiences that aim to evoke beliefs about God or God's activity . . . [I]nstead . . . there are important elements that contribute to the loosening of the grip of the sin-disorder that operate—at least in large measure—at a sub-doxastic level, below the level of understanding or belief." Cuneo, *Ritualized Faith*, 195.

28. Johnson, *Human Rites*, 56.

If this is right, then it provides a helpful way of thinking about the role of the Eucharist in trauma recovery. Participating in the Eucharist is unlikely to change the beliefs of those who are recovering their sense of safety overnight—it doesn't seek to *immediately* persuade anyone that the community of the church is a safe place to be and that God is a source of kindness and goodness, rather than malevolence. But the simple acts of joining ourselves to Christ and therefore to all of those who belong to Christ's body might slowly and subconsciously retrain the body to see the world as God intends it, rather than how it is currently perceived. This conclusion is significant not only for the traumatized, but for all of us. For as we have seen repeatedly, the outward forms of the church do not reflect its objective reality as a body united in Christ and with one another. The continuation of the Eucharist is vital for our regaining of this reality and the shifting of our perception.

We must also remember that the Eucharist is not the sum total of what the church can offer for trauma care. But the Eucharist provides a paradigm for entering the sacramental worldview of the Christian life because it points to a ritual that summarizes the Christian approach to the whole world. On Sunday morning the celebrant blesses God with the eucharistic bread and wine and the whole church feeds on Christ at God's table. But on Monday through Saturday the blue-collar Christian is sent out into the world to replicate this act by learning to be hungry for God at every moment of every day:

> You do not remain and are not to remain at the Communion table . . . [W]hen you follow him, you do indeed leave the Communion table when you go away from it, but then it is as if the Communion table followed you, for where he is, there is the Communion table—and when you follow him, he accompanies you. What earnestness of eternity, that wherever you go, whatever you do, he still accompanies you . . . [D]o not forget that where he is, there is the altar, that his altar is neither on Moriah nor on Gerizim, or any visible there, but that it is where he is. If this were not so, then you of course would have to remain at the Communion table, take up residence there, never budge from the spot, but such superstition is not Christianity.[29]

So, while the Eucharist is a unique sacrament that mediates God's love in the church for the traumatized, God's love can be manifest in eucharistic

29. Kierkegaard, *Christian Discourses*, 273–74.

ways in the church beyond the confines of Sunday morning.[30] For example, survivors may find the care of God in a number of mundane events like a refreshing evening walk, loving relationships, a hot cup of tea before bed, the love of animals, the relaxing scent of a favorite candle, or a fun night out with a safe friend. Or, survivors and carers alike may feel God's special presence in volunteer ministries where meaning is made from suffering by loving Christ in the face of the poor at a local outreach shelter. Even a simple prayer at mealtimes can invite God's trauma-safe love. The important point is that in the Eucharist we are not given an exclusive medicine but a balm that is inclusive of all the events of our daily life. After all, *eucharistia* simply means "thankfulness." Wherever we can learn to "give thanks" to the Lord for the feeling of being safely loved and recovering safe boundaries, we are participating in a sacramental approach to the world that recovers safety after trauma. In all of this the church is a community of safety that promotes even more safety for survivors in the world.

Towards a Model of the Trauma–Safe Church

This chapter has considered some of the important theological underpinnings of the practical work that will be developed in the next chapters. We have tried to highlight the areas of obvious contact to the practical discussion, but the full extent of our practical proposal will not be made apparent until the end of chapter 8. This ordering is intentional. While our aim is to offer concrete and practical suggestions for ministering and belonging to a trauma-safe church, these depend on us seeing the theological grounding of such suggestions. Our proposal is rooted in a conviction that the church is the primary way in which God ministers to the world, and therefore to those who recover from trauma. But as we have shown, this claim is liable to be misunderstood and even misappropriated by those who are agents of harm. Having a robust Trinitarian account of the church is vital if we are to see how the church, the church of Christ, can be a source of healing, wholeness, and goodness in the world.

---

30. Dru Johnson makes a relevant point that not just church but all of life is made up of rituals. See Johnson, *Human Rites*, 126.

Part 3 _____

Creating Trauma–Safe Churches

8

Principles of a Trauma-Safe Church
The Hippocratic Church

Turning toward the Dawn

We have seen so far that our life is lived east of Eden. We live in a world that is not only fallen but also full of horrors and trauma. In the aftermath of horrors and trauma we lose a sense of safety in our relationship with God and one another. This involves a loss of secure attachment in our connections with others that are designed for maximal flourishing. We are either not safely loved by others through neglect or we are not afforded the safe boundaries that keep others from violating our honor and disempowering us. When these horrors become traumatic, we feel unsafe in our bodies and unsafe in the world. In Jeremiah's words, trauma survivors see "terror all around" (Jer 20:4, 10).[1]

It is also important to remember that horrors and trauma are not always obvious. We may have encountered them so often that we become numb to their effects on others and accept them as commonplace or just "the way it is." Take for example a story of racial trauma told by Esau McCaulley:

> I was eight years old the first time someone called me a nigger. It all began around midmorning when I started to feel sick at Rolling Hills Elementary School. I was not a kid prone to escape the classroom. My mother worked during the day, and there was no one to take care of me if I fell ill . . . I dutifully went to the school office, where they dialed the number . . . I asked to speak to Laurie McCaulley, but the speaker said that I had the wrong number and

---

1. O'Connor, *Jeremiah*, 33, 133.

abruptly hung up the phone. I told the office manager to try again
. . . Again, I nervously asked for Laurie McCaulley. The man on
the other line angrily said something along the lines of "I told you
that you have the wrong number . . . Can't you niggers even use
the phone?" . . .

I remember wondering how he could tell that I was Black
without seeing me . . . I also recall the rage building alongside my
awareness of my powerlessness. I knew I had been emotionally
assaulted, but there was no way to respond . . . I was infuriated by
my own powerlessness.[2]

Tragically, horrors like these are commonplace. Yet despite their prevalence
they are no less damaging. We must avoid growing numb to stories such as
this. This story painfully illustrates trauma and the loss of safety it creates.
Trauma is at root an experience of violence in which one is powerless to
escape and as a result of this lives with terrifying reminders of the experience. While not all go on to develop post-traumatic stress after such events,
many survivors suffer in silence with overbearing feelings of rage, helplessness, despair, and terror. These survivors are in our midst. They are in our
churches.

However, we have also considered how God the Trinity helps us recover a sense of safety after trauma. Through God's Trinitarian works, we
can feel safely loved, recover safe boundaries, recover a big picture sense
of safety, and feel safe in our bodies. In an earlier chapter we captured this
approach with the metaphor of a "dawn of Sunday," which involves straddling the boundary between Holy Saturday and Easter Sunday, having one
foot planted in the horrors of trauma and loss while having the other firmly
rooted toward the hope of healing. This approach involves a *double witness*
where we are honest about the losses and laments of trauma while remaining open to God the Trinity's works of healing, life, and love. We can find
healing through being safely loved in our losses while also recovering safe
boundaries that offer new life after trauma. Because healing should take
place where the wound has occurred, we know that this double witness
involves tending to our whole selves as we live in our bodies and have a
larger perspective on a big picture of the world. We have seen that God's
primary means for helping us recover safety after trauma is through God's
community of safety, the church. It is crucial to be open to creating church
communities that are trauma-safe.

2. McCaulley, *Reading While Black*, 118–20.

In the face of our world's violence the proposal to create trauma-safe church can sometimes feel amusing at best or a cruel joke at worst. How could healing possibly come about in our churches for stories like that of Esau's? Are we not beyond the hope of healing with such violence? Returning to racial trauma as an example, consider the following words of Martin Luther King Jr. to the bereaved families of a racist bombing of an Alabama church:

> So in spite of the darkness of this hour we must not despair. We must not become bitter . . . I hope you find consolation from Christianity's affirmation that death is not the end. Death is not a period that ends the great sentence of life, but a comma that punctuates it to a more lofty significance . . . It has its bleak and painful moments . . . but through it all, God walks with us. Never forget that God is able to lift you from the fatigue of despair to the buoyancy of hope . . . Dawn will come.[3]

A trauma-safe church is able to face the darkness with eyes open and ready to see that "dawn will come." Trauma-safe churches offer a double witness to both trauma and healing. We have to believe that no matter the horrors God is still the God of his church and that we can join his Trinitarian works to create trauma-safe spaces.

Given the reality of horrors and trauma and God the Trinity's healing work to recover safety in the church, how are we to begin fostering trauma-safe spaces today? In this chapter we wish to outline four criteria for a trauma-safe church. We will offer the tentative definition that a church or community is trauma-safe *if it is a place where those vulnerable to trauma are protected and where trauma healing can take place*. For a church to be a trauma-safe space there must be at least the following four criteria: trauma-safe churches

(1) do no harm,

(2) listen to survivors tell their stories of trauma,

(3) take action to empower restoration, and

(4) engage and bless the bodies of their members.

These four criteria roughly correspond to the four senses of safety we have been exploring in each chapter (big picture safety, being safely loved,

---

3. King, "Eulogy for the Martyred Children" and "A Knock at Midnight," cited in Cone, *Cross and the Lynching Tree*, 87–89.

safe boundaries, and safety in the body). Of course, these four criteria are not sufficient to make a community completely immune to all forms of trauma or to respond perfectly to the traumatized. That may be a goal that no community can fully realize this side of glory. But we do think that a church will never be trauma-safe without these criteria, at least. More can be added but we need these to start.

We hope that these four criteria can do a couple of things for you the reader. For everyone, let these become *guiding principles* for any community or church that wishes to become trauma-safe. If you are a survivor, we offer you these principles as a guide to determine whether your community or church is a safe place for your story and recovery. For pastors, we urge you to implement these principles in the ethos of your local church. For carers, please use these principles in your relationships and groups you lead where it is helpful. For families, remember these principles as you interact with your loved ones. Lastly, you do not have to be a Christian for these principles to be a source of trauma-safe community. For example, they would be helpful for thinking about how to make any workplace trauma-safe.

First, Do No Harm: A Hippocratic Church

Many medical doctors take some form of the Hippocratic Oath as an entry into their profession of healing and care. A fundamental principle that has often been attributed to the Hippocratic tradition is "first, do no harm." While there have been many changes recently in how the medical community understands this principle, the basic premise of "non-maleficence" remains important and is a fundamental principle for biomedical ethics and licensed therapists today.[4] The idea is simple and intuitive. If we are to create safe spaces, we must create spaces where no harm is done. We must not inflict intentional harm on others, and we must always weigh potential benefits against potential harm when making decisions in order to ensure we do no harm. This is the first principle of a trauma-safe church. Above all else we must do no harm.

This principle is obvious enough for the purpose of creating trauma-safe churches. Recall the first part of our above definition that a church is trauma-safe if it is a church where *those vulnerable to trauma are protected*. A church cannot be trauma-safe if it is a church where its members are being actively traumatized. Our churches today can learn a valuable lesson

4. Beauchamp, *Standing on Principles*. See also *Code of Ethics*.

from doctors and therapists in this respect. Nothing outweighs the importance of safety for members of the church. What have we profited if we gain the whole world for our churches but lose trauma safety once people are inside? We must realize that trauma-safe churches are Hippocratic churches; they are spaces where safety is valued as a first priority.

Disaster occurs when a church's first priority is not "above all, do no harm." This is especially clear when trauma happens not only in the church but at the hands of its leaders. Because clergy often hold positions of power it is imperative that we prioritize doing no harm to avoid the trauma of malicious leaders as well as accidental retraumatization from well-meaning pastors. To see the urgency for pastors to do no harm, consider the story of Elaine Heath, who tells her experience in receiving the Eucharist as a survivor of sexual abuse:

> Some of us survivors, especially if we experienced ritual abuse, may never be able to participate in the Eucharist . . . If this is the case for us, be patient with our struggle. Some of us cannot allow male pastors or priests to put the communion bread into our open mouths because . . . the body memories are too strong. We may or may not be able to tell you just why we cannot do this. If that is our reality, be kind. Put the wafer or bread into our hands. Let us control what we put into our mouths. Respect our boundaries. Many of us, given the right teaching and companionship, could find significant healing of sexual wounds and shame through the Eucharist. For that to happen, we need pastors, teachers, counselors, and friends who understand the real meaning of the Eucharist. By participating in the sacred meal, we Christians declare our oneness with one another and with the God who made us.[5]

As this story indicates, establishing safety must be our first priority. Otherwise, we will be traumatizing or retraumatizing the members of our own church body. Traumatization must be avoided in the church at all costs. If we are be trauma-safe churches we must first and above all do no harm. Trauma may happen but we must first stop the bleeding in our midst, or we cannot offer hope to others. "Occasions for stumbling are bound to come, but woe to anyone by whom they come! It would be better for you if a millstone were hung around your neck and you were thrown into the sea than for you to cause one of these little ones to stumble" (Luke 17:2).

---

5. Heath, *We Were the Least of These*, 145.

A trauma-safe church is a Hippocratic church; a Hippocratic church prioritizes the avoidance of ongoing traumatization of its members. Unless they know that the community prioritizes the safety of its members, survivors will not feel safe or be able to recover safety for themselves. Recall here that trauma is an event of powerlessness that continues to terrify survivors throughout their lives. Survivors feel like the trauma of the past is still taking place in the present. Recovery therefore involves soothing the traumatized perspective by reassuring persons that the trauma is over and in the past. This can never happen so long as our churches harbor the predators of trauma. We can't begin to help survivors realize the trauma they feel is over if abuse is still occurring in our midst. For this reason, any suspicion of predatory behavior must be addressed. This sends the signal that all abuse is taken seriously. A trauma-safe culture has its origins in mutual awareness and establishing group safety. Jesus the Good Shepherd warned us against many types of predators—they are wolves in sheep's clothing who ravage the flock and break people away from life-giving relationships with one another and Jesus: "the wolf attacks the flock and scatters it" (John 10:12). In the name of the Good Shepherd, all Christians are called to protect Jesus' precious flock from those who would come to take what is not their own: to "steal and kill and destroy" (John 10:10). Jesus' followers are not hirelings who run away or turn a blind eye to abuse but are dynamically included in the Shepherds' works that defend the flock against wolves who come to destroy. Two key images from John 10 help us conceptualize what this work involves: building up the sheep pen to protect the sheep and listening to the voice of Jesus. Building the protective sheep pen's wall around the flock is a helpful image for the defensive and life-ensuring policies, people, and DNA of a trauma-safe church. In this chapter and the next we will focus on building up the church's sheep pen as we listen to the voice of Jesus through the wisdom that he has given a number of secular organizations as well as the church as it has navigated recent abuse crises.

When trauma-safe churches prioritize the principle "above all, do no harm," this creates an environment where survivors and the vulnerable can begin to recover a sense of *big picture safety*. In a trauma-safe space, I know that my peers, leaders, and those I lead all have my back. I can trust them because they have bought into a culture whose guiding ethos is "non-maleficence," or not doing harm. In an environment like this I can learn again to see God's bigger perspective on the world, that horrors and trauma are not the last word even if they are an abiding word. The wounds of the past may remain, but I can recover a sense of safety in a community that values safety as the highest priority. Trauma-safe churches prioritize doing no harm above all else and thereby create a fundamentally safe space where survivors can recover a big picture sense of safety in the world.

One of the biggest takeaways on what we are calling the "Hippocratic principle" is that *trauma-safe churches never value the social image of the church above the safety of its members*. Remember "Sco-Mo's handshake"? This involved the Australian Prime Minister valuing forced photo opportunities with fire trauma survivors above engaging with them, witnessing their losses and laments, and then helping them. In this case, staged public relations were more highly valued than people who were also trauma survivors. Whenever "moral failing" happens at the hands of our church leaders we must expose these horrors without condition, without apology, without timidity, and with all haste. "God is light and in him is no darkness at all. If we say that we have fellowship while we are walking in darkness, we lie and do not know what is true" (1 John 1:5–6). If we claim to be the church but we fail to act swiftly and publicly to bring the darkness to light when leaders are traumatizing members, we may as well pack up and go home, for we are kidding ourselves. Trauma-safe churches are never shy to bring darkness to light even when this may hurt the reputation or finances of our institutions. The safety of our members is always more important. The defense that this might ruin our public witness to the world is no good reply either, because "by this everyone will know that you are my disciples, if you have love for one another" (John 13:35) and this love is absent unless we act to help the vulnerable among us. "How does God's love abide in anyone who has the world's goods and sees a brother or sister in need and yet refuses to help?" (1 John 3:17). Caring for the safety of our members is our greatest witness to the world that God's love abides with us.

It is important to note that the commitment to "do no harm" and to take decisive action when harm has been done is not enough. We must not only be guided by a principle of non-maleficence but also by one of "beneficence" or doing good. Like medical doctors the Hippocratic church does not merely avoid harm but *actively seeks the good of its members* and weighs these together when making decisions. We are called by Jesus to be "the light of the world" and "the salt of the earth" so that "they may see your good works and give glory to your Father in heaven" (Matthew 5:13–16).

By adopting the Hippocratic principle to "first do no harm" and the further principle to proactively do good we can take the first step to create a trauma-safe church. With this first step we can ensure that our church is not traumatizing itself. If trauma does happen in our communities, we must take swift action to publicly address the harm. We must not "keep it in the family" because only by *public* action to expose harm can we be a witness of God's love to the world. Trauma-safe churches have nothing to hide and everything to gain by prioritizing safety to do no harm. The recent words of Pope Francis regarding a case of sexual abuse by clergy summarizes the Hippocratic principle well:

> "If one member suffers, all suffer together with it" (1 Cor 12:26). These words of Saint Paul forcefully echo in my heart as I acknowledge once more the suffering endured by many minors due to sexual abuse, the abuse of power and the abuse of conscience perpetrated by a significant number of clerics and consecrated persons. Crimes that inflict deep wounds of pain and powerlessness, primarily among the victims, but also in their family members and in the larger community of believers and nonbelievers alike. Looking back to the past, no effort to beg pardon and to seek to repair the harm done will ever be sufficient. Looking ahead to the future, no effort must be spared to create a culture able to prevent such situations from happening, but also to prevent the possibility of their being covered up and perpetuated. The pain of the victims and their families is also our pain, and so it is urgent that we once more reaffirm our commitment to ensure the protection of minors and of vulnerable adults.[6]

Second, Listen to Survivors: A Compassionate Witness

Survivors need to tell their stories. Trauma healing cannot take place without some level of being able to tell one's story of harm and to have that story faithfully heard by a compassionate witness. This is the second criteria and principle of a trauma-safe church; it is a church that is not threatened to hear survivor stories but welcomes them and wants to witness harm with compassion.

Telling trauma stories has been recognized as an effective means for healing trauma because it allows a safe space where survivors can counter the isolating and silencing effects of trauma with testimony and the

---

6. *Report on the Holy See's Institutional Knowledge,* 449.

accompaniment of safe witnesses.[7] Trauma is an isolating experience because survivors feel alone in their powerlessness; against this, telling one's story is a powerful way to bring comfort to loneliness. Trauma also literally silences survivors because during traumatic events the language center of the brain (the "Broca's area") shuts down which makes it difficult to put one's trauma into words and this happens again and again every time survivors feel triggered as though the trauma were happening in the present.[8] Against this it is powerful for survivors to learn to *speak their trauma out loud to others* because it restores power where the harm has silenced them. Where they felt alone and silenced, telling one's story can be a powerful healing step that brings survivors' shameful hiding out into the liberating light of acceptance and love.

As we saw in chapter 3, shame is one of the biggest hurdles that keeps survivors from even admitting that they have survived trauma. If we are survivors, we often feel like we failed to protect ourselves or others, whether in war, childhood sexual abuse, domestic abuse, or emotional assaults.[9] The powerlessness feels shameful. Too shameful to say out loud. And every time a survivor feels triggered in the present this shame is felt *just like it was the first time it was experienced.* Through a slow, safe, structured, careful process we can begin to create safe spaces where the shame of traumatic powerlessness can be lessened *by acknowledging it.* Somehow, just naming the trauma can sap some of its overwhelming power. To understand this, consider the story of Mrs. K, a Nazi holocaust survivor:

> The turning point in Mrs. K's treatment came when she "confessed" that she had been married and then had given birth to a baby in the ghetto whom she "gave to the Nazis." Her guilt, shame, and feeling "filthy" were exacerbated by "well-meaning people" that said that if she told her new fiancé, he would never marry her. The baby, whom she bore and kept alive for two and a half years under the most horrendously inhumane conditions, was torn from her arms and murdered when his whimper alerted the Nazi officer that he was hidden under her coat . . .
>
> The K family started sharing their history and communicating. It took about six months, however, of patient requests for her to repeat the above incident . . . until she was able to end her story with "and they took the child away from me." She then began to

7. Herman, *Trauma and Recovery*, 182ff.

8. Van der Kolk, *Body Keeps the Score*, 43.

9. Rothschild, *8 Keys for Safe Trauma Recovery*, 76–80.

thaw her identificatory deadness and experience the missing . . . emotions of pain and grief . . .

Her ability and longing to love were really resurrected . . . No longer formally in therapy, Mrs. K says, "I have myself back, all over again . . . I wasn't proud. Now I'm proud. There are some things I don't like, but I have hope."[10]

For trauma survivors like Mrs. K, the shame of feeling powerless during the traumatic event is experienced again and again, and it feels like the trauma is still happening. This makes it feel impossible to talk about the trauma. But we can also see in this story that with the right context of safety and compassionate witness, such as a trusted friend, therapist, or pastor, the shame can be lessened by putting words to it. In her testimony we hear the place of recovery that we call the Dawn of Sunday: she laments the horrors and may yet grieve at the losses these involve, yet she has hope for life in the present.

As we have seen previously, shame is one of the biggest prohibitors to being in safe relationships with others. "Shame loves secrecy. The most dangerous thing to do after a shaming experience is hide or bury our story. When we bury our story, the shame metastasizes."[11] This kind of sharing that overcomes shame requires *vulnerability* from both the teller and the hearer. The emotional risk to tell the truth of our story is an antidote to the secrecy of shame. When thinking of ourselves most of us perceive vulnerability as gross weakness but when we see it in others, we perceive this as courageous. That is a double standard. The truth is that vulnerability is our most accurate measure of courage and our greatest source of connection and wholehearted living with others.[12] We can see this by looking at God the Trinity. "In the Trinity we see something that we must pay attention to: God does not leave. The loving relationship shared between the Father, Son and Spirit is the ground on which all other modes of life and creativity rest. In this relationship of constant self-giving, vulnerable and joyful love, shame has no oxygen to breathe."[13] It is this communion and love, one that snuffs out shame, that we are invited into through safe people and the gifts of the Spirit in God's church. In a trauma-safe community being safely loved by God the Trinity allows for us to enjoy life again by sharing our

10. Herman, *Trauma and Recovery*, 194.

11. Brown, *Gifts of Imperfection*, 10.

12. Brown, *Daring Greatly*, 2.

13. Thompson, *Soul of Shame*, 125.

stories with others who are safe witnesses. Where trauma has isolated and silenced, we can find accompaniment and be empowered through vulnerability with others. We can invite others into our stories of harm.

Being vulnerable is often a terrifying idea for survivors because it feels like the powerlessness of trauma. Talking about trauma will not be easy for survivors and carers alike. With this level of shame, it almost always feels better to shut down emotions and to numb oneself than to enter into admitting the truth. This is why trauma survivors are often at higher risk for substance abuse, because these provide outlets for shutting off the terrifying sensations.[14] We must learn to have mercy on these coping mechanisms and not be quick to judge them. We must also never rush survivors to talk about their trauma. It is their story to tell. It may be better to wait through the process. You never know what pain is behind someone's behavior. This is not an excuse, but it gives a context to help care for the wounded among us. We can learn to bless negative coping mechanisms such as self-protective distancing from others, aggressive styles of relating, and even binging on food and entertainment for the ways these have helped someone survive in the past while also inviting persons to healthier styles of relating in the present. Eventually, being a blessing to survivors will involve naming the trauma that has driven us to addictive coping behaviors.

Trauma-safe churches are places where survivors are free and invited to tell the truth of their harm. Without being open to the testimony of survivors we can never learn to be trauma-sensitive communities because we need these stories to learn what we don't know about the kinds of harm we haven't endured. For those who *have* experienced trauma we need a safe space where the healing available through bringing shame out of hiding can take place. Trauma-safe churches offer a compassionate witness to trauma stories and trauma survivors by recognizing that *you cannot heal what you have not named.* "What is forgotten is unavailable, and what is unavailable cannot be healed."[15] If we are to create communities that witness to the healing works of God the Trinity after trauma this must start with learning to listen to the trauma of our church members. A church that cannot name its own trauma cannot be a trauma-safe church.

For us to create trauma safety in our churches we must learn to be open to, encourage, and not be threatened by the testimony of trauma survivors. Their stories must be heard for their healing and for us to become

14. Van der Kolk, *Body Keeps the Score*, 327.

15. Nouwen, *Living Reminder*, 22.

safe communities. For the telling and listening of trauma stories to be healing our posture must be one of "compassionate witness."[16] This involves, among other things, actively listening with care and responding with compassion to the testimony of the other.[17] For example, if someone discloses a history of sexual abuse we must not wince with disgust but empathize with kindness, or if another is triggered by a loud noise and overreacts we must care more for restoring safety to the survivor in this moment than being concerned with how we are inconvenienced. A compassionate witness involves more than just audibly hearing tales of harm but is concerned with how we can "bear one another's burdens" by living with survivors as they navigate the effects of harm. All the while we must prioritize showing kindness and mercy. "In this way you will fulfill the law of Christ" (Gal 6:2). A compassionate witness like this allows survivors to be truly known and *to have a real experience of being safely loved by others.*

A few very important caveats are needed on offering a "compassionate witness." First, this does not mean valorizing the suffering of survivors or running a fine-tooth comb through morbid details of trauma in a public forum. That would do more harm than good, and we must take care to "first do no harm." For example, it would be harmful to have a survivor stand before a public congregation on Sunday morning and openly share details of their trauma. Not only can this trigger others in an unhelpful way but it can be counterproductive for the survivors in our midst. What is needed is a safe, structured, private, accessible, guided setting where survivors feel safe to share and disclose in a context where trust has been built and oversight is maintained.[18] In these settings the goal is not a detailed account of the trauma; without a trained therapist this will only aggravate PTSD symptoms. Remembering and telling *everything* is *not* required.[19] Instead the goal is to create a safe space on the terms of survivors where a simple acknowledgment of the trauma can be witnessed by a compassionate group of carers and other survivors.

Second, we must take care not to place survivors on a pedestal in a way that would patronize their suffering. Consider the words of a female survivor from a play written about the Holocaust:

---

16. Weingarten, *Common Shock.*

17. See this fully discussed in Hunsinger, *Bearing the Unbearable,* 22–41.

18. Herman, *Trauma and Recovery,* 217.

19. Rothschild, *8 Keys to Safe Trauma Recovery,* 41.

Whenever I am introduced as "a survivor," I am little bit uncomfortable. I mean, what do people want? What do they expect? In the beginning, until just a few years ago, nobody wanted to hear from us . . . Now, today, everybody makes a big deal out of it. I mean, they don't just invite us to speak, but they turn us into some kind of heroes. They talk about the special wisdom we're supposed to have . . . What is this, a Bar Mitzvah? A celebration of our Jewish roots? I mean, we, whose roots were totally destroyed . . . we, who can hardly speak at all, are supposed to tell you our fabulous tales and legends? In the beginning people were silent. Today, they are stupid.[20]

Listening to the testimony of survivors and inviting their story can keep us from silence. But a *compassionate* witness can keep us from the stupidity of romanticizing suffering. A trauma-safe church allows for stories to be told in a way that honors them with reverence and sees they are holy ground worthy of being loved in safety.

Third, we must acknowledge the danger of "compassion fatigue" and burnout. We need to recognize our limits as carers of others and acknowledge that no one is immune to the "vicarious trauma" that comes from hearing stories of violence. Consider Deborah van Deusen Hunsinger, who tells her story of experiencing this kind of burnout. She describes a time when she and her husband were researching and advocating against political torture in the United States: "One evening some time ago, as I went to him to say good night, he began to tell me about what he was reading . . . No longer able to keep my heart open, I told my husband with considerable energy that I *just could not bear* to hear one more story of trauma."[21] This is entirely reasonable. No one but God can handle all the world's trauma. All we can do is our best. And unless we take time to recover, we will burn out from caring for others. A trauma-safe church is not only safe for survivors but safe for carers, and this is true trauma safety. Importantly this applies to survivors as well. We cannot handle our own story all the time either. Witnessing trauma with compassion is like deep-sea diving. Eventually we have to come up for air. That is an important part of compassionate witnessing; it cares for compassion fatigue through realistic expectations for what is possible in listening and witnessing.

---

20. *Remnants*, cited in Greenspan, "On Testimony, Legacy, and the Problem of Helplessness in History," 44–45.

21. Hunsinger, *Bearing the Unbearable*, 72.

Fourth and finally, a compassionate witness does not only listen to survivors but *believes* them. It is easy to look at the trauma of others and see them as "overreacting" or to judge them by our own standards of resilience. But we must remember that what is only stressful for one person can be traumatizing for another and this changes from person to person. "No matter how frightening an event may seem, not everyone who experiences it will be traumatized."[22] This will seem strange until we realize that "*none of us ever actually has the same experience* because our minds organize our experience in a completely idiosyncratic way."[23] My experience is not your experience. We all see the world differently.

One of the most harmful responses to trauma is to belittle it or not believe or affirm survivors. This response sends the message that we do not take suffering seriously or that we think survivors are weak for having been traumatized. That is counterproductive because the way to engage healing is to promote safe vulnerability in trusting relationships. We must take survivors at their word, believe them, affirm their suffering, and seek healing, care, and justice on their behalf. "*A traumatic event needs to be treated as valid, regardless of how the event that induced it appears to anyone else.*"[24]

One of the biggest takeaways from the principle of listening to survivors and believing them is that *trauma-safe churches never value the freedom of one person over the safety of another*. When a survivor reports harm we must not only listen and believe them but act accordingly. We must act with the assumption that the story is true *until we find out otherwise*. This ensures trauma safety. This does not mean that accusations against others are believed with no questions asked. But it does mean that accusations are always taken at face value. While it may be true in a court of law that people are innocent until proven guilty, this does not apply to our practices and procedures to protect the vulnerable. If a survivor reports either past or ongoing trauma we listen, we believe, and we take decisive action to stop any *possible* ongoing harm *before we even have all the facts*. It is always better to be safe than sorry. For example, when someone shouts "Look out!" do we turn around with an unshielded face to see what the fuss is about? No. We crouch, cover our face, close our eyes, and brace for impact. Even if the person who shouted was mistaken, we are glad we covered up because

22. Levine, *Waking the Tiger*, 28.

23. See this whole topic and the relevant sources brilliantly discussed in Hunsinger, *Bearing the Unbearable*, 5.

24. Yoder, *Little Book of Trauma Healing*, 10.

we would have been protected. The same is true of listening to survivors and believing them. A compassionate witness not only invites survivor stories, not only believes them, but acts accordingly until all is well again.

Creating a culture where vulnerability can be fostered takes time. Churches that invest heavily in cultivating a certain pristine image (through social media, or heavily airbrushed leadership models) will likely find it harder to create a space with permission for people to make mistakes. If the emphasis is on image over truth, then hearing accusations will always be too costly. If we care more about the perception of the church from the outside, then it will be difficult to take seriously those who have been wounded by the church. Trauma-safe churches do no harm and are open to hearing the stories of survivors and meeting these stories with compassion and kindness. They believe survivors. Trauma-safe churches are not threatened to witness violence but are bold and ready to hear the real stories of its members and to act to protect the vulnerable. Our stories need to be told and heard in safety and love.

So then, these are the first two principles of a trauma-safe church: (1) above all else, do no harm, and (2) listen to survivors with a compassionate witness. A trauma-safe church is a Hippocratic church and one that witnesses the stories of survivors. As we tell our vulnerable stories with compassionate witnesses who do no harm, we can begin to heal. While we may fail from time to time in this journey, God is the perfect compassionate witness who never fails to accompany us in safety and love through all the trauma of our world. Before turning to the next two principles of a trauma-safe church, we offer this prayer for what has been explored so far:

> O Lord, many of us have tears deep down inside of our lives, because we've been hurt in ways that go to the very core of our being, and some of the hurts we carry around have been there for a long, long time—even for years. We experienced a loss from which even today we have not really recovered.
>
> O God, you are the one who looks way down deep inside all of us. You see and know what no one knows, no one at all except we ourselves. And, not only do you see us and know us, but you also feel things along with us, even the very painful stuff, the deep stuff along with us, and we feel a strange kind of healing taking place. For it's like you care and understand . . . and we're no longer left alone with our burdens.

Today, those of us who are struggling inside—who've been broken and hurt and still feel the tears within—we thank you for being there and sharing with us what we cannot bear alone.[25]

25. Lutz, "Prayers of the VA Chaplaincy."

9

Principles of a Trauma–Safe Church

Healing Together

Do Something Together: Empowering Restoration

I t is not enough to listen to trauma. Return to the image of a Sunday dawn and the double witness. Listening to survivors is the witness to loss and laments and the one leg planted in the horror of Holy Saturday. But what about the witness to God's Trinitarian works of healing and life, and the other leg stepping toward the light of a dawn of Sunday? How do we move from listening to trauma toward the hope of healing?

The answer is so simple it is almost too good to be true. Do something. Do almost anything. Take action of some sort to empower restoration. But whatever you do, do it *together*. Trauma-safe churches do not sit idly by but follow the lead of survivors to try new practices that can alleviate post-traumatic stress by empowering survivors for the journey of healing. This is the third principle of a trauma-safe church: it *does something* about the trauma of its members. And what is done encourages a mutually consented alliance between survivors and carers on how best to proceed. Trauma-safe churches take restorative action that empowers survivors by doing something about the trauma together. Taking action together allows us to recover safe boundaries in the aftermath of harm.

At first this might sound aggressive or ambitious. It might sound like a reckless approach to find "quick fixes" that are clean and tidy to resolve the trauma or make it go away. Or it may come across as though "we" are the helpers and "they" are the ones who need helping. Nothing could be further from the truth. The second principle (listening to survivors) can help us avoid triumphalism or naivety because we know that no matter the hope of healing you have to name the horror, and healing that cannot stomach the real details of trauma is not true healing. We have one foot in Holy Saturday. We also know that trauma is no respecter of persons and that we are *all* vulnerable to violence and we all know *something* of the horrors of life east of Eden. With these recognitions we can work together toward imagining how to receive the healing of God the Trinity in a trauma-safe church. This must involve taking action to empower restoration.

A helpful way to begin implementing this third principle of trauma-safe church is to recognize it as a form of "restorative practice." Restorative practice is an internationally studied form of peacemaking in communities between persons of varying power dynamics. Deborah Hunsinger defines restorative practice as "a commitment . . . to working *with* people in order to deepen community ties instead of doing things *to* them or *for* them (or alternatively, not doing anything at all)."[1] From the perspective of restorative practice, there are no experts at the healing journey. Rather, we are all on the same level working toward a common goal and negotiating our perspectives to reach one another's flourishing. "Those 'in authority' do not own the process; the community as a whole owns it."[2] This approach to recovery levels the playing field and is seen as helpful for the post-traumatic context because "the fundamental premise of restorative practices is that people are happier, more cooperative and productive, and more likely to make positive changes when those in authority do things *with* them, rather than *to* them or *for* them."[3]

Trauma-safe churches do something *with* survivors, not *to* or *for* them. Anything less than a cooperative alliance like this will undermine survivor flourishing because of the nature of trauma itself. Recall that the fundamental thing about a traumatic event is the powerlessness of the event. "Psychological trauma is an affliction of the powerless. At the moment of trauma, the victim is rendered helpless by overwhelming force."[4] Because trauma takes power away, empowerment must be the guiding principle of taking action to restore safety after trauma. "The core experiences of psychological trauma are disempowerment and disconnection . . .

---

1. Hunsinger, *Bearing the Unbearable*, 125.

2. Hunsinger, *Bearing the Unbearable*, 126.

3. International Institute of Restorative Practices, cited in Hunsinger, *Bearing the Unbearable*, 125.

4. Herman, *Trauma and Recovery*, 33.

The first principle of recovery is the empowerment of the survivor."[5] So long as we continue to approach trauma with the mindset of a hierarchy of expertise, we cannot be trauma-safe because we are starting on the wrong foot. Restorative action that empowers one another involves recovering safe boundaries that are *mutually negotiated*. Where trauma has taken power the trauma-safe church restores power. Without this no healing can take place and survivors will likely feel unsafe. The language of being an ally to one another is helpful at this point. An ally is an empathetic, helpful companion who witnesses to our losses and laments, as well as to the room for hope in our lives. An ally is with us through difficult times and beyond. For example, an ally has been vitally important for Brent, who suffers from psychosis. Amidst the scary voices he hears and their "barrage of negativity, Brent found an ally: a welcoming voice that was supportive, caring, and kind; a friendly voice that gave him hope."[6]

Practically, this means that survivors often have an intuitive sense of what might be good for their own healing and what might be counterproductive. This may seem surprising at first, but it is absolutely central to recovery. Trauma shatters a person's sense of self-worth and self-determination; recovery restores autonomy to the individual. To look with suspicion on survivors sends them the message that we think they are incapable, incompetent, and this only reinforces the stigmatized identity that is in need of transformation. What is needed is for us to say, "I see you; I believe you . . . Now, *how can I join you* in your journey of healing?" Trauma-safe churches bestow the dignity trauma has robbed back to the survivors by inviting them to be the arbiters of what is good for their healing. Recovery that is trauma-safe always puts the survivor in the driver's seat.[7] Safe boundaries cannot be recovered *for* other people, only *with* them and their own initiation of the process.

Again, important caveats are needed. Of course, this does not suggest that survivors have all the answers, nor does it put all the pressure on them or take away responsibility from carers. We all have a role to play and no one bears the burden alone. Neither does this suggest that survivors always know what is best or have unilateral say over all circumstances. That would be equally as counterproductive to trauma safety. Rather, this approach of empowerment means that *in creating trauma safety we defer to*

5. Herman, *Trauma and Recovery*, 133.
6. Swinton, *Finding Jesus in the Storm*, 128.
7. Rothschild, *8 Keys to Safe Trauma Recovery*, 2.

the perspective of the survivor because as we have seen it is the individual perspective that determines whether an event is traumatic. Just as trauma varies from person to person, so does the path of healing. There is no one size fits all. We need to follow the lead of survivors to create trauma safety in our churches.

A trauma-safe church is a restorative church: a restorative church invites the broken to a position of power that plots the course for recovering safe boundaries. Empowerment of all members and joint action are the goal of a restorative practice. For example, if you are a pastor and someone discloses in your office that they are a survivor of sexual abuse, you may offer to sit across from them in an ordinary chair rather than stay behind an intimidating scholar's desk. Changing our posture can send powerful positive messages that we do not think we are above someone else. Importantly, in this scenario you would first ask if they felt comfortable before moving closer to them. Empowerment and autonomy are key. Or take another example. Rather than inviting a "put-together" professional who has not been "dirtied" by trauma to lead a recovery group, you might invite one of the brave and vulnerable survivors in your church to co-facilitate and lead a support group. Trauma-safe churches are willing to take risks that show survivors we do not see them in the stigmatized way that they see themselves. We see them as capable and competent for their healing. Oftentimes it is this simple message and gesture that ends up renewing the self-confidence necessary for survivors to experience restoration. If we set a bar for persons that they must live up to before they are invited to the planning table of recovery, we send the message that we do not trust people with their own story. That only reinforces the powerlessness and shame of trauma. Nothing could be further from the truth or from what trauma safety requires. Each person's story is their own to tell and their own to invite us into.[8]

When we adopt a posture of recovery "with," not "for or to" the traumatized among us, we enable the kind of empowerment that ignites renewed imagination and inspires possibility that survivors may have never

---

8. It is important to see that medication for trauma-related mental health challenges, such as depression, bipolar disorder, or psychosis, opens us up to new social/biological/psychological possibilities in life, as well as to spiritual ones: "It is Robert's medication that helps him find a spiritual place, which he could simply not inhabit without its assistance. For Robert, the taking of medication is much more than an engagement with pharmacological products. Taking medication functions as a deeply spiritual act." Swinton, *Finding Jesus in the Storm*, 104.

hoped was possible. This kind of autonomy may be so new for some that it feels scary, because having power restored means it could be taken away again. But the hope of God the Trinity in the church is that persons can dare to hope again that life is better lived with a full heart than with the paralysis of traumatization. To create trauma safety in our churches that invites empowering restoration we must invite survivors to the table and "regard others as better than ourselves" (Phil 2:3).

To see this, consider the story of Andrew, an adult survivor of childhood sexual abuse who had to find a new church after his previous one had ostracized and disciplined him for failing to reconcile with his unrepentant abuser. That was a church not safe for trauma. The elders thought they knew what was best and were not open to Andrew's perspective that forgiveness and reconciliation are not the same thing. He had a better experience with his new pastor:

> I met with the pastor of the new church for a face-to-face. He asked me about my story. At this point, some of my lines were rehearsed—but the warm tears weren't. I sat across from him, drowning my face but knowing that I need not wear a scarlet *A* either. Then . . . he started crying too. *I'd never seen any church leader or pastor cry with me over my story!* His pastoral demeanor took me in. He looked at me with a shepherd's empathy. Then, shaking his head, he began repeating, "Not on my watch! Not on my watch!" I found a man who not only wept with me but knew how to sit in pain, both his own—his wife had just passed away from cancer—and the pain of others.
>
> Then he asked me if I would help him with the survivors of his own congregation. He asked me to help the broken of his flock. His tears opened my heart. His words welcomed me to a new home. I told him I would probably fall back into obscurity; he asked me not to. His trust helped me build a new identity. This broken sheep had found a shepherd who also knew how to talk with a wet face.[9]

We can see in this story that the leaders of trauma-safe churches empathize with the stories of others and consider their own points of connection in a way that levels the field for the process of recovery. Even if we lack the emotional intelligence to know how to respond in situations like these, being able to use a few simple words that show that you are listening and you care is crucial. All are welcome to plan the healing. All are empowered for

---

9. Schmutzer et al., *Naming Our Abuse*, 87.

the journey. No one has a monopoly on establishing trauma safety. We are in this together.

One of the biggest takeaways from the third principle of a trauma-safe church (empowering restoration with action) is that in these settings *survivors are safely invited to explore their healing and own it for themselves.* This restores dignity and autonomy and runs directly counter to the disempowering, stigmatizing experience of trauma. It helps to recover truly safe boundaries. This is similar to what earlier chapters have seen as recovering boundaries in the larger sense of owning one's responsibility for one's own personhood. We are all dignified with the making our own choices and no one else chooses for us. This creates a community where real mutual love can take place because everyone consents for themselves. This kind of honor is necessary for true vulnerability and secure attachments with others and with God. Trauma-safe churches invite survivors and carers alike to take action in a way that empowers one another for restoration.

Get Moving: Engaging and Blessing the Body

The last principle of a trauma-safe church must include something about the body because as we have seen "safety always begins with the body."[10] Trauma brings about a loss of bodily integrity for most survivors and this means that recovering safety must involve creating a space in which survivors can restore a sense of calm and regulation back to their bodies. If we are to create trauma-safe spaces, we must create churches where the bodies of those among us are engaged in safety and blessed for the wounds and terrifying sensations that burden them daily. This is the last principle of a trauma-safe church: it does not ignore the body but incorporates physical practices to help survivors get moving again with others; this is done by blessing the fears we feel in our bodies and finding creative ways to restore safety. Where trauma has paralyzed bodies, recovery invites fresh movement and offers kindness to the bodies of the traumatized. Trauma-safe churches are not afraid of embodiment. Trauma-safe churches help survivors to get moving again after trauma by encouraging survivors to engage and bless their bodies within the church community.

One of the greatest advances in our understanding of trauma in recent years is that for survivors "the body keeps the score."[11] What this means

10. Herman, *Trauma and Recovery*, 269.

11. Van der Kolk, *Body Keeps the Score.*

is that trauma does not work like regular memory or like other ordinary events we experience in our bodies. With most other life experiences, we can remember events like a normal story: there is an orderly beginning, middle, and end. Even if these experiences were difficult or involved some pain, we can usually recall these experiences without excessive emotional angst, and we can consider the way our bodily senses felt during those events. For example, we may remember a time when we felt very loved by another, such as an evening sunset picnic with a loved one on a beach or in a local park. We may remember that it was bright when we arrived, dark when we left for the night, and that we felt especially loved when we sensed the warmth of our significant other's hand brushing against our arm. The memory is orderly, and we recall our body's senses. Or take for instance a more painful event. Perhaps we had a bicycle accident as a child. We may remember getting on the bike, riding halfway along the trail, and then hitting a rock and flying over the handlebars. We may recall the smell of the forest trail, the texture of the dirt on our face from falling, and the sting of our scrapes and wounds afterward. But for both the evening picnic and the cycling accident, we can recall the story's sensory details in an orderly way and without being thrown into emotional or visceral chaos and fear.

Traumatic memory does not work like this. During trauma, the parts of our brain that create orderly narratives and organize our bodily senses (the hippocampus and thalamus) become dormant and stop working properly. Instead, the part of our brain that registers potential sources of danger and threats in our environment (the amygdala) goes on full alert.[12] The result of these changes in the brain is that during trauma survivors "dissociate" from their bodily senses. Dissociation is essentially an extreme narrowing of perception that allows us to survive events of extreme stress by dulling the terror of our bodily senses. A very low-grade and innocuous example of this is the "white-line syndrome" that we may experience during long road trips. Have you ever been driving for hours and hours so long that all of a sudden you "wake up" and find that you were "zoning out" because the landscape and road felt so repetitive and tedious? Of course, you never fell asleep, you just sort of had a blank stare that dulled out your senses. For a moment you dissociated from the experience of driving.

Traumatic events do something similar, only much worse. Instead of dulling our senses to a boring situation, traumatic dissociation allows our minds to "get through" something horrible by dulling our senses so

12. Van der Kolk, *Body Keeps the Score*, 44–71.

that we do not have to fully perceive all the horror of what is happening. In dissociation we are able to escape the unbearable bodily sensations of trauma. For example, for a soldier in war this may cause a bodily numbing that allows the soldier to survive the battle. Or for a survivor of childhood sexual abuse this may enable a child to escape the horrifying sensations of the worst moments of personal violation during abuse. Survivors frequently describe dissociation as a kind of "out-of-body" experience where they have the perception of floating above their own bodies, as if they were watching the trauma happen to someone else. Through such experiences "the helpless person escapes from [one's] situation not by action in the real world but rather by altering [one's] state of consciousness . . . This altered state of consciousness might be regarded as one of nature's small mercies, a protection against unbearable pain."[13] When people are powerless to flee a traumatic event, dissociation is a last-ditch effort to avoid the physical pain that cannot be escaped. Close your eyes, grit your teeth, and just try to avoid the horror you feel *in your body*.

We now know that, tragically, when traumatic events are dissociated, they remain unprocessed; as a result, they are continually relived in the present. When a survivor is "triggered" through some bodily sensation that reminds them of the trauma, the brain is literally "rekindled as if the trauma were actually occurring."[14] It is important for us to recognize that when survivors feel the pain of past trauma in their bodies or "get jumpy" from physical contact, they are not just recalling an unpleasant experience. They are feeling the trauma in their bodies all over again, *just like it was felt the first time they suffered.*

What all of this means is that for survivors of trauma the terror of the past is felt in their bodies over and over again in the present. It is like going through a haunted house. Terrors jump out at you unexpectedly, left and right, and you never know when you might feel on edge by something that seems so innocent to everyone else. Your body is remembering the terror of the past your mind has forgotten. Your body needs to be cared for. The body keeps the score.

Trauma-safe churches recognize the role of the brain and the body for trauma survivors. We need to be aware that healing and safety can never be recovered without restoring a visceral sense of well-being for survivors among us. Because trauma terrifies survivors through bodily sensations

13. Herman, *Trauma and Recovery*, 87–88.
14. Van der Kolk, *Body Keeps the Score*, 44.

such as physical touch or loud noises, recovering safety must involve tending to these sensations with intentional care. Bringing care and restoring movement to the body is one of the best ways to restore safety for many trauma survivors. For example, you might implement a rule in your church where it is understood that the policy is "always ask before touching." That is one practical step that every church can implement immediately, and this would bring an effective level of care to even the most anonymous survivor among us. Or you might offer earplugs to church members who find the worship music overwhelming and overstimulating. The goal is to help people calm their bodies to restore a sense of safety. We want people to feel safe where it matters most, in their bodies.

However, restoring calm is not the only goal. Most people tend to think that traumatized persons are delicate and need to be treated with velvet gloves or that the primary goal of care should be to help ease the hypervigilance of post-traumatic stress through soothing techniques and relaxation. While there is some truth to this, we need to go further. "Though most people would assume relaxation is the state that helps trauma recovery most, a good portion of traumatized individuals do not do well with relaxation. In a relaxed state, they may actually become more anxious or even panicked."[15] Simply listening to trauma and encouraging calm can heighten PTSD symptoms because it can sometimes feel very similar to the powerlessness of the original trauma. For survivors this is a terrifying notion. Sometimes still and calm is not the answer—it feels like dissociation, it feels like the freeze of trauma. Sometimes the answer is to learn to move and get the blood pumping again.

Instead of only inviting calm we can encourage survivors to engage their bodies in a way that empowers them. For example, physical exercise is often a powerful mode for many people to feel strong and restored. For me (Preston), learning to run three miles several times a week has been instrumental in my journey of recovery and managing PTSD symptoms. Others may find a local regiment of self-defense classes to feel extremely refreshing and invigorating. For example, consider the following story told by Serene Jones:

> I helped to lead a self-defense class that met on Thursday nights in the all-purpose room in the parish house basement of my church . . . During the twelve weeks that we met, the dozen or so women gathered rarely spoke of things theological; mostly, we moved our

15. Rothschild, *8 Keys to Safe Trauma Recovery*, 119.

> bodies, learned to hit hard, scream loudly, and kick with force . . .
> All told, it was a wonderfully bonding and empowering event, and
> its force was lodged firmly in the physical world, where we fought
> together to empower our bodies against the wounds inflicted by
> the world.[16]

This story shows that for some learning to fight helps counter the ways trauma immobilizes people and this can happen when we can encounter danger in a structured and safe setting like a group class. Still others may incorporate yoga or alternative tension stretching exercises as a powerful way to "get moving." In all these examples the important point is simple. Trauma and dissociation bring about a freeze response in which survivors feel paralyzed and stuck in the terror that their bodies are feeling. Recovering safety involves learning to "get moving" again and to bring vitality back to the body.[17] Trauma-safe spaces encourage this kind of movement. Simply asking those in your community what would help them and how the church might serve them (rather than assuming that you know how best to help) is an excellent place to start.

Trauma-safe churches are not threatened by the wounds that bodies carry and the special care this requires. We must not be inconvenienced by what trauma safety requires of us. We must learn to accommodate to the bodily sensitivities of our church members and not see this as weakness or a lack of resilience. We must learn to honor the ways that dissociation has helped people survive horrifying violence and help to promote calm when people still feel terrorized in their bodies. However, we must also invite survivors to engage their body with movement and power. We must not be threatened by the exhilaration of restoring agency that many survivors find extremely refreshing to counter the paralysis they have felt for so long.

This leads to one final element for how trauma-safe churches invite people to engage their bodies. We must not only soothe trauma terrors and engage fresh movement. We must also *bless* our bodies. This may seem vague or abstract, but it is extremely important. Most survivors carry a profound self-disgust about how their bodies respond to the world around them. They may feel like a nuisance to others for being overly sensitive or they may hate the ways they find it hard to physically interact with others. They may carry shame if they prefer baggy clothing in social settings or prefer a corner seat with their backs covered to feel safe. They might rather

16. Jones, *Trauma and Grace*, 75–76.
17. Rothschild, *8 Keys to Safe Trauma Recovery*, 115.

sit near the exit, so they can see everyone in the building, or need a support animal to feel safe. In all this self-contempt there is a deep level of shame for the avoidance response that traumatized bodies carry.

In these settings a trauma-safe church is not afraid to recognize this shame and to invite kindness and blessing in its place. Where people have learned to hate their bodies a trauma-safe church blesses the bodies of its members. We must bless our bodies for the ways they have survived and the wounds they carry. For example, we may teach our members that the sign of the cross is a Trinitarian blessing over our bodies as much as our hearts and minds. Or we may encourage liturgical practices that help us get the body moving in worship of God the Trinity. Or we may communicate to the traumatized among us that we do not view their body triggers as weakness but as a testament to their strength for how they have survived past harm. In all of this our posture must be one of welcome, hospitality, and unconditional blessing. Without learning to accept our scars and bless them we can make no progress in healing.

One of the biggest takeaways from this principle (engaging and blessing the body) is that trauma-safe churches *are not threatened by bodily engagement but view this as central to trauma recovery and the wholeness and goodness of human flourishing.* God made us with bodies, and he called them good. Trauma disrupts the goodness of our bodies at the deepest levels of how our brains function with our nervous system. Recovering safety involves affirming the goodness of human bodies and God's design for how these bodies flourish in community with others. Trauma-safe churches acknowledge the role of the body in recovery.

In fact, many survivors of trauma have a better understanding of the importance of their bodies in the church than those who have not experienced trauma. Traumatized people don't have the luxury of being gnostic. While many people in our congregations may think of themselves as minds in bodies, those recovering from trauma know that their spirituality involves their whole selves. This can be a useful insight to see traumatized people not just as wounded people to be healed, but as those we can minister *with*. There is much that survivors of trauma have to offer to the ministry and leadership of the church. The assumption that they need to be "fixed" (whatever this means) to minister to others will ultimately mean none of them can serve the church.

Toward Practical Next Steps

In the last two chapters we have explored four criteria of a trauma-safe church that serve as principles for the recovery of safety. First, do no harm. Second, listen to survivors. Third, take action together. Fourth, never forget to engage the body. Trauma-safe churches attend to all these principles. This leaves open the question of where to go from here. In the next chapter we will consider some more concrete practices and ideas that we can implement to get started with trauma safety in our churches and communities today. As we turn to practical next steps, we offer the following prayer to God for help in getting started with trauma safety.

> God of all newness, we come to you this day in daring hope,
> For healings we want yet to receive, believing in them,
> While the world says "not possible" . . .
>
> God of Exodus and Easter, God of homecoming and forgiveness,
> God of fierceness and peaceableness,
> We are finally driven to your miracles.
> This day hear our urgency and do among us
> What none of us can do.
> Do your Friday-Sunday act yet again and make us new.
> We pray out of the shattering death and shimmering new life of
> Jesus, whose name we bear. Amen.[18]

18. Excerpted from "While the world says 'not possible,'" in Brueggemann, *Awed to Heaven, Rooted in Earth*, 121–22.

10

Practical Next Steps

Getting Started with Trauma Safety

Practices for Recovering Safety

R ecovering safety after trauma is not a linear process. It is messy. It is full of twists and turns and requires immense patience, diligence, perseverance, and grace. But the incredibly good news is that trauma recovery is possible, it is doable, and it can start today with small, concrete, attainable steps. Little by little, we can all learn to be a little more trauma-safe in our relationships and in our churches. Getting started with trauma safety can pay significant dividends for countless people in our churches today.

We return to an image from *The Lord of the Rings*. Earlier we saw how Gollum is a character who illustrates the withering effects that horrors and trauma can have on persons. Horrors and trauma are aimed at undermining the relational, moral, creative, and perceptive capacities that all humans possess as image-bearers of God's triune life and love. As with Gollum, post-traumatic stress can leave us feeling isolated, ghostly, and fixated on past terrors in a way that keeps us from fully enjoying our attachments to others in the present.

The hope of recovery means that this is not the only option. Surviving trauma does not have to doom us to its withering effects. Trauma may likely be a lifelong burden for many survivors, but it does not have to be totally debilitating. "From what I've seen, it's not like it ever goes away, but somehow it loses its gripping quality, its ability to stop you in your tracks and make you feel completely undone. It loses its power."[1] Bilbo, who is also a character from *The Lord of the Rings*, is a helpful alternative character to

---

1. Herman, *Trauma and Recovery*, 228.

illustrate this. Unlike Gollum, Bilbo was not totally overwhelmed by the dark ring that nearly destroyed Gollum but was eventually able to surrender some aspects of his burden in relationship with Gandalf. This positive coping with overwhelming burdens and fears did not happen without a struggle. Although he suffered greatly and was changed due to the heaviness of the burdens he carried, the results were not ultimately withering ones, as they were in the case of Gollum. Without denying the heaviness of the ring, he was able to find peace in relationship with others. In fact, Bilbo grew in unforeseen ways after the life-altering and traumatic events that accompanied the burden he endured. He grew in terms of his length of life, his understanding of other peoples and their sagas, his friendships, and he gained a much richer and broader picture of the world. Finally, he was able to help others in ways that would previously have been impossible for him if he had remained in his comfortable hole in the ground. Bilbo can be seen here as an illustration of the positive and surprising life that can take place in post-traumatic recovery. One leg is in Holy Saturday but the other really reaches for the dawn. Recovering safety after trauma is possible.

In this chapter we wish to consider some simple, concrete, doable practices that anyone can implement to help create trauma safety. Getting started with some of these practices can help us to create trauma-safe churches. In what follows we will offer roughly two practices for each principle discussed in the previous chapter. There are certainly more than two practices one could adopt to get started in creating a church that does no harm, listens to survivors, empowers restoration, and engages the body. But these practices are ideal starting points for churches today to consider adopting to start becoming trauma-safe.

Two Practices for Doing No Harm

We have seen a trauma-safe church is a Hippocratic church that first does no harm. One of the most obvious questions might be: how can we create churches that are safe not just for current survivors but also for those vulnerable to trauma, who have yet to experience horrors? First, we must consider how we can structure our churches with strong accountability for those in positions of authority to avoid the abuse of power. Sadly, we have learned in recent years that churches are not immune to scandals of sexual abuse, emotional manipulation by powerful leaders, and perpetuating narcissistic cultures that breed disaster for parishioners.

> We've all seen the news. Power in God's house has been abused in God's name by notorious pastors and leaders who have been sexually involved with multiple sheep, who have used money fraudulently, who have been verbally nasty and demeaning and controlling of others . . . It is crucial that we pay attention and understand the issues involved in order to protect God's sheep, proactively train shepherds who will not damage the sheep of God, and wisely come alongside those who have been victims of abuse in God's family.[2]

As this quote indicates, there are a number of avenues we may consider to begin protecting God's sheep. But here we will consider one simple practice that may prove useful for trauma. In Scott's church (Anglican Church of Australia), there are expressly stated codes of conduct and policies in place to ensure the protection and safety of children. For example, there is a church statute that requires "mandatory reporting," which means that "if a prescribed Church worker believes on reasonable grounds that a person has suffered harm, or is at risk of harm . . . they must as soon as possible report the matter to the Director of Professional Standards."[3] Note how reporting harm in the body is not an option here. It is required by church law. People who fail to comply with training to do with child safety and with the practices of reporting are removed from leadership positions in the church regardless of whether they are bishops, priests, deacons, or lay ministers. This is an example of a practice that can be implemented for trauma safety. Additionally, we should encourage all our church members to follow the state laws for mandatory reporting. Trauma-safe churches have nothing to hide from the laws of justice and are not afraid to bring darkness to light. They are concerned with protecting the vulnerable.

Importantly, practices like these require people who are willing to serve in reporting capacities that can help establish trauma safety. In this example, there is an appointed person ("Director of Professional Standards") whom everyone knows is available for bringing mandatory reports of wrongdoing. Placing someone in a public, official capacity to safeguard against harm sends a powerful message to our members and to the world that we prioritize trauma safety. In Scott's church, there is an additional "Child Safety Policy" that provides clear definitions of child abuse and outlines a clear procedure for reporting. One of the procedures is not only a

2. Langberg, *Redeeming Power*, 126.
3. *Code of Conduct for Child Safety*, 6.

global Director but a local "Child Safety Officer" who is a local point of contact in each individual church for anyone who has concerns about suspicions of wrongdoing.[4] In addition to this person, there are signs in every church bathroom and office that have the telephone numbers for reporting abuse of any kind. The big message is "we do not tolerate abuse, we will find out about it, and root it out of our churches—predators are not welcome to prey in our church."

For our purposes, we suggest that every local church body consider appointing a "Trauma Safety Advocate." This does not have to be a trained professional, paid staff, or even an ordained minister. The purpose of the advocate is to have someone who can speak in two directions: on the one hand, they advocate on behalf of those who report harm, and on the other hand they also advocate for trauma-informed theology in church practices. This role aligns with the "double witness" that we have explored throughout this book—speaking on behalf of those who have suffered loss and lament and pointing toward God's hopeful work. Listening to every person's story and becoming aware of a congregational culture are the key aspects of this role. Discernment requires wisdom from God, channeling the insight and comfort from the Holy Spirit as the advocate.

While some form of training or credential for effective trauma care is preferred for the person who would fill this role, it is better than nothing to just have someone available for people to talk to about their journeys of trauma and recovery. The Trauma Safety Advocate would be the key person in the church who ensures that trauma is reported as well as ensuring that there is a vital double witness to the losses and hopes that arise within and after trauma for both survivors and their caregivers. This might also involve a more proactive role in the congregation to facilitate conversations around trauma: leading healing services, training others in the congregation, inviting experts to speak and train the congregation, and instigating support groups of peer support or professional support. So, the role of Trauma Safety Officer would be both responsive to reports of harm as well as proactive in researching and consulting to establish safe practices, develop a network of mental health resources for parishioners, and serve as an overall point of contact to bring the darkness, shame, and secrecy of trauma into the light. Again, at the local level, creating an official title and point of contact person sends a powerful message that our churches are not ignorant of trauma and want to first do no harm.

4. *Child Safety Policy*, 5.

These are two simple practices to consider for creating a Hippocratic church: (1) to develop and implement a policy of mandatory reporting both within church statutes and according to national authorities and (2) appoint a Trauma Safety Advocate who can serve as a safe liaison for persons who suspect wrongdoing as well as being an ally who can steadily walk alongside people and groups as they move through the long journey of recovery. Trauma-safe churches are not afraid to expose injustice and have appointed persons to help aid the processes of recovery from these injustices.

Two Practices for Listening to Survivors

Survivors who have processed through their trauma to some degree often feel passionately about justice. For those who still feel dissociated from their memories of harm, justice may not be a concern because they have yet to face the horror of their story. But as we continue to tell our story of trauma, we will continue to realize the injustice of what we have suffered and the importance of communal justice for recovering safety. A safe community is a just community, and as survivors tell their story and are listened to by the community, it is important that we share a passion for justice and the goodness of the right ordering of God's creation.

One important practice we can implement related to this is to explicitly teach in our churches the truth that justice and forgiveness are not at odds with one another. Rachael Denhollander, a former USA gymnast and survivor of sexual abuse in the Larry Nassar case, has made this point powerfully in her advocacy and public speaking:

> Frequently, victims report that leaders, parents, and even the abusers themselves appeal to forgiveness as a reason why everyone should simply move on. Handwaving toward forgiveness is sometimes used by Christians to excuse themselves from getting involved in the messes created by abuse. If the victim has forgiven, everyone can just move on and the problem has disappeared.[5]

In this scenario forgiveness is thought to be a shortcut proof that healing has taken place and that the demands of justice have been foregone, and that any subsequent pursuit of justice would involve annulling the original offer of forgiveness. On this way of thinking justice and forgiveness are

5. Denhollander and Denhollander, "Justice," in *Christ and Trauma*, forthcoming.

opposites. You can have one or the other but not both. If survivors pursue justice instead of instantaneous forgiveness, they are thought of as vindictive or bitter.

This is a destructive myth that has been perpetuated in Christian circles for far too long. It fails to truly listen to the testimony of survivors. The truth is that although expressing anger toward perpetrators is a necessary step in the healing process, most survivors do not ultimately long for retribution. "Rather than either retribution or reconciliation, the goal most frequently sought . . . was exposure of the perpetrator. It was more important, in their view, to deprive the perpetrator of undeserved honor and status than to deprive him of either liberty or fortune."[6] More often than not, survivors simply want justice for the isolating silence of trauma. They just want to be heard and believed and for restitution to be made. They want the darkness to come to light and evil to be exposed for what it is.

We can take a significant step in our churches today toward listening to survivors by teaching that forgiveness does not undermine the demands of justice but is consistent with them. Insofar as human justice reflects God's justice it is a good to be pursued. When we report wrongdoings to authorities, we participate in an orderly legal process that actually renounces the personal claim to vengeance by taking part in a communally ordained procedure to punish wrongdoing. Throughout, we can maintain all the virtues of forgiveness that God ultimately requires. Above all, we must take dire care to teach more in our churches on the process of healing than the pressure to "forgive and forget." Trauma-safe churches listen to survivors in their desire for justice and do not pit this against cheap forms of quick forgiveness. Trauma-safe churches are not threatened by engaging the messiness of a real healing process. Teaching the goodness of justice in our churches is one practical way we can communicate to survivors that we see them, we hear them, we believe them, and we care about what they care about. So the first practice is listening without rushing to promote "forgiveness."

A second practice we can all implement today for listening to survivors with a compassionate witness is to take great care how we use words like *trauma*, *traumatize*, and *PTSD*. We noted in the previous chapter that listening to survivors' testimony of trauma is a principle of trauma-safety founded on the simple truth that *you cannot heal what you have not named*. One reason it is imperative to name trauma appropriately is because this can

6. Herman, "Justice from the Victim's Perspective," 593.

alleviate the isolation caused by the shame one feels from having survived an experience of extreme powerlessness. Where trauma isolates, telling the story of harm and listening with compassion can begin to heal shame. But there is another reason that is also important. Naming trauma properly allows the larger community to honor survivors by affirming that they have survived something that is unlike anything else. Surviving trauma is not the same as being depressed, having anxiety, being highly sensitive, or passing through ordinary stressful events. Trauma is a unique experience and ought to be properly named only when it actually occurs.

Naming trauma properly points to "the power of diagnosis."[7] Posttraumatic stress has a long history of being misdiagnosed and confused with other labels such as "hysteria," "masochism," "psychosis," and even "multiple" and "borderline personality disorder."[8] Even though the establishment of PTSD as a formal diagnosis has helped many survivors name their trauma properly for the sake of recovery, this category doesn't cover the unique effects of chronic childhood trauma for which dependable diagnostic labels are still being developed. The road to naming traumatic stress properly is a long journey that clinicians and survivors alike are still figuring out.

While we are all still learning exactly in what ways various events count as traumatic and what are the long-term effects of these on survivors, we know that there are some things that are definitely *not* traumatic. For example, it is categorically not traumatic to undergo a stressful event with which one can adequately cope. This is not traumatic because trauma is *by definition* an event that *overwhelms* one's coping mechanisms. So, it is improper to say "that was so traumatic" in a passing manner if one is referring to an ordinary stressful event. For example, spilling coffee on the way to work on a new favorite shirt, watching a mentally disturbing but bearable horror movie, or a loving parent playfully scaring a child—these are all events that may cause stress but are not traumatic. No matter how effective it feels or how common it is to jokingly communicate one's stress in overstated terms, calling something traumatic when it isn't is improper and inappropriate. It is improper because it is untrue. But it is inappropriate because it dishonors those who actually live with post-traumatic stress.

Just as it has become offensive to call things "retarded" because this term has been taken out of its original medical context and become a

7. Van der Kolk, *Body Keeps the Score*, 142ff.

8. Herman, *Trauma and Recovery*, 116–29.

pejorative slang, it is likewise offensive to call something "traumatic" when it is not.[9] Although most people who misuse the term *trauma* probably do not have ill intent, the effect is the same on survivors. Misusing the term only perpetuates the isolation, alienation, and shame that survivors feel. Even when we dishonor others by accident, we are still dishonoring them. No matter our intent, this is unjust, sinful, and must be avoided.[10]

This does not mean we should walk on eggshells and avoid naming trauma. It just means we need to take care wherever possible to name trauma appropriately. Not only is it true that you cannot heal what you have not named; you also cannot heal what's name has been sold to something else. We can take a huge step in our churches today toward listening to survivors by stealing back the word *trauma* from its current sloppy usage in everyday jargon and reserving this as a term of honor for those who have survived unbearable violence. Changing how we speak will not be enough by itself, but it is a very important first step. Naming trauma appropriately allows us to hear the real testimony of survivors with compassion by honoring the wounds they carry.

These are two practices to get started in listening to survivors with compassion: (1) teach the good news that justice and forgiveness are completely compatible and (2) take great care to use the term *trauma* properly. In this way we can listen to survivors and honor them.

Two Practices for Empowering Restoration

We have seen that listening to survivors with a compassionate witness needs to move toward empowering survivors by taking action with one another together. One very practical and simple way we can empower survivors for restoration in our churches is to create support groups.[11] For me (Preston) participating in a support group had a huge impact early on in my journey to recovery and healing. I felt so alone, isolated, and afraid to face the horror of my traumatic memories and story. I was invited by one

9. On the terminology surrounding intellectual disability (such as "retarded"), see Albert et al., "Sticks, Stones, and Stigmata."

10. Thomas Aquinas makes this point by saying that "reviling" others can be a "mortal sin" that "deserves the eternal punishment of hell" even when one "did not intend to dishonor the other." See *Summa Theologiae*, 2–2.72.2.

11. For details on how to get started with support groups and what forms they may take, see Herman, *Trauma and Recovery*, 214–36.

of my undergraduate Bible professors to recruit other brave and vulnerable men who would be interested in participating in a support group for survivors of abuse. So, we dreamed up a group together. I found other men who needed support. We met every few weeks and just talked. We shared about our trauma, our fears, our hopes, our triggers. In a safe context of shared trust, we imagined what healing could look like in our lives. We wept together. We negotiated boundaries with one another. I had never felt less isolated from trauma than in that group. And it made a huge difference that my professor invited me to help create and lead the group and that he was a survivor himself. He was not healing us. We were all healing together. We were in the muck and mire with one another and we were all on a level playing field. PhD and BA alike, we were healing *with* one another, not *for* or *to* one another.

Starting support groups like this does not have to be complicated and does not require the highest levels of trained professionals to do good work. Half a century ago, Vietnam veterans were running "rap groups" to talk about their trauma, long before psychiatrists knew how to diagnose it properly.[12] More often than not, it is the brave survivors who feel empowered by one another and other advocates to take restorative action that precedes and enables professionals to learn the ropes themselves. We can take a big step in our churches today toward empowering restorative action for trauma healing by simply inviting survivors to start a support group for one another. It sends a powerful message that we trust survivors with their story and want to come alongside them to empower their journey of restoration. This may require at least one more mature member who is further along the road to healing than the others and can help guide the process of the group. We recommend that for every support group started that at least one of the members has participated in a support group previously. This will ensure that there is some level of guidance and experience so that the group is not confused in getting started and avoids engaging counterproductive dialogue by accident. But there should still be no agenda. It should just be a safe space where trauma survivors can meet and talk and offer one another support. These groups should be closed, prioritize anonymity, and be structured for a specific time and place that will not be interrupted. It needs to be treated as sacred because it is a space for holy and supernaturally aided healing. What is said in the group should stay in the group unless life-threatening or generally harmful details need to

12. Herman, *Trauma and Recovery*, 26ff.

be disclosed to a caring professional for the purpose of someone's safety. The group should also know its limits and not seek to replace professional counseling or therapy. And the group should adopt a policy where nothing is off-limits and everything is welcome, in the context of mutually agreed standards of discussion.

Any church can take a simple step like this to empower restoration for survivors. Importantly, we must remember the "with" not "to" or "for" principle when initiating these groups. For example, a pastor could post in a public church newsletter that the church wants to become more trauma-safe and is seeking a survivor who may be interested or willing to start up a group for others, and that any interested persons can reach out anonymously to the pastor or the Trauma Safety Advocate. This sends the message that a church is open to survivors' needs and gifts and is actively seeking these out. We are actively seeking ways to empower survivors for their own journey of healing. Groups like this can offer a safe context where survivors can recognize and bless negative coping patterns for the ways they helped them survive in the past while also acknowledging the need for new styles of relating in the present. Support groups offer a safe space to practice new skills for restoration and healing.

In addition to creating support groups for survivors, a second practice for empowering restoration is to invite survivors into positions of leadership, agency, and active ministry within our churches. We must not only engage "with" (not "for" or "to") the traumatized for *their* well-being. We must also engage with survivors *for the well-being of the broader church community*. Inviting survivors into active ministry in the church is empowering because it shows that surviving trauma does not preclude one's ability to minister in God's kingdom. In fact, it may often be the case that survivors possess unique gifts and abilities from which we all can and must learn. Survivors have something to offer "us" just as much as we have something to offer "them."

For example, survivors of chronic childhood trauma may have heightened senses of social awareness and in such cases may be specially gifted for ministries of counseling, prayer, and spiritual direction. Or a male veteran of war may have a valuable perspective on how men may learn to relate intimately with God after experiences of extreme powerlessness. Or a survivor of natural disaster may have a special appreciation for both the destructive and life-giving power of water and this may give them a unique perspective for how to administer baptism with special pastoral care for other survivors of disaster. These are just hypothetical examples and should not be taken as typical patterns to expect. We must avoid generalizing survivors into clean-cut categories. Every experience of surviving trauma is unique. However, these examples show that survivors of all stripes should not be stigmatized for the trauma they have endured, but should be welcomed for the unique gifts they may possess in their recovery journey.

The truth is that splitting people into groups of either "helpers" or "wounded" is a false dichotomy. More often than not, ministering to others is a reciprocal process that simultaneously helps both people involved. This is also true in trauma therapy. "The helper gains from the act of helping as much or more than the helpee."[13] To see this, consider the story of Francine, who survived a violent bank robbery and witnessed the shooting of two of her coworkers. Francine's therapist tells the story of how her journey to recovery involved learning to help others:

> I grew increasingly concerned for Francine's isolation. She could not motivate herself to get together with friends . . . Sometimes she would briefly, if superficially, chat with adults or children she met on the street . . . [W]hen she talked about these kids she became much more animated that at any other time during our contacts. I waited a while before pointing this out . . . An idea was beginning to take shape in my mind . . . Were there any of them who might be able to use a little help with their math homework? Francine suspected all of them did, but zeroed in on a 12-year-old girl who also seemed somewhat neglected . . . Our dialogue turned into strategizing how she might approach the girl with an offer of free tutoring . . .
>
> The next week Francine looked more lively than I had ever seen her. The girl had been shy, but interested . . . They had a first tutorial and made a date for a second. Through the following weeks, Francine's emotional state improved. She began going to church again, taking the girl with her. They were a good fit, so their relationship grew. The girl provided Francine with companionship and purpose. In return, she gradually became a kind of safe harbor for the girl . . . Francine's was not an unusual situation. I have heard similar stories from many . . .[14]

Francine's story shows how survivors have gifts to offer in their own journey of recovery that is not only good for others but good for themselves as

13. Rothschild, *8 Keys to Trauma Safe Recovery*, 137.
14. Rothschild, *8 Keys to Safe Trauma Recovery*, 137–38.

well. When we welcome the traumatized into helping relationships with others, we can join them to feel empowered and restored with a new sense of agency that counters the powerlessness of trauma.

Inviting survivors into active ministry toward others lets them know that we do not see them as fundamentally flawed, broken, or incapable of good in the world. Rather, we see them as beautiful people with valuable gifts to offer. Survivors often feel branded by the violence they have suffered and carry a deeply stigmatized identity. They may feel like they are at base incapable of giving or receiving love. They may feel like their post-traumatic stress makes them inevitably dangerous to others. It is our responsibility as the church to bear witness to God's Trinitarian works of life and love and to show all people that they are made in the image of God and that nothing can destroy this image. The truth we must proclaim in word and deed is that trauma survivors are capable of brilliant glory, goodness, and service in God's kingdom. Recovery is possible. To the extent that we resist integrating survivors in our ministries because their post-traumatic stress appears atypical to us, or we do not want to be "stained" by their suffering, we are participating in the kingdom of darkness. This perpetuates the stigma of trauma that survivors carry deep inside. Where trauma has stigmatized, we must empower restoration by telling survivors we value their contribution to our common church life.

We can make our churches more trauma-safe today by inviting survivors into active ministry, especially when the survivor feels that their trauma history prevents them from being qualified for this. Importantly, we must never pressure anyone into ministry activities that feel unsafe or uncomfortable. And because trauma-safe churches are safe for everyone, the ministry of survivors must be tailored to their current stage of recovery. For example, it would be unwise to invite a trauma survivor who has just escaped a situation of domestic abuse to immediately counsel others. An extensive season of personal recovery would be needed first. But this is no excuse to keep those who have suffered in a stigmatized state and avoid seeking ways they can grow into their God-given gifts. "I say to everyone among you not to think of yourself more highly than you ought to think . . . For as in one body we have many members, and not all members have the same function, so we, who are many, are one body in Christ, and individually we are members of one another. We have gifts that differ . . ." (Rom 12:3–6). As the church we are called to nurture the unique gifts of *every* member.

Nurturing the gifts of the traumatized in our churches helps to restore a sense of agency to survivors. As we have seen, trauma is essentially an experience of powerlessness. Recovery involves restoring agency. To illustrate this, we return to a story from earlier in this book in chapter 2, the story of Serene and her friend Wendy, who experienced a traumatic miscarriage. Serene describes a moment of restoration when she and Wendy were digging in Wendy's garden:

> As Wendy and I dug into the dirt in her yard that morning, for the first time in several days Wendy felt that she was doing something she had control over. She felt like an agent whose intentional actions, even the simple action of turning over mud, were controlled and had measurable consequences. This momentary feeling of control and agency stood in stark contrast to the radical loss of agency she experienced in the midst of her miscarriage.[15]

Restoring agency to survivors can be a dirty process—literally so for Serene and Wendy. It involves getting down into the muck and debris of harm and finding creative ways to celebrate even the smallest outlets for survivors to reclaim their capacity for bringing life and joy to others.

What we must do then is to remove everything that hinders the flourishing of the traumatized in our midst and the ways their gifts can bring flourishing to others. If someone has been traumatized, they are not disqualified from leadership, from ministry, or from full participation in the church. There may be limits to what shape this activity takes for the good and safety of all. But the active ministry is there, nonetheless. This can be as simple as inviting a member with PTSD to lead a prayer, preach a sermon, visit a sick church member, or any other ministry. People with PTSD are just like normal people in many ways: they have hopes, fears, dreams, aspirations, and desires. We are called to nurture these and to provide outlets for ministry. The larger point here is simple: survivors are more than the sum of their PTSD.[16] Behind the diagnosis, they are images of God who have a number of valuable gifts to offer others. We need to invite and nurture what they have to offer, in their time and with their permission. In this way we can empower restoration.

15. Jones, *Trauma and Grace*, 134–35.

16. See Swinton, *Finding Jesus in the Storm*, 12–18. While Swinton downplays the role of the demonic in cases of mental illness and trauma (195), we don't rule out the possibility that demonic forces may be at work in at least some people's experience of trauma and recovery. For some people, recognizing the role of nonhuman malevolent forces is important for their journey of mourning and recovery from harm.

So, these are two practices for empowering restoration: (1) create support groups for survivors to chart their own path to healing and (2) invite survivors into active ministry within the broader church community. The goal of both these practices is to restore agency to survivors and to honor their recovery journey by dignifying their autonomy. Whether traumatized or not, we are all on a journey of healing from the effects of sin in our world. We can all help one another in a joint effort to this end.

Two Practices for Engaging and Blessing the Body

Trauma safety requires us to create communities that engage and bless the bodies of the traumatized. To become trauma-safe churches that promote healing we must find creative ways to get our bodies moving in safety and blessing the wounds they carry. This poses a problem for many churches today. All too often in our worship services "a few songs merely function as a preface to a long sermon, the goal of which is the dissemination of information to brains-on-a-stick, sitting on their hands . . . where the only adornment [is] often scriptural texts emblazoned on the walls."[17] Settings like this inadvertently promote dissociation. Where traumatized people have learned to chronically escape the terrifying sensations their bodies carry, churches that do not engage the body can compound the problem of ignoring the body and its sensations, and thus impede the recovery of safety. We need more sights, more sounds, more smells, more movement. But we need to ensure these are not overwhelming. We need bodily movement to be structured, safe, regulated, and accessible on the terms of each individual.

One very simple practice we can adopt to engage and bless the role of the body in our churches is to implement liturgies, especially those that incorporate the power and practice of lament. In the Psalms, lament is repeatedly expressed with visceral language that engages the body. "I am poured out like water, and all my bones are out of joint; my heart is like wax; it is melted within my breast; my mouth is dried up like a potsherd, and my tongue sticks to my jaws; you lay me in the dust of death" (Ps 22:14–15). Lament like this takes in the whole body; it reaches into one's guts and the deepest bowels of emotion. It is expressive and requires movement. It engages the body. In certain safe settings, prostration and kneeling may enhance the power of the spoken words of lament.

17. Benson, *Liturgy as a Way of Life*, 9–10.

It is extremely important to incorporate lament into our public worship in the church. Of all the Psalms—the great biblical hymnbook of the church—nearly one-third is made up of laments. Sadly, laments are not frequently part of public worship today; sadness does not sell. But we desperately need forms of worship that can speak the whole range of human emotion and that can engage the wounding experiences of life. We need songs that resonate with "an anatomy of *all* parts of the soul."[18] As Walter Brueggemann states, "My expectation is that pastors, liturgically and pastorally, most need to provide opportunity and script for lament and complaint and grief for a long time."[19] We must allow people to engage the rich complexity of inner emotional life and the ways this must be expressed through the body after horrors and trauma. In time and without rushing, this can facilitate a cathartic space where healing can occur because pain has been named in safety. "By permitting an unrelieved descent into the raw emotions of grief within the secure boundaries of ritual space, hope and trust may be paradoxically restored."[20]

Scripture reading is a central element of many lament liturgies. But reading Scripture can pose challenges for trauma safety. There is a tension in engaging with *all of Scripture,* since many passages in Scripture may be triggering (think how the story of Mary's conception may be read by victims of rape, for instance). If we wish to hold on to the rich tradition and authority that we have been given in the pages of Scripture while making space for trauma-safe church, we have to deal creatively with its contents. This may be as simple as giving "trigger warnings" when discussing or reading passages which are difficult for some members of the congregation to hear. It may sometimes mean finding passages that say the same thing but in different ways (consider how much softer Luke's depiction is of Mary's encounter with the angel Gabriel, for example).

But we must also wrestle with the fact that some passages in Scripture are difficult to hear, even for those who have suffered communal rather than individual trauma. Acknowledging this is crucial. Esau McCaulley, in exploring how African American Christians might engage with passages of Scripture which have been used as weapons of oppression to Black communities in the past, writes, "The path forward is not a return to the

---

18. Calvin, Preface to Commentary on the Psalms, emphasis ours. See Jones, *Trauma and Grace*, 43ff.

19. Brueggemann, cited in Swinton, *Raging with Compassion*, 121.

20. Hunsinger, *Bearing the Unbearable*, 20.

naivete of a previous generation, but a journeying through the hard questions while being informed by the roots of the tradition bequeathed to us. I propose instead that we adopt the posture of Jacob and refuse to let go of the text until it blesses us."[21] Adopting the posture of Jacob is fitting for lament. It involves protesting evil, wrestling with God, and resolving to be blessed—a movement from pain to grace. Central to this process is an honest acknowledgment of the trauma. "Traumatized communities must be able to tell God the truth about what they feel. We must trust that God can handle those emotions. God can listen to our cries . . . It gives us permission to remember and feel."[22]

There are a number of resources for creating and implementing lament liturgies in our churches. Several denominations already use liturgies for healing, such as anointing the sick, which can apply to mental distress no less than physical ailments. For example, the Anglican Church offers several rites of healing and lament for the sick and dying. One of the prayers reads:

> May God the Father bless you, God the Son heal you, God the Holy Spirit give you strength. May God the holy and undivided Trinity guard your body, save your soul, and bring you safely to his heavenly country; where he lives and reigns for ever and ever. Amen.[23]

Another prayer comes from the ministry of committing those who have died into the care of God. It is a prayer that is also used on Holy Saturday in the liturgical calendar and is resonant with themes of lament, suffering, and reaching for God in times that feel like death. For me (Preston) this has been one of the most nourishing prayers to offer to God in lament when my post-traumatic stress feels especially overwhelming:

> Man born of woman has but a short time to live, and is full of misery. He springs up, and is cut down like a flower; he flees like a shadow, and never continues the same.

> In the midst of life we are in death; of whom may we seek for help, but you, O Lord, who for our sins are justly displeased?

> Yet, O Lord God most holy, O Lord most might, O holy and most merciful Savior, deliver us not into the pains of eternal death.

21. McCaulley, *Reading While Black*, 21.
22. McCaulley, *Reading While Black*, 126.
23. *Book of Common Prayer (2019)*, 233.

> You know, O Lord, the secrets of our hearts; shut not your ears to our prayer; but spare us, Lord most holy, O God most might, O holy and merciful Savior, most worthy Judge eternal; do not let us, in our final hour, through the pains of death, fall away from you.[24]

Other denominations and parachurch groups have created liturgies specifically designed for PTSD and trauma survivors.[25] One liturgy opens with a call to worship and uses the following questions:

> People of God, why are you gathered? . . . People of God, are you wounded? . . . People of God, what is your hope?

And answers:

> To worship the Lord who comforts us in our pain and distress, hears our cry for justice when we are wronged, and breaks the walls of silence that keeps the truth from being heard . . . Yes! We are wounded when children are neglected and abused. We are wounded when the weak are assaulted and oppressed . . . Our hope is in God who has promised to be with us in our suffering.[26]

Many of these liturgies involve creative gestures of washing, lighting candles, and burning memorials of the past trauma. One nondenominational liturgy opens with an imprecatory litany to condemn evil: "Cursed be the violence of the strong . . . cursed be the evil power of secrecy . . . cursed be our collusion and cowardice."[27] Another liturgy opens with a call to worship and a simple litany that can be used in any church service for survivors and non-survivors alike:

> God of compassion, you feel our pain and cry with us in our passion. God of justice, you rage with us against the injustice of our experience. Be with us today.
>
> We gather today in sadness to remember all [who have survived] violence . . .
>
> [Leader]: Come, all who are weary and heavy-laden; come, all who seek God's rest and peace.

---

24. *Book of Common Prayer (2019)*, 260, 579.

25. For a full list that is very helpful, see Gould, "Healing the Wounded Heart."

26. Church of the Brethren, Health Promotion Sunday Resources, cited in Gould, "Healing the Wounded Heart," 301–2.

27. Evans, *Healing Liturgies*, 206–17, cited in Gould, "Healing the Wounded Heart," 302.

People [Together]: We come with reluctance, knowing the pain and suffering and fear of our lives, fearing that they may be revealed.

[Leader]: Come before our God, who knows the hidden depths of each heart, and knowing, loves us completely.

People [Together]: We come with expectation, seeking out of our confusion and fear the light and hope of God's love.

[Leader]: Come, all who seek transformation. Let us worship God who offers us new life.[28]

More specifically, there are also liturgies designed for small groups of survivors outside of public church gatherings, including for use on retreats. These small group liturgies are intended to make the ministry of church services available to those who may not be able to rejoin yet because of a trauma history or similar factors. In time, these small group services can help survivors who feel alienated from the church to rejoin in public worship. These liturgies are especially creative in facilitating lament by using open-ended questions and multiple-choice answers as free responses for survivors to exert their own agency. For example, one liturgy offers the question of whether an individual has forgiven an abuser or believes that God loves them. While most traditional liturgies would be quick to script a positive answer, these liturgies allow the free and honest space of lament for participants to acknowledge in the negative. Open and safe spaces like this for honest reckoning with pain can be extremely cathartic and create surprising avenues for intimacy with God. For example, one liturgy reads as follows:

Survivor: God, I confess that I hide from myself and others, and try to hide from you.

Leader: God, help him/her not to fear your healing light. Help him/her to dare to approach you as he/she is, trusting in your promised love for him/her.

Congregation: Have mercy on us, O God . . .

Survivor: God, for wholeness, as much as I experience now, I am thankful.

Congregation: We also give thanks, O God.[29]

28. Evans, *Healing Liturgies*, 191–92.

29. Summers, "A Service of Celebration and Thanksgiving for Healing," 13–25, cited in Gould, "Healing the Wounded Heart," 306.

Because of the vulnerable and direct nature of these more intimate small group liturgies, it is important for significant trust and rapport to be established before such programs are used in a closed group.[30] These liturgies must only be used with the greatest discretion, no coercion, and free consent by all involved.[31] They may all be adapted as desired. For instance, a support group could eventually implement these small group liturgies, if desired by all, for a renewed sense of healing, group lament, and movement toward recovery.

Any of the above prayers or liturgies of lament and healing can be creatively and strategically used in a variety of worship settings. No decisions for proceeding should be made unilaterally by a single leader but should always be negotiated by the free consent of all participants. We must lament "with" one another, not "for" or "to" one another. If your church or group is not used to lament, you can take more simple steps such as replacing the monopoly of upbeat praise songs with more reflective and contemplative songs that invite emotions of mourning in relationship with God. If your church does not often use intentional liturgies, you might consider hosting a weekly small group to recite a simple litany of suffering that incorporates an antiphonal call and response pattern. Almost anything will do. The point is not doing it perfectly but to get started with expressing suffering.

One powerful way of listening well to one another and of listening to God on behalf of one another is to perform of double witness to loss and hope together: this is a *Dawn of Sunday* liturgy.[32] Dawn of Sunday liturgies involve joining together in a time, place, and space dedicated to God, so that by drawing upon each other's witness we can together before God with both and all of our pain and shame, as well as our trust in possibilities and new light for life. By means of together affirming loss and life as a sacred and spiritual gift, we will deeply benefit from "a liturgical imagination that seeks to capture the fullness of the emotions that are present within the body of Jesus."[33] Amidst elements—such as various kinds of prayers, the double witness, the Lord's Supper, hearing from the Scriptures—the aspect of lament within these gatherings "demands a mode of liturgical inclusivity that does not insist that happiness and lack of anxiety are the hallmarks of the presence of God. Lament puts the lie to those who insist that 'praying

---

30. See this importantly underscored in Herman, *Trauma and Recovery*, 218ff.

31. See this point further elaborated in Hunsinger, *Bearing the Unbearable*, 137ff.

32. See our future volume on *Liturgies of Loss and Hope*.

33. Swinton, *Finding Jesus in the Storm*, 86.

harder' will bring blessing defined as a release from our present sufferings . . . Lament allows honesty and mystery—'Life is horrible, and I have absolutely no idea where you are, God.'"[34]

Importantly, many trauma survivors will find liturgy very powerful even if lament is absent. Survivors often feel terribly uncomfortable and not at home in their bodies. With PTSD it feels hard to know what to do with your body. Liturgy is an incredible balm in this situation because it gives clear guidelines and expectations for what to do, where to move, and how to be postured. It takes the pressure off the individual. It offers a safe and structured frame of reference for how to join the rest of the church members to worship God together. With clearly outlined liturgy and simple bodily movements—whether crossing oneself, kneeling, bowing, tasting, sipping, or walking—it is hard to feel lost and is easy to engage. Liturgy is like a "how-to" for worshippers feeling stuck in their bodies. This doesn't mean that only *traditional liturgies* will be of use to a trauma-safe church; all churches have liturgies, and most traditions use bodily movement of some kind in these liturgies, even if this is as simple as standing and sitting, eating and drinking. Finding ways to make worship both bodily and ritualized is the crucial point. Worship that is bodily and ritualized helps you get the blood pumping, get the body moving, and all in a safe and structured way. Leading our churches in even the smallest liturgical directions can prove powerful and transformative for those burdened with trauma.[35] Liturgy is not about training the mind to know certain theological claims are true; liturgy teaches us how to engage with God in a distinctively bodily way. Slowly, this can have the power of changing how we relate to God and relate to the world. This can have a significant effect for trauma survivors who lack language for their feelings, a condition called "alexithymia" that is often tied up with post-traumatic stress.[36] In the context of those who have experienced these effects through moral injury, liturgy provides a new frame of reference for speaking again about one's feelings of both loss and hope. Where trauma feels "unsayable," liturgy can give us a new vocabulary to voice the unbearable sensations involved in overwhelming loss.[37] These words are not just humanly constructed words of comfort; liturgy is typically an organizing and ordering of Scripture so that we can hear God's

34. Swinton, *Finding Jesus in the Storm*, 86–87.

35. Schmutzer, "Spiritual Formation and Sexual Abuse," 79–81.

36. Van der Kolk, *Body Keeps the Score*, 98ff.

37. O'Connor, "Stammering Toward the Unsayable."

words spoken into our lives through the daily patterns of prayer the church has practiced for centuries.

Aside from liturgy/lament, there is one other practice that we must consider for getting started with bodily trauma safety in our churches. We must always honor the autonomy of each individual over their own bodies. We have noted several times how trauma-safe churches are places where the rule is "always ask before touching." Surprisingly, while this may sound intuitive and a commonsense rule for being considerate of others, many churches are not known for being safe places in this way. In some churches today you may find overly aggressive or invasive leaders or people who assume that touch is always received by others as a sign of welcome and hospitality. This is not always the case. For survivors in particular, touching without asking can often feel highly triggering and can be overstimulating and heighten PTSD symptoms. We must learn to care for the bodies in our midst, and survivors can teach us all a valuable lesson in this respect. Each person's body is their own to invite for physical contact. We must never assume it is okay to touch. We must ask permission before hugging. Initiating touch with someone else may seem innocent, but if it is unwanted most survivors will feel so frozen and paralyzed by their trauma that they will not even be able to express in the moment that they need space. Where trauma has silenced the autonomy of survivors and shut down their ability to speak for themselves, we must create spaces that are safe. Every church today can implement this simple practice. It would go miles for survivors everywhere who are suffering in silence. It would impede narcissistic leaders from grooming vulnerable persons. Touch is never okay without explicit invitation and consent. Never. Trauma-safe churches create spaces where people own their bodies for themselves in relation with others. Always ask before touching.

The importance of asking permission before touching has been important for Preston in his own journey to safe trauma recovery. Consider the tradition in many churches of "passing the peace." For me, this has always been my least favorite portion of the church liturgy. I cannot tell you how many times I have been in church and my whole body begins to cringe when the pastor invites the congregation to stand in preparation for personal greetings with one another. It is almost the same experience every time. My heart rate is elevated, my shoulders hunch over, and I begin a mental panic of fight or flight. I know I am about to suffer through social expectations where free touch among one another is normalized. It feels like a sensory nightmare of hyperarousal and overstimulation. I remember one when my wife (who knows this is a struggle for me) warned me as some family friends approached me from behind to embrace me. I was not prepared in time. These people stroked my shoulder and rubbed down my arm for a solid five seconds. It felt like an eternity to me. I was triggered and just wished they had asked first. Then I might have been able to prepare and my whole day would not have been spent trying to recover from a single moment of gnawing interior discomfort. Although awkward, it became an important part of my recovery journey to subsequently approach these individuals and calmly explain my trigger and my need for their special care to engage with my body in ways that honor and respect boundaries. You never know what the simple gesture of asking someone before touching them can do in helping them feel safe. And because we are often unaware of which people are traumatized and which aren't, we must never assume it is okay one way or another. It is always better to be safe than sorry. Our churches can become trauma-safe by implementing this rule. Always ask before touching.

These are two simple practices we can implement to create trauma safety for the traumatized bodies in our churches: (1) implement liturgies that help the body get moving, especially those that incorporate the power and practice of lament, and (2) implement an explicit policy for church leaders and lay members that the rule of all our socializing is "always ask before touching." These simple practices can help us become a little more trauma-safe and they can help us restore wholeness and healing for the bodies of our church members.

Practicing Safety on Sunday Morning

In this chapter we have considered some basic practices that every church can use to get started with trauma safety. These practices can begin to create more safety on Sunday morning for so many trauma survivors in our midst. We have seen two practices for each principle of a trauma-safe church. These are but a sample of possible options to consider. There are many more practices to be used and we encourage you to explore these in conversation with survivors, carers, pastors, and others. Much of this may seem daunting but it is well worth our efforts. Most trauma survivors have suffered in silence for so long that even our failed attempts will be met with appreciation, so long as they are sincere. The point is to get started. We can all begin to create churches and communities that are more trauma-safe today than they were yesterday. Sunday morning can become trauma-safe again by God's help.

> Lord, make me an instrument of your peace: where there is hatred, let me sow love; where there is injury, pardon; where there is discord, union; where there is error, truth; where there is doubt, faith; where there is despair, hope; where there is darkness, light; where there is sadness, joy. O divine Master, grant that I may not seek so much to be consoled as to console, to be understood as to understand, to be loved as to love. For it is in giving that we receive, it is in pardoning that we are pardoned, and it is in dying that we are born to eternal life. Amen.[38]

38. Prayer of St. Francis, *The Book of Common Prayer* (2019), 672.

Afterword

We end where we began, straddling the borderline between the death of Holy Saturday and the life of Easter Sunday. We think this is a fitting metaphor for trauma. With one leg standing in the pains of death we can always be honest about how trauma is the suffering that remains, that persists, that is not quite healed. We can listen to the survivors in our midst with a compassionate witness and acknowledge their wounds and how they shape us in lifelong ways. We can look at horrors and trauma full in the face and avoid quick fixes, offering instead principles and practices for being safely loved in our pain. We have seen that God the Trinity—Father, Son, and Holy Spirit—comes alongside us all in unique and surprising ways to restore a big picture sense of safety and to safely love us right where we are after trauma.

Yet while one leg is planted in death, the other is reaching toward life. We think that healing is possible, and hope is plenteous through God's Trinitarian works among us. Through God the Trinity's works in his church, the community of safety, we can offer a double witness to the wounds of trauma. We can affirm the way that suffering remains and acknowledge trauma's losses and laments while also bearing witness to God the Trinity's healing works of life, light, and love. We can help survivors and all of us to recover safe boundaries in our relationships. We can begin to thaw out our frozen bodies and bless them for the wounds they carry. We can learn to get moving again and empower restoration by imagining together what healing may look like in our trauma-safe communities. The Father, Son, and Spirit are ready and eager to join us in this good work to create trauma safety in the church.

We know that this work will not be easy. But it is necessary, and God the Trinity makes it possible. Through God's Trinitarian works and love we can see that God is abundantly able and ready to meet us with healing at every level that trauma safety requires. We can trust this God for creating trauma safety. The work is not easy but through God the Trinity's works in the church it is possible, it is doable, it is good. Returning to our dawn of Sunday metaphor, creating trauma safety with the Trinity means that although darkness is all around us, we have our face set eastward and we see inklings of light breaking just over the horizon. This is what trauma healing feels like. The darkness is fading but the light is not yet full; we are still in a shroud of black, but we think we can see the sun just beginning to rise. It is right here that the death of Jesus was vindicated by God's mighty resurrection power through the Spirit. Right here is where our death today can begin to turn to life. We think that the dawn of Sunday is a good place to be to begin creating trauma safety with the triune God and the church.

Every sun that rises has a setting and every dawn will turn to dusk. After all our efforts at creating trauma safety have come and go, we must maintain a single posture of offering these efforts to God in petition and thanksgiving. As we have seen only God creates safety in his Church and it is ultimately God's work before it is ours. In closing, we think it is fitting to include the following prayer "O Gladsome Light," as an offering and petition that God the Trinity continue his good work of healing among us from the sun's rising to its setting.

O Gladsome Light

O gladsome light,
pure brightness of the everliving Father in heaven,
O Jesus Christ, holy and blessed!
Now as we come to the setting of the sun,
and our eyes behold the vesper light,
we sing your praises, O God: Father, Son, and Holy Spirit.
You are worthy at all times to be praised by happy voices,
O Son of God, O Giver of Life,
and to be glorified through all the worlds.

Glory be to the Father, and to the Son, and to the Holy Spirit;
as it was in the beginning, is now, and ever shall be,
world without end. Amen.

Bibliography

Adams, Marilyn McCord. "The Coherence of Christology: God, Enmattered and Enmattering." *Princeton Seminary Bulletin* 26, no. 2 (2005) 157–79.

———. "Plantinga on 'Felix Culpa': Analysis and Critique." *Faith and Philosophy* 25, no. 2 (2008) 123–40.

Albert, Avery B., Holly E. Jacobs, and Gary N. Siperstein. "Sticks, Stones, and Stigmata: Student Bystander Behavior in Response to Hearing the Word 'Retarded.'" *Intellectual and Developmental Disabilities* 54, no. 6 (2016) 391–401.

Allender, Dan. *Healing the Wounded Heart: The Heartache of Sexual Abuse and the Hope of Transformation.* Grand Rapids: Baker, 2016.

———. *How Children Raise Parents.* Colorado Springs: Waterbrook, 2003.

———. *The Wounded Heart: Hope for Adult Victims of Childhood Sexual Abuse.* Colorado Springs: NavPress, 1995, 2008.

Aquinas, Thomas. *Summa Theologiae.* Translated by Fathers of the English Dominican Province. 10 vols. London: Burns Oates and Washbourne, 1920–1922.

Arel, Stephanie N., and Shelly Rambo, eds. *Post-Traumatic Public Theology.* Cham, Switzerland: Palgrave Macmillan, 2016.

Augustine. *Confessions.* Translated with an introduction by R. S. Pine-Coffin. London: Penguin, 2015.

Barrett, Justin L. *Cognitive Science, Religion, and Theology: From Human Minds to Divine Minds.* West Conshohoken, PA: Templeton, 2011.

Bass, Ellen, and Laura Davis. *The Courage to Heal: A Guide for Women Survivors of Sexual Abuse.* New York: Harper and Row, 1990.

BBC News. "Australia fires: PM Scott Morrison sorry for Hawaii holiday during crisis." December 22, 2019. https://www.bbc.com/news/world-australia-50879850.

Beattie, Melody. *Codependent No More: How to Stop Controlling Others and Start Caring for Yourself.* Center City, MN: Hazelden, 1986.

Beauchamp, Tom L. *Standing on Principles: Collected Essays.* New York: Oxford University Press, 2010.

Benson, Bruce Ellis. *Liturgy as a Way of Life: Embodying the Arts in Christian Worship.* Grand Rapids: Baker Academic, 2013.

Bernard of Clairvaux. *Saint Bernard on the Love of God.* Translated by S. Patmore and C. Patmore. London: Burnes and Oates, 1884.

Blocher, Henri. *Evil and the Cross: An Analytical Look at the Problem of Pain*. Grand Rapids: Kregel, 2004.

Blue Knot Foundation. "What is Complex Trauma?" National Centre of Excellence for Complex Trauma. Accessed May 15, 2020. https://www.blueknot.org.au/Resources/Information/Understanding-abuse-and-trauma/What-is-complex-trauma.

Bonhoeffer, Dietrich. *Letters and Papers from Prison*. New York: Touchstone, 1997.

The Book of Common Prayer (2019). Anglican Church in North America. Huntington Beach, CA: Anglican Liturgy, 2019.

Boothby, E. J., M. S. Clark, and J. A. Bargh. "Shared Experiences Are Amplified." *Psychological Science* 25, no. 12 (2004) 2209–16.

Boothby, E. J., L. K. Smith, M. S. Clark, and J. A. Bargh. "Psychological Distance Moderates the Amplification of Shared Experience." *Personality and Social Psychology Bulletin* 42, no. 10 (2016) 1431–44.

Bowlby, John. *A Secure Base: Parent-Child Attachment and Healthy Human Development*. New York: Basic Books, 1999.

Boynton, Eric, and Peter Capretto, eds. *Trauma and Transcendence: Suffering and the Limits of Theory*. New York: Fordham University Press, 2018.

Brison, Susan J. *Aftermath: Violence and the Remaking of the Self*. Princeton, NJ: Princeton University Press, 2002.

Brown, Brené. *The Gifts of Imperfection: Let Go of Who You Think You're Supposed to Be and Embrace Who You Are: Your Guide to a Wholehearted Life*. Center City, MN: Hazelden, 2010.

———. *Daring Greatly: How the Courage to Be Vulnerable Transforms the Way We Live, Love, Parent, and Lead*. New York: Penguin, 2012.

Brueggemann, Walter. *Awed to Heaven, Rooted in Earth: Prayers of Walter Brueggemann*. Minneapolis: Augsburg Fortress, 2003.

Burns, Judith. "'My mum killed my dad with a hammer but I want her freed.'" *BBC*, January 3, 2019. https://www.bbc.co.uk/news/education-46111655.

Byers, Andrew J. "The One Body of the Shema in 1 Corinthians: An Ecclesiology of Christological Monotheism." *New Testament Studies* 62, no. 4 (2016) 517–32.

Calvin, John. *Institutes of the Christian Religion*. 2 vols. Edited by John T. McNeill and F. L. Battles. Philadelphia: Westminster, 1960.

Carlson, Nathaniel A. "Lament: The Biblical Language of Trauma." *Cultural Encounters* 11, no. 1 (2015) 50–68.

Carr, David M. *Holy Resilience: The Bible's Traumatic Origins*. New Haven, CT: Yale University Press, 2014.

Carroll, Noël. *The Philosophy of Horror, Or, Paradoxes of the Heart*. New York: Routledge, 1990.

Caruth, Cathy. "Introduction." In *Trauma: Explorations in Memory*, 3–12. Baltimore: Johns Hopkins University Press, 1995.

———. *Unclaimed Experience: Trauma, Narrative, and History*. Baltimore: Johns Hopkins University Press, 2016.

Caruth, Cathy, ed. *Trauma: Explorations in Memory*. Baltimore: Johns Hopkins University Press, 1995.

Cassidy, Jude, and Phillip Shaver, eds. *Handbook of Attachment*. New York: Guilford, 2016.

Chan, Simon. *Liturgical Theology: The Church as Worshipping Community*. Downers Grove, IL: IVP Academic, 2006.

Child Safety Policy. Australia: Anglican Church of Australia, Anglican Diocese of Melbourne, 2018.

Cloud, Henry, and John Townsend. *Boundaries: When to Say Yes, How to Say No to Take Control of Your Life*. Grand Rapids: Zondervan, 1992.

Code of Conduct for Child Safety. Australia: Anglican Church of Australia, Anglican Diocese of Melbourne, 2018.

Code of Ethics. Alexandria, VA: American Counseling Association, 2014.

Collins, Natalie. "Broken or Superpowered? Traumatized People, Toxic Doublethink and the Healing Potential of Evangelical Christian Communities." In *Feminist Trauma Theologies: Body, Scripture, and Church in Critical Perspective*, edited by Karen O'Donnell and Katie Cross, 195–221. London: SCM, 2020.

Cone, James H. *The Cross and the Lynching Tree*. Maryknoll, NY: Orbis, 2011.

Cuneo, Terence. *Ritualized Faith: Essays on the Philosophy of Liturgy*. New York: Oxford University Press, 2016.

DeGroat, Chuck. *When Narcissism Comes to Church: Healing Your Community from Emotional and Spiritual Abuse*. Downers Grove, IL: InterVarsity, 2020.

Denhollander, Rachael, and Jacob Denhollander. "Justice: The Foundation of a Christian Approach to Abuse." In *Christ and Trauma: Theology East of Eden*, edited by Preston Hill. Eugene, OR: Pickwick, forthcoming.

Drevokovsky, Janek. "Bushfire victim slams Scott Morrison for walking away." *The Sydney Morning Herald*, January 3, 2020. https://www.smh.com.au/national/nsw/bushfire-victim-slams-scott-morrison-for-walking-away-20200103-p530mq.html.

Dudley, Dominic. "Where And Why The World Is Getting More Dangerous." *Forbes*, June 6, 2018. https://www.forbes.com/sites/dominicdudley/2018/06/06/why-the-world-is-getting-more-dangerous/?sh=3568511c5a6d.

Durand, Emmanuel. *Les Émotions De Dieu: Indices D'engagement*. Paris: Cerf, 2019.

Enright, R. D. *Forgiveness Is a Choice: A Step by Step Process for Resolving Anger and Restoring Hope*. Washington, DC: American Psychological Association, 2001.

Evans, Abigail. *Healing Liturgies for the Seasons of Life*. Louisville: Westminster John Knox, 2004.

Fahy, Thomas Richard. *The Philosophy of Horror*. The Philosophy of Popular Culture. Lexington, KY: University Press of Kentucky, 2010.

Farley, Wendy. *Gathering Those Driven Away: A Theology of the Incarnation*. Louisville: Westminster John Knox, 2011.

Faulkner, Doug. "Coronation Street: Coercive control is 'all of our business.'" *BBC*, May 5, 2020. https://www.bbc.co.uk/news/uk-52502409.

Fee, G. D. *The First Epistle to the Corinthians*. Grand Rapids: Eerdmans, 1987.

Fosha, Diana, Daniel J. Siegel, and Marion Solomon, eds. *The Healing Power of Emotion: Affective Neuroscience, Development, and Clinical Practice*. New York: W. W. Norton, 2009.

Freedman, Suzanne. "The 'F Word' for Sexual Abuse Survivors." *And He Restoreth My Soul Project*, February 23, 2019. https://andherestorethmysoulproject.org/2019/02/23/the-f-word-for-sexual-abuse-survivors/.

Gostecnik, Christian, Tanja Repic Slavic, Sasa Poljak Lukek, and Robert Cvetek. "Trauma and Religiousness." *Journal of Religion and Health* 53 (2014) 690–701.

Gould, James B. "Healing the Wounded Heart Through Ritual and Liturgy: Accompanying the Abused in their Healing." In *The Long Journey Home: Understanding and*

Ministering to the Sexually Abused, edited by Andrew Schmutzer, 293–313. Eugene, OR: Wipf and Stock, 2011.

Granqvist, Pehr, and Lee Kirkpatrick. "Attachment and Religious Representations and Behavior." In *Handbook of Attachment*, edited by Jude Cassidy and Phillip Shaver, 919–41. New York: Guilford, 2016.

Greenspan, Henry. "On Testimony, Legacy, and the Problem of Helplessness in History." *Holocaust Studies* 13, no. 1 (2007) 44–45.

Greven, Philip. *Spare the Child: The Religious Roots of Punishment and the Psychological Impact of Abuse.* New York: Vintage, 1992.

Guardian News. "'I don't really want to': Scott Morrison's attempts to shake hands in Cobargo rejected." *Guardian News*, January 2, 2020, video. https://www.youtube.com/watch?v=kePvZkV-Zcs.

Harrower, Scott. *God of All Comfort: A Trinitarian Response to the Horrors of This World.* Bellingham, WA: Lexham, 2019.

Hay, David, with Rebecca Nye. *The Spirit of the Child.* Rev. ed. London: Jessica Kingsley, 2006.

Heard, Dorothy, Una McCluskey, and Brian Lake. *Attachment Therapy with Adolescents and Adults: Theory and Practice Post Bowlby.* Rev. ed. London: Routledge, 2012.

Heath, Elaine A. *We Were the Least of These: Reading the Bible with Survivors of Sexual Abuse.* Grand Rapids: Brazos, 2011.

Herman, Judith. "Justice from the Victim's Perspective." *Violence Against Women* 11, no. 5 (2005) 571–602.

Herman, Judith Lewis. *Trauma and Recovery: The Aftermath of Violence—From Domestic Abuse to Political Terror.* New York: Basic, 1992.

Hill, Preston, ed. *Christ and Trauma: Theology East of Eden.* Eugene, OR: Pickwick, forthcoming.

Hopkins, Gerard Manley. "God's Grandeur." In *The Poems of Gerard Manley Hopkins*, edited by W. H. Gardner and N. H. MacKenzie, 47–48. 4th ed. New York: Oxford University Press, 1967.

Hunsinger, Deborah van Deusen. *Bearing the Unbearable: Trauma, Gospel, and Pastoral Care.* Grand Rapids: Eerdmans, 2015.

Johnson, Dru. *Human Rites: The Power of Rituals, Habits, and Sacraments.* Grand Rapids: Eerdmans, 2019.

Johnson, Marcus Peter. *One with Christ: An Evangelical Theology of Salvation.* Wheaton, IL: Crossway, 2012.

Jones, Serene. *Trauma and Grace: Theology in a Ruptured World.* Louisville: Westminster John Knox, 2009.

Joseph, Stephen, and Kate Hefferon. "Post-Traumatic Growth: Eudaimonic Happiness in the Aftermath of Adversity." In *The Oxford Handbook of Happiness*, edited by Susan A. David, Ilona Boniwell, and Conley Ayers, 926–40. Oxford: Oxford University Press, 2014.

Kalsched, Donald. *The Inner World of Trauma: Archetypal Defenses of the Personal Spirit.* New York: Routledge, 1996.

Kierkegaard, Søren. *Christian Discourses: The Crisis and a Crisis in the Life of an Actress.* Translated by Edna Hong and Howard Hong. Vol. 17 of *Kierkegaard's Writings.* Princeton, NJ: Princeton University Press, 1997.

―――. *Discourses at the Communion on Fridays.* Translated by Sylvia Walsh. Indiana Series in the Philosophy of Religion. Bloomington, IN: Indiana University Press, 2011.

Knabb, Joshua J., and Matthew Y. Emerson. "'I Will Be Your God and You Will Be My People': Attachment Theory and the Grand Narrative of Scripture." *Pastoral Psychology* 62, no. 6 (2013) 827–41.

Langberg, Diane. *Redeeming Power: Understanding Authority and Abuse in the Church.* Grand Rapids: Brazos, 2020.

Lembke, Jürgen Jian, and Julianne Funk. "Feeding the Hungry Spirits: A Socially Engaged Buddhist Response to the Distortion of Trauma." In *Trauma and Lived Religion: Transcending the Ordinary,* edited by R. Ruard Ganzevoort and Srdjan Sremac, 177–202. Cham, Switzerland: Palgrave Macmillan, 2019.

Levine, Peter. *Waking the Tiger: Healing Trauma.* Berkeley, CA: North Atlantic, 1997.

Lewis, Alan E. *Between Cross and Resurrection: A Theology of Holy Saturday.* Grand Rapids: Eerdmans, 2001.

Lewis, C. S. *The Problem of Pain.* New York: Macmillan, 1947.

―――. *The Voyage of the Dawn Treader.* London: HarperCollins, 2014.

Luther, Martin. *Luther's Works.* 55 vols. Edited by Jaroslav Pelikan and Helmut T. Lehman. Philadelphia: Fortress; Saint Louis: Concordia, 1955–1986.

Lutz, Richard A. "Prayers of the VA Chaplaincy." Presentation at Department of Veteran Affairs, 12th Annual Chief's Convocation, Washington, DC, December 6–9, 1997.

Mannion, Lee. "Most people think world is more dangerous than two years ago: survey." *Reuters,* July 11, 2018. https://www.reuters.com/article/us-global-security-poll/most-people-think-world-is-more-dangerous-than-two-years-ago-survey-idUSKBN1K02I8.

Martin, Dale. *The Corinthian Body.* New Haven, CT: Yale University Press, 1999.

Mascall, E. L. *Christ, the Christian, and the Church: A Study of the Incarnation and Its Consequences.* Peabody, MA: Hendrickson, 2017.

McCaulley, Esau. *Reading While Black: African American Biblical Interpretation as an Exercise in Hope.* Downers Grove, IL: IVP Academic, 2020.

McGrath, Alister. *Theology: The Basics.* 3rd ed. Chichester, UK: Wiley Blackwell, 2018.

Mikulincer, Mario, and Phillip R. Shaver. "Adult Attachment and Happiness: Individual Differences in the Experience and Consequences of Positive Emotions." In *The Oxford Handbook of Happiness,* edited by Susan A. David, Ilona Boniwell, and Amanda Conley Ayers, 834–46. Oxford: Oxford University Press, 2013.

―――. *Attachment in Adulthood: Structure, Dynamics, and Change.* New York: Guilford, 2007.

Mitchell, Stephen A., and Margaret J. Black. *Freud and Beyond: A History of Modern Psychoanalytic Thought.* New York: Basic, 2016.

Moffitt, David M. *Atonement and the Logic of Resurrection in the Epistle to the Hebrews.* Supplements to Novum Testamentum 141. Leiden: Brill, 2011.

Moltmann, Jürgen. "Sun of Righteousness, Arise! The Freedom of a Christian—Then and Now—for the Perpetrators and for the Victims of Sin." *Theology Today* 69 (2012) 7–17.

Mullen, Wade. *Something's Not Right: Decoding the Hidden Tactics of Abuse—and Freeing Yourself from Its Power.* Carol Stream, IL: Tyndale Momentum, 2020.

Muller, Richard. *Divine Will and Human Choice: Freedom, Contingency, and Necessity in Early Modern Reformed Thought.* Grand Rapids: Baker, 2017.

Murray, N., E. Koby, and B. van der Kolk. "The Effects of Abuse on Children's Thoughts." In *Psychological Trauma*, by Bessel van der Kolk, 89–110. Washington, DC: American Psychiatric Press, 1987.

The Nature and Scope of Sexual Abuse of Minors by Catholic Priests and Deacons in the United States 1950–2002: A Research Study Conducted by the John Jay College of Criminal Justice, The City University of New York. Washington, DC: United States Conference of Catholic Bishops, 2004.

Nouwen, Henri J. M. *The Living Reminder: Service and Prayer in Memory of Jesus Christ*. New York: HarperCollins, 1977.

———. *The Way of the Heart: Desert Spirituality and Contemporary Ministry*. New York: Seabury, 1981.

O'Connor, Kathleen M. *Jeremiah: Pain and Promise*. Minneapolis: Fortress, 2011.

———. "Stammering Toward the Unsayable: Old Testament Theology, Trauma Theory, and Genesis." *Interpretation* 70, no. 3 (2016) 301–13.

O'Donnell, Karen. *Broken Bodies: The Eucharist, Mary, and the Body in Trauma Theology*. London: SCM, 2018.

Panchuk, Michelle. "The Shattered Spiritual Self: A Philosophical Exploration of Religious Trauma." *Res Philosophica* 95, no. 3 (2018) 505–53.

Parker, Jarrod. "Jarrod Parker." In *Crisis: 40 Stories Revealing the Personal, Social, and Religious Pain and Trauma of Growing Up Gay in America*, edited by Mitchell Gold, with Mindy Drucker, 83–90. Austin, TX: Greenleaf.

Rambo, Shelly. "Spirit and Trauma." *Interpretation* 69, no. 1 (2015) 7–19.

———. *Spirit and Trauma: A Theology of Remaining*. Louisville: Westminster John Knox, 2010.

Reid, J. K. S. *Our Life in Christ*. Philadelphia: Westminster, 1963.

Report I of the 40th Statewide Investigating Grand Jury. Commonwealth of Pennsylvania: Office of Attorney General, 2018.

Report on the Holy See's Institutional Knowledge and Decision-Making Related to Former Cardinal Theodore Edgar McCarrick (1930–2017). Vatican City State: Secretariat of State of Holy See, 2020.

Rogers, Carl. *On Becoming a Person: A Therapist's View of Psychotherapy*. Reprinted with introduction by Peter D. Kramer. New York: Houghton Mifflin, 1995.

Root, Andrew. *The Grace of Dogs: A Boy, a Black Lab, and a Father's Search for the Canine Soul*. New York: Convergent, 2017.

Rothschild, Babette. *8 Keys to Safe Trauma Recovery: Take-Charge Strategies to Empower Your Healing*. New York: Norton, 2010.

Sartor, Daniel C., Cara Cochran, Amanda M. Blackburn, Mary K. Plisco, and Jama L. White. "The Role of Attachment in Spiritual Formation at Richmont Graduate University." *Journal of Spiritual Formation and Soul Care* 11, no. 2 (2018) 253–70.

Schmutzer, Andrew J. "Spiritual Formation and Sexual Abuse: Embodiment, Community, and Healing." *Journal of Spiritual Formation and Soul Care* 2, no. 1 (2009) 67–86.

Schmutzer, Andrew J., ed. *The Long Journey Home: Understanding and Ministering to the Sexually Abused*. Eugene, OR: Wipf and Stock, 2011.

Schmutzer, Andrew J., Daniel A. Gorski, and David Carlson. *Naming Our Abuse: God's Pathway to Healing for Male Sexual Abuse Survivors*. Grand Rapids: Kregel, 2016.

Schore, Allan N. *Affect Regulation and the Origin of the Self: The Neurobiology of Emotional Development*. Hillsdale, NJ: Lawrence Earlbaum, 1994.

Seligman, Martin E. P. *Flourish: A Visionary New Understanding of Happiness and Well-Being*. London: Atria, 2011.

"The Serenity Prayer." *A. A. Grapevine*, 1950.

Shengold, Leonard. *Soul Murder: The Effects of Childhood Abuse and Deprivation*. New Haven, CT: Yale University Press, 1989.

Shoop, Marcia Mount. "Body-Wise: Re-Fleshing Christian Spiritual Practice in Trauma's Wake." In *Trauma and Transcendence: Suffering and the Limits of Theory*, edited by Eric Boynton and Peter Capretto, 240–54. New York: Fordham University Press, 2018.

Siegel, Daniel J. *Pocket Guide to Interpersonal Neurobiology: An Integrative Handbook of the Mind*. New York: Norton, 2012.

Smith, James K. A. *You Are What You Love: The Spiritual Power of Habit*. Grand Rapids: Brazos, 2016.

Stern, Daniel. *The Interpersonal World of the Infant: A View from Psychoanalysis and Developmental Psychology*. New York: Basic Books, 1985.

Stringer, Jay. *Unwanted: How Sexual Brokenness Reveals Our Way to Healing*. Colorado Springs: NavPress, 2018.

Stump, Eleonore. *Atonement*. Oxford Studies in Analytic Theology. New York: Oxford University Press, 2019.

———. "The Atonement and the Problem of Shame." *Journal of Philosophical Research* 41 (2016) 111–129.

———. *Wandering in Darkness: Narrative and the Problem of Suffering*. New York: Oxford University Press, 2010.

Summers, Bonnie. "A Service of Celebration and Thanksgiving for Healing." *Journal of Religion and Abuse* 8 (2006) 13–25.

Swinton, John. *Finding Jesus in the Storm: The Spiritual Lives of Christians with Mental Health Challenges*. Grand Rapids: Eerdmans, 2020.

———. *Raging with Compassion: Pastoral Responses to the Problem of Evil*. Grand Rapids: Eerdmans, 2007.

"This Is My Father's World." In *The Presbyterian Hymnal Companion*, edited by Lindajo H. McKim, 209. Louisville: Westminster John Knox, 1983.

Thompson, Curt. *The Soul of Shame: Retelling the Stories We Believe About Ourselves*. Downers Grove, IL: InterVarsity, 2015.

Tietje, Adam. *Toward a Pastoral Theology of Holy Saturday: Providing Spiritual Care for War Wounded Souls*. Eugene, OR: Wipf and Stock, 2018.

Tisby, Jemar. *The Color of Compromise: The Truth About the American Church's Complicity in Racism*. Grand Rapids: Zondervan, 2019.

Torrance, J. B. *Worship, Community and the Triune God of Grace*. Downers Grove, IL: InterVarsity, 1996.

Travis, Sarah. *Unspeakable: Preaching and Trauma-Informed Theology*. New Studies in Theology and Trauma. Eugene, OR: Cascade, forthcoming.

Underhill, Evelyn. *Collected Papers of Evelyn Underhill*. New York: Longmans, 1949.

———. *Worship*. London: Nisbet, 1936.

Van der Kolk, Bessel. *The Body Keeps the Score: Brain, Mind, and Body in the Healing of Trauma*. London: Penguin, 2014.

———. *Psychological Trauma*. Washington, DC: American Psychiatric Press, 1987.

Vander Zee, Leonard J. *Christ, Baptism, and the Lord's Supper: Recovering the Sacraments for Evangelical Worship*. Downers Grove, IL: IVP Academic, 2004.

Vorster, Nico. *The Brightest Mirror of God's Works: John Calvin's Theological Anthropology*. Eugene, OR: Pickwick, 2019.

Waterford, Jack. "Scott Morrison's handling of Brittany Higgins rape allegations lack empathy." *The Canberra Times*, February 20, 2021. https://www.canberratimes.com.au/story/7133899/once-again-the-pm-has-shown-he-has-no-empathy-for-human-emotions/.

Weingarten, Kaethe. *Common Shock: Witnessing Violence Every Day*. New York: New American Library, 2003.

Williams, Rowan. *Christ the Heart of Creation*. London: Bloomsbury Continuum, 2018.

Worthington, Everett. *A Just Forgiveness: Responsible Healing without Excusing Injustice*. Downers Grove, IL: InterVarsity, 2009.

Yoder, Carolyn. *The Little Book of Trauma Healing*. Intercourse, PA: Good Books, 2015.

Index

A

abandonment, 46–47, 49, 64

abuse, 17, 21–24, 27–28, 37, 43–44, 46, 50, 52–53, 72–74, 78, 79, 97, 115–18, 120–21, 140, 157–58, 160–61, 163–64, 172–73, 176, 182–85, 192

Adams, Marilyn McCord, 26, 76

agency, 6, 29, 58–59n2, 64, 69, 73, 95, 97–101, 107, 113, 117, 121, 125–28, 146–47, 178, 190, 192–94, 198

animals, 4, 84–85, 149

anxiety, 34, 38, 43, 46, 79, 106, 109, 177, 187, 199

Aquinas, 24, 67, 188

attachment, 23, 31, 33–45, 47–50, 58, 62, 67, 69, 81, 89–90, 95, 98, 101, 107, 110, 117, 122–23, 131, 134, 137, 153, 174, 181
  insecure, 31, 41–45, 47–50, 123, 131, 138
  secure, 32, 36, 38–39, 41–43, 48–50, 58, 67–69, 74, 81, 89–90, 107, 117, 131, 137, 153,
  theory, 34, 36, 41, 89

B

baptism, 77, 139, 190

body, 10, 20, 23–25, 27, 29–31, 33–36, 52–53, 59–60, 72, 84–85, 94–95, 100, 103, 105, 107, 113–15, 125, 131, 156–57, 174–80, 182–84, 192, 194–96, 200–202
  of Christ, 6–8, 11, 82–82, 88, 101, 122, 130–34, 136, 139–42, 144–48, 199

boundaries, 34, 36, 40–44, 51, 57, 68, 70–74, 91, 95–101, 103, 114, 117–20, 122–26, 128, 131, 134, 143, 149, 153–54, 156–57, 169, 171–72, 174, 189, 195, 202, 205

brain, 30, 37n11, 68–69, 84, 103, 112, 144, 161, 175–76, 179, 194

C

Calvin, John, 58n1, 82, 195

carers, 131, 136, 149, 156, 163–65, 169, 171, 174, 202

Christ, 5, 7–8, 11, 15–16, 21, 49, 58–59, 62, 69, 71, 76–77, 80, 82–88, 93–95, 98–99, 101–2, 104, 113, 118, 120–22, 124–25, 128, 130–34, 136, 138–42, 144–49, 164, 192, 206

Christians, 5, 11, 48, 57, 63–65, 67–68, 75, 77, 85–86, 94–95, 101, 110–11, 113–14, 120–23, 132, 134, 136–37, 142, 157–58, 185, 195

Made in the USA
Columbia, SC
14 March 2023

13749218R00140